MW00475463

Wedded to the Land?

Post-Contemporary

Interventions

Series Editors:

Stanley Fish and

Fredric Jameson

Wedded to the Land?

Gender, Boundaries, and

Nationalism in Crisis

Mary N. Layoun

Duke University Press

Durham and London

2001

© 2001 Duke University Press
All rights reserved
Printed in the United States of America on acid-free paper ∞
Typeset in Melior by Keystone Typesetting, Inc.
Library of Congress Cataloging-in-Publication Data
appear on the last printed page of this book.

For Niko

Contents

Acknowledgments

Silences are melodies
Heard in retrospect
—Christopher Okigbo,
"Lament of the Silent Sisters"

The pages that follow would not have been possible without the help, support, and encouragement of many people. To say that I am indebted to their kindness and generosity is scarcely adequate—and an impoverished metaphor in any event. Although intellectual work is often not specified as collaborative, it unquestionably is. We neither think nor write nor read in a vacuum—even if we often seem to be in isolation. The books, articles, conversations, questions, dialogues, arguments, and challenges by which we seek to engage one another shape the work that any one of us does.

So I am the grateful beneficiary of excellent work already done by others, some of it well-known (as in the case of the work of Edward Said, Gayatri Spivak, and Fredric Jameson), some of it less known (as in the case, for example, of the Greek historian Nikos Psyroukis or the Cypriot writer and intellectual Leandros Nearkhos). Without the work of scholars and intellectuals such as these, I could not have begun to conceptualize what follows. Nor would some fundamental formulation of the questions and suggestions of *Wedded to the Land* have been possible without the literary and cultural work of those whose novels, short stories, films, poems, and artwork are taken up here, as well as the work of a good many other writers and artists whose work is not. Although *Wedded to the Land* is not by any means an exhaustive treatment of each of the three instances of cultural responses to crises of nationalism, I have tried to responsibly draw the outlines of the historical crises and of social and cultural responses to them. But, in each instance, I have deliberately discussed in more detail those national crises that seem to be less familiar or closer to forgetfulness in our own moment in the United States at the beginning of the twenty-first century. And I have elaborated on those aspects of the crises and responses to them that seem to me to make the most productive offering in a debate on the issues of gender, nationalism, culture, and citizenship.

In the past twenty years, for example, there has been, sometimes fierce opposition notwithstanding, far more foregrounded work produced in the United States on Palestine, Palestinian culture, and Palestinian history than on the Asia Minor exchange of populations or on the Cypriot situation. The intellectual richness of the work on Palestine owes an immeasurable amount to the indefatigable and decades-long efforts of Edward Said, to the equally steadfast and important work of Ibrahim Abu-Lughod and the late Eqbal Ahmad, to the translation projects of Salma al-Jayyusi, to the outstanding English-language journal *MERIP*, to the individual and collective work of scholars, intellectuals, and activists such as Ella Shohat, Zachary Lockman and Joel Beinin, Janet Gunn, Rashid Khalidi, and Antun Shammus. The list is long and distinguished and it is impossible to do it justice here. But the cases of Cyprus and Asia Minor are less familiar, less often taken up in the United States, and so I devote attention to those historical and cultural instances for their rich possibilities in contributing to the debates on the nation, gender, culture, and citizenship or communal membership. The conjuncture of these three examples allows the construction of a series of suggestions about nationalism and gender, about culture and (a reconceptualized) citizenship that no single example allows. Although nationalisms claim uniqueness and noncomparability, there is no necessary imperative to accept that claim at face value. In fact, it is in their comparability that we begin to understand their specificity—if not "uniqueness."

If the conceptualization of *Wedded to the Land* owes a great deal to scholars, intellectuals, and literary and cultural workers, the specific workings of it owe no less to the generosity of spirit, time, and intellect of the librarians, archivists, and curators of those places that granted me access to their holdings and archives. To the librarians and archivists and workers in Estia Neas Smyrnis in Athens, Greece, and in the Cypriot Press and Information Office and the PLO Cultural Center in Nicosia, Cyprus, I am deeply grateful. In the course of researching *Wedded to the Land,* I came to even more fiercely appreciate the committed and often undervalued work of the keepers of archives and libraries. Sadly enough, the testimonials, documents, photographs, and newspapers that might suggest alternative (and, to some, undesirable or unsavory) accounts of historical events are too often "lost" from state archives precisely because of their challenge to official histories. In a related fashion, controversial or nonhegemonic accounts of history and culture are "lost" from private archives because of the disappearance of state or private funds to ensure the preservation of their now crumbling newspapers and pamphlets or rapidly fading photographs or because of the willful desire of someone with enough power and control to enforce such a "loss."

Such disappearance or willful loss of materials notwithstanding, individual women and men who lived through the historical and cultural events recounted here are also keepers of archives of a different sort—archives of memory. For their generously and sometimes painfully shared memories and stories I am immeasurably grateful. As the introduction suggests, without those stories, *Wedded to the Land* would probably have had a rather different shape. I hope I have been able to do some justice to the suggestions and desires of their memories and experiences. And to have listened not only to what was said but also to what was not or could not be said—or heard.

I am grateful for the financial support of the institutions that have underwritten much of my work over the past few years: the University of Wisconsin–Madison, the Fulbright Foundation, the Institutes for Research in the Humanities at UW Madison and UC Irvine; and to the colleagues and their departments and institutions who have invited me to present versions of these chapters at various stages of development and from whose comments and questions I have learned a great deal. And I have learned no less from the kind and patient support and insightful questions and comments of Ken Wissoker at Duke University Press.

In that vein of helpful comments and questions and in the context of intellectual community, I am most deeply thankful to the graduate and undergraduate students I've had the privilege and pleasure to work with closely over the past years: Amy Brooks, Elyse Crystall, Joy deStefano, Anneka Kmeicik, Helen Leung, Kristin Pitt, Najat Rahman, Jeff Shalan, Kiko Benitez, and Mia Zamora. To those whose names I've inadvertently omitted, my apologies and my gratitude nonetheless. I hope I have been able to do some justice to the suggestions of their questions and experiences.

My colleagues in the Department of Comparative Literature at UW Madison have also been steadfastly supportive, both personally and intellectually. I am grateful for their support and encouragement. So too, my colleagues in other departments have made living and working here during these past years an education, in the best sense of the word, and a pleasure.

Last, but never least, I dedicate this book to Niko, my partner in all things of the past three decades. To my sons, Odysseas and Kyo, my love and gratitude for the lessons they've taught and learned. To my mother-in-law and second mother, Eleni Athanasidi Lodopoubu. To the memory of my father, who would have loved to be a man of books, if he could have. To my mother, who took me to my first libraries. I hope I have been able to do some justice to the suggestions and desires of their memories and experiences. And to have listened not only to what was said but also to what was not or could not be said—or heard.

Wedded to the Land?

Introduction:
Culturing the Nation

A coffin clad with the face of a child
A book
Written on the bowels of a crow
A wild animal advancing, bearing a flower

A boulder
Breathing with the lungs of a madman:

This is it
This is the Twentieth Century.
—Adonis, "Mirror for the
Twentieth Century"[1]

I will tell you something about stories,
[he said]
They aren't just entertainment,
Don't be fooled.
They are all we have, you see,
all we have to fight off
illness and death.

You don't have anything
if you don't have the stories.
—Leslie Marmon Silko, *Ceremony*

Memories of history are born not from
a need to determine the past but from
a need to shape the future.
—Anand Patwardhan[2]

The Lebanese women and their children had left the apartment across the yard. Able to afford a few months' respite in Cyprus—away from the Lebanese civil war (1975–1992), the water shortages and electricity outages, the car bombs and gun battles in the streets—they had now gone back to Lebanon. I had come to know the tall, dark-eyed, younger woman in particular. She would sit on the narrow balcony of their apartment, clutching her hands and looking out over the dusty park next door. She had knocked quietly on my door late one morning to tell me she'd heard me talking to my children while I hung out the clothes. She thought I might be Lebanese. Her next-door neighbor had told her I was writing a book about refugees. She thought I should hear what had happened to her. I did, over coffee or orange juice on mornings when I didn't leave early for the library or one of the archives. And our kids played together, trading their stories of life in the midwestern United States and in Beirut. I thought I had to let her know that I wasn't writing about Lebanon nor even about refugees in particular. She insisted it made no difference. She would visit and tell me about her neighbors and neighborhood in Beirut, her family elsewhere in Lebanon, the other women and children who had come to Cyprus with her. And she would ask about how I lived in the United States, what I was doing in Cyprus, how I came to teach literature, about my family, neighbors, and friends.

Now standing in her place on the balcony was a thin old woman dressed in black. She watched me closely as I hung out the clothes, a little surprised when, after a while, I greeted her in Greek.

—You're from America, aren't you? A teacher, right, who's writing a book?

(Information circulated rather efficiently in the neighborhood among its diverse residents—Lebanese, Palestinians, Cypriots.) And then, after a short pause:

—I have to talk to you.

In a few minutes, she came over carrying a large plastic bag. When I offered her coffee, she smiled and asked for orange juice instead. (Later she admitted with an unabashed laugh that she wasn't sure at first whether I knew how to make Cypriot coffee, so orange juice seemed a safer choice.) She introduced herself as the owner of the flat across the yard, in Nicosia on a five-day "leave of absence" from her enclaved village in the north.[3] I introduced her to my mother-in-law, who had come to spend a couple of months with us in Cyprus. While I got coffee and orange juice, they talked about daughters-in-law, about the effects on younger women of their access to education, and about the lace tablecloth that my mother-in-law was crocheting. As I reentered the room, the old woman called out.

—So, your mother-in-law makes lace, you make books, is that it?

This distinctly pleased my mother-in-law, Eleni. The daughter of a village schoolteacher from northern Greece, she is proud of her six years of formal education.

In a strong Cypriot dialect, the old woman proceeded to describe the school that her sons and daughters had attended in their now enclaved village on the Karpassian peninsula in the Turkish-occupied north of Cyprus. She was in Nicosia to see her daughter and grandchildren and get medication for her husband, who was too ill to make the long bus trip to the south. She rather matter-of-factly catalogued life under Turkish occupation: the harassment and daily indignities, the shortages of basic necessities and inaccessibility of medical care, the isolation and loneliness of being cut off from family and friends who had left or been forced out of their village, the frequent cancellations of their monthly passes to unoccupied Cyprus. With the help of substantial government subsidies for resettling refugees, her children had purchased the apartment across the way for her and her husband. But the old couple had never moved south to the unoccupied half of the capital city. They had had different plans. At this point in her story, tears quietly began to creep down the old woman's wrinkled brown face.

—In the beginning, we old folks thought we would stay in the villages to take care of things, to defend what was ours. Until everything went back to the way it was. It wouldn't be long, we thought. The [Cypriot] government urged us to resettle in the meantime, assured us that there would be a quick resolution by the UN to the "Cyprus problem" and that all refugees would then return to their homes. But [unlike the younger villagers] we didn't have children to send to school, work to take care of. We had our pensions, our gardens with vegetables, and an orange tree or two. So we stayed. We tried to keep things up. And we managed in the beginning. But we were already old to start with and fifteen years have gone by. Now we can barely manage. Me, of course, I'm younger than my husband.

The old woman smiled faintly with a touch of pride.

—Fifteen years ago, we thought . . . we would hold out against the in-vaders. We old folks would be the "front line."

She paused for a moment and smiled again, a little more sadly this time.

—Then we stopped talking so much about everything going back to the way it was. We knew, anyway. And the oldest of us started dying off. We had trouble preparing and burying the dead. It got harder to take care of our houses, of the vegetable gardens that we depended on.

The old woman stopped again and looked at me almost fiercely.

—Are you going to put this in your book? Will you remember? You write that we weren't fooled. We knew. We knew things weren't going back to the way they were before. But we stayed anyway. No matter what the [Cypriot] government said; we told them we would hold out in the north. No matter what the Turkish military authorities threatened; we told them we were old and could cause them no harm, that they had nothing to gain by forcing us out. No matter how much we would rather have been close to our children; we told them we would wait for their return to our village. And we weren't wrong. Or maybe we were. But we weren't fooled. We knew.

She broke off for a moment, wiping her eyes almost angrily. And then she began again, telling us now about her house, her children, her family and covillagers, the things they had and the way they lived before the invasion. Looking often at my empty hands, she punctuated her story with

—Do you understand me? Will you remember what I say?

My mother-in-law, feeling, I think, compelled to defend the absence of some visible recording tools (tape recorder or paper and pencil), reassured the old Cypriot woman that I had a great memory, that I could remember telephone numbers and addresses from years ago. And then, pointing out her own experiences in the Balkan wars, WWII, the Greek civil war, the dictatorship that followed, and the loss of virtually everything that she had known as a young woman, my mother-in-law added that nothing is the way it was before. Old people have only their memories of a better time. At this, the old Cypriot woman straightened up in her chair and answered firmly.

—The memories aren't just ours. We have to think it was a better time. We have to say it was a better time. We have to keep telling the younger ones stories about that better time.

She cast a meaningful look in my direction.

—And maybe it will be that [better time] for them in the future.

With that she drew her plastic bag close and pulled out a bag of fresh-hulled lima beans.

—Now I've told you what I have to say to you. Wouldn't you like some fresh limas? I grew them myself, beans from occupied Cyprus. Two liras a kilo. Here, just look at what fine beans they are.

We laughed; I bought the beans. And she went back to her enclaved village two days later. Though we made arrangements to meet the following month when she hoped to be allowed to return to the south, I never saw her again. Six weeks later her flat was rented out to an old Lebanese couple and their grandchildren.

The old Cypriot woman's story is suggestive testimony: to the simultaneous though not uncontradictory telling of personal and official history; to the crucially gendered matrix of the telling and of its audience; to the utter imbrication of the private (home, family, village) in the public (the political, the state and nation, the Turkish invasion of Cyprus and resistance to it); to the vocal accounts of lived human experience that productively challenge the putative quiet of texts and archives.[4] In the context of sifting through the remnants, textual and otherwise, of nationalism in crisis for traces of alternative ways of defining community, gender, nation, and ethnicity, there are two facets of the old woman's narrative that seem particularly significant. One is her insistence on her own wide-ranging authority in the narrative present in which she tells her story. What seemed most important to her, what she emphasized over and over, was her ability in the narrative present to tell the larger story as well as her own past experiences, and the preferred manner in which she told both. In retelling her narrative, I privilege, as she seemed to do in the telling, her claim to and distinctive style of narrative authority. Of course, her story or, more properly, stor*ies,* were important to her telling. They were set in two past moments separated from one another by the Turkish invasion—a distinctive "before" and "after." That is, life in her village before the invasion, her home and possessions then, her relationships with family and covillagers then *and* life in her now-enclaved village in the occupied north of Cyprus, (the creeping loss of) her home and possessions, her relationships with her family and covillagers, most of whom are now separated from her by death or by exile as refugees in unoccupied Cyprus. But as important as the content of her stories was her strategic construction of narrative authority. It was this authority, the perspective from which she could and did tell her own and the larger stories, that she insisted on most adamantly. In this, she was perhaps more forceful than many of the other women I spoke with—a comment on her age and its privileges as much as anything else. But her insistence was not qualitatively different from theirs. Her narrative authority and strategy included the attempt to carefully and relatively directly implicate her audience in the telling. And this implication of her audience (in this instance, my mother-in-law and I) was not simply an attempt to direct the reception of her narrative but to generate other narratives for which hers might provide a suggestive story and style. She, as many of the other women with whom I spoke, was concerned not just to relate her own story but to question the reasons for, and influence the context of, what she thought might be my retelling of her story.

At first, the conversations over mid-morning or late afternoon coffee seemed simply a gendered part of living in the neighborhood. I welcomed the company, a distraction from the tensions of archival work on sensitive topics. And I was familiar enough with this ritual among women, with the appointed times for coffee, gossip, jokes, and personal and social concerns. My mother-in-law and I were objects of neighborhood "fieldwork" as well, curious transitory members of a neighborhood that was only too familiar with passers-through, refugees, and researchers. Later, I came to think of the occasions of the women's stories as a way to check that what I saw in political and cultural texts were not only figments of desire or imagination. But it became increasingly clear that these were also and simultaneously occasions for other women to speak their piece, "to say what I have to say to you." There was perhaps even a chance that their stories might collectively and individually reach a different audience and effect a change in their circumstances. Their stories did effect a change in my understanding of the project in which I was engaged and of its direction. Their stories and sometimes trust and brief friendship in exchange for coffee (or orange juice) were unabashedly predicated on my privilege as someone who could come and go at will, who could gather stories or read texts and retell them to a different and differently empowered audience. There was less recrimination in their pointed observations about that privilege than a resolute insistence that it be used to convey something of their own determination, resourcefulness in duress, and expectations for change.

My reading or listening and retelling, then, does not "re-present" or substitute for theirs. To the contrary. There are other stories to be told as well. But their narrative strategies suggest that the battle over who gets to tell the story of what happened—and in the telling critically shape the what-happened itself—is a complex and variously waged one. It is one that is, finally, perhaps only provisionally won. In that battle, however apparently decisive its outcome at a given moment, other narratives of what happened do not necessarily or inevitably just fold up and disappear.

They sometimes manage not only to survive at the margins, they even insinuate themselves in the heart of dominant narratives themselves. This possibility is scarcely certain or unwaveringly predictable, either in sociocultural contexts or in more properly textual or literary narratives. But it is nonetheless clearly the case—a case we know even from a careful reading of the apparently less flexible literary narrative—that leaders or narrators, characters or actors, narratees or audiences do not inevitably perform the narrative and their roles within it in precisely the ways that the narrative structure (or authorial intention) would appear to direct. This is the case not only in fictional literary narratives but also in the not-necessarily-literary stories that are part of the dominant narrative of nationalism.[5] In those contexts, the role of the state or dominant political organization or leader as authoritative narrator is constantly challenged. Not just from without—from other, competing "foreign" or "outside" narratives—but from within: from other, competing tellings of (not quite) the same story. The old Cypriot woman's narrative account of her personal and metapersonal histories contradicts the notion that narrative theorizing and potential narrative alteration (and, more arguably, structural transformation) are unavailable to characters or narratees within the narrative. In a more traditional understanding of narrative, that authority resides with the author and/or the narrator. Yet the old Cypriot woman articulated in performance, in her telling, a complexly strategic practice and theory of narrative. She accounted for the nonidentical calls of the Cypriot government, the Turkish occupation forces, her family and covillagers, and for her necessarily nonidentical responses to those calls. She recognized, was called out by, and participated—or was forced to participate—in various narrative accounts of her place in the dominant order of things. And implicated variously in those narratives, she constructed from within more than one position from which to strategically narrate back. From those positions, she reiterates her own agency as partial narrator—not just as victimized character—in a narrative not predominantly of her own making. The apparently incontrovertible and fixed order of a military occupation, a national(ist) government, a village society, or family organization is at least disputed and arguably even recast. A similar effort is exerted or at least attempted in relationship to the future narratives of her audience as well.

And so, I recall her strategic narrative authority here perhaps because she insisted on it—a variant claim to some sort of narrative realism on my part. Or as a dutiful testimony to her efforts to shape a future narrative. But more important, her strategic narrative authority suggests what became overwhelmingly apparent in the more textual and archival focus of rereading nationalism and the stories of the peoples and nation(s) in nationalism. That is that in spite of, or at least simultaneous with, the boundary fixations that specific nationalisms in crisis would call forth, the peoples of the nation often negotiate that nationalism and its boundaries in far more various and inventive ways than they are given credit or apparent narrative license for. The specifics of those negotiations and their implications suggest that, in the consideration of relations between the state and its societies and, more specifically, between culture and the state or between oppositional and dominant cultures or between culture and citizenship, to consider only official or ruling party or governmental or international proclamations, laws, documents, or statements of intent and to read them literally, as statements of fact and unflinching intention, is to forget the ways in which they construct fact, the ways in which they are sometimes desperate attempts to constrain fact. But more crucial, it is also to forget—or ignore—the ways in which the very peoples those proclamations and documents and laws claim to, and undoubtedly *do* partially, represent do not read, live, or theorize them as statements of literal fact.[6] Attention to the ways people narrate the stories in which they are involved is, then, as important as attention to the stories they tell. But the retelling of those stories here (or the attempt at antiliteral readings of official and unofficial stories) do not neatly coincide with either the "original" tellings or readings. More likely, various responses to the question of what is or was happening for Greeks or Cypriots or Palestinians at moments of nationalism in crisis bump against each other, sometimes uneasily, perhaps sometimes in concert.

There is a second suggestion of the old Cypriot woman's strategic narration that I would like to foreground: her assertion of the necessity of telling stories—stories of "a better time," of a different time, in the past—in the hope of a better future. That assertion holds out, with rather distinct urgency in her instance and in the instances of many like her, for the possibility of things being different, of there being something other than the endless repetition of the same in the present. On the one hand, her insistence on her own narrative authority in telling stories claims an agency in the narrative present in retelling narratives that would not seem to grant her license for that authority. On the other hand, the stories of the past (or pasts) and their telling in the present point to, hold out for, a future of something better and different when neither the narrative present nor the stories past would seem to allow that authority either. Here, telling stories is not just a way of constructing an arguably renegade authority in the present or simply of nostalgically remembering a better past. It marks the desire for, the attempt to point at (but not necessarily to directly represent or narrate), a different future. It is an effort to hold a space open for something whose precise contours and contents are not known, perhaps cannot be known.[7] It also marks the desire for what, lacking a better word, we might call confrontation. That is, to resolutely bring to the fore, to get in the face of the audience with, an ignored story and/or narrative perspective on a story and to point out, or create, the implication of the audience in that narrative. Thus, as the old Cypriot woman insisted, not just the narrator and her characters but the narratee, the implied reader, the real reader and listener are variously implicated in the telling.

The more explicit assertion here, then, is about the organization of nationalism as a narrative[8]—not nationalism *and* narratives but nationalism *as* narrative—and about the importance of both the rhetoric and the grammar, or order, which that narrative constructs and exerts, with varying degrees of success. Nationalism—at a given time, in a specific space, and in the name of particular nationally defined and constituted peoples—constructs and professes a narrative of the nation and of its relation to a projected potential or already existing state. In doing this, nationalism lays claim to a privileged narrative perspective on the "nation" (the "people[s]") and thus justifies its own capacity to narrate—to organize and link the diverse elements of—the nation. It is from this often third-person and implicitly omniscient perspective that the claims of nationalism are organized and articulated as a narrative. That is, the story of a national history, of a past usually identified as continuous and persevering, is told as the legitimation of and precedent for the practices of the national narrative present. By the early twentieth century, and especially in the post-WWI period with the crises of earlier experiments with constituting national citizens from diverse populations,[9] the discrete boundaries of nations were presumably marked by the boundaries of a linguistic community. The inhabitants of that common language constituted a national people with rights to self-determination. In fact, self-determination, in spite of its remarkable contradictions in concept and practice, was the key concept of the post-WWI League of Nations.[10]

Whether it is nationalism or a nation conscious of itself as such or conscious of itself through language that is the originary or generative moment is of less relevance here, though this question of origins can clearly be the topic of considerable concern for historians of nationalism.[11] It might well be that the origin is far more diverse and complex than an either/or proposition would suggest, than either the notion that the nation as such constitutes nationalism or that nationalism constitutes the nation (conscious of itself) as such. Identifying an originary moment for nationalism does not necessarily shift the process whereby nationalism narrates, and in the narrating proposes links among diverse and often discontinuous elements or stories. That it does so in the name of a single language and a single community does not allay the frequent historical reality of radical linguistic, cultural, religious, and social diversity on the part of the nation. In that profoundly contradictory process (and scarcely accidentally), nationalism as narrative privileges—indeed *must* privilege—the authority of its own position as a presumably reliable narrator.[12]

National narratives propose and articulate, then, a *rhetoric* of the nation at the same time that they propose and enact a *grammar* of the nation—the "correct" or orderly placement and use of the constituent elements of the nation. The latter—national grammar—suggests the ordering line (*gramme*) as well as the letter and language (*gramma*) of the nation. The *rhetoric* of nationalism as narrative calls out and persuades its audiences, both national (the narratees) and international (the implied audience) of the efficacy and desirability of its terms and of the natural relationship between (the order of) those terms. It appeals not just as the letter and word of national truth and order (as *grammar*) but, with letters and words and images, as persuasion and likely possibility (as *rhetoric*). And, because no rhetoric or grammatical order is ever all-inclusive and utterly effective, the specific workings of national rhetoric and grammar in a given instance also point to the silences of that which is effaced or excised from the national narrative. Or their specific workings suggest that which escapes or refuses to be incorporated into the national narrative.

There is no easy fit or simple relationship between nationalism and the nation(s) or peoples nationalism claims as its own. Though at a given moment, the call of nationalism may have tremendous and broad appeal, and may marshal masses of people in the name of the nation, there is no simple or tidy commensurability between the rhetoric or the grammar of nationalism and the peoples that it calls out and organizes. This incommensurability does not necessarily alter its appeal. In fact, it is often in the concrete interest of people to respond to the call of nationalism as a means to better their conditions and quality of life. But at times of national crises, people's willingness to overlook contradictions and gaps in the nationalist narrative is often severely strained. The very premises on which the call of nationalism is based stand out as impossible or traitorous. In this context, efforts to articulate alternative pasts and to consider alternative futures to the present are powerfully evident. Thus, instead of maintaining or even exacerbating normative positions, crises can generate radical or exceptional insights into social and cultural organization and possibility.

In the spring of 1993, in the aftermath of the Gulf War, with the apparent impasse of the Palestinian intifada, the increasing impoverishment, incarceration, and death of Palestinians in the Occupied Territories, and the crisis in "peace" negotiations, political scientist Fouad Moughrabi gave a public lecture outlining three possible responses to the contemporary critical juncture by Palestinians and their supporters.[13] The "peace" talks could be used as a forum for public relations and education about the Palestinian situation; the "peace" talks could be refused altogether. And both of these possibilities were, in fact, put into practice by different groups of Palestinians. Or, Moughrabi continued, Palestinians could demand the complete annexation by Israel of the Occupied Territories with full and equal rights of Israeli state citizenship for all residents. Moughrabi himself proposed the latter option as the most desirable, with its de facto implication of a unified, democratic (and, by implication, secular or at least multireligious) state of Israel that included both Jews and Palestinians as equals. This latter proposition has not yet been taken up in the policy sphere. Moughrabi's alternative to the "peace" talks might have seemed provocative at the time; it might still seem so now. It was certainly, though, a radical challenge to both the status quo of the "peace" talks and to the status quo of various Israeli and Palestinian nationalisms. For both talks and nationalism(s) were predicated on separate states or at least spaces for separate peoples. Yet, polemical as it might have been, Moughrabi's im/possible proposal was also an astute analysis of and challenge to a moment of intense crisis in a dead-ended process. His proposal is distinctly in keeping with the propositions and challenges made to nationalism in crisis that are the subject of the chapters that follow. Yet if Moughrabi confronts the dominant narratives of nationalism(s) in crisis as an articulate and disciplinarily qualified intellectual (i.e., as a political scientist in a U.S. university), many of the challenges considered here are less those of people disciplinarily concerned with the "science of politics." Instead, they are of witnesses to, objects of, and participants in the crises about which they speak. Their testimonials occupy the cultural and literary fields; they take the form of testimonials proper, newspaper articles, cartoons, short stories, novels, poetry, and films. Yet, these diverse forms are no less disciplined attempts to negotiate dominant narratives of nationalism in which they participate and the boundaries that those dominant narratives draw and seek to maintain.

Such narrative negotiation is contestatory *and* complicit, often simultaneously. If nationalism is articulated as a narrative, the tactical and strategic maneuvers *of* and *within* those narratives and *among* contesting narratives are a significant commentary on the workings of nationalism as it is told, heard, and retold. A crucial part of negotiating nationalism is located in the complexity of this narrative process; in the generic (i.e., of genre) interruption of the narrative; in the construction, deconstruction, and reconstruction of (perhaps only parts of) the national narrative. The rhetorical attempt of nationalism as narrative—perhaps of narrative in general—is to give the impression of coherence, of the legitimate authority of the narrator (however that authority might be construed, even as non- or antiauthoritative), of the "truth" of the story told. And, not least of all, nationalism as narrative attempts to situate its narratees and its implied narrative audience/listener/reader in a particular fashion. Clearly, that attempt is always contradictory, full of slippages and gaps. Therein lies the vulnerability of nationalism as narrative, perhaps of any narrative. But there too, in those moments of narrative slippage and contradiction, lie possibilities of recasting or at least renegotiating the specific order (the "grammar") of nationalism. Those moments or spaces of possibility can be manifest as much in the literary or cultural register as in the self-proclaimed political.

In commonsense understanding, the relationship between nationalism and the political seems apparent, of course, even "natural." But nationalism and culture are no less axiomatic; their intimate relations are, at the turn of the century, again conspicuous. Culture, variously understood and formulated, is privileged by nationalism as a primary mode of iterating and reiterating collective identity, seeming more than occasionally to jostle contentiously against broader and more explicitly political demands for social and economic justice, democratic citizenship, equality, and an open and accessible organizational or state structure. Demands for independence, statehood, sovereignty, or self-determination, though not abandoned, are certainly more skeptically and even cynically invoked than the demand for recognition of distinct cultural integrity. In some ways, in the beginning of the twenty-first century, this retrenchment is unsurprising. Historical memory might be myopic but not *that* myopic. The grand claims to modern, rational (the one typically implying the other) social and political organization made in the name of distinct and independent states for distinct and independent peoples—whether formulated by self-assured European colonial powers at the rivalrous height of their imperial power or by anticolonial peoples struggling for justice and independence against those self-assured European powers—have not generated an un-equivocally more just and equitable world or even more just and equitable *parts* of the world. If, though, the claims of an all-encompassing national-ist politics and state are problematic, the claims of nationalist culture are no less so at the beginning of the twenty-first century.

Yet, the necessary relations between nationalism and culture were no less in the forefront for late-eighteenth- and nineteenth-century western Europe. Culture was presumed to display the distinct and unique charac-ter of a people. It formulated and mobilized a past and its tradition that illustrated, indeed verified, cultural perseverance and continuity. And thereby the unified identity of the nation was articulated. Nationalist claims were legitimized on the edifice of that national culture and its put-ative unified identity. Further, as, for example, Matthew Arnold's un-abashed formulation in *Culture and Anarchy* makes abundantly clear, cul-ture was the guarantor of the authoritative stability of the state and its guardian functionaries. This stabilizing function of national culture is still fiercely debated.[14] Twentieth-century commentators on and historians of nationalism often marshal a similar notion of culture as one of the distinc-tive elements on which nationalism bases its claims and its appeals.

But there is an even more fundamental principle on which nationalism depends, one to which, until recently, not as much attention has been paid. That is the gendered construction of the national citizen—and, by extension, of the noncitizen—and of his or her sexuality. The thoughtful insights of George Mosse's *Nationalism and Sexuality* demonstrate the importance of the regimentation of the gendered body, of homosociality, of fierce gender divides in nationalism—in Mosse's later work, most specifi-cally in the case of German nationalism. No subsidiary category or second-ary concern of nationalism, particular and specific boundaries of gender and sexuality are, rather, its sine qua non. They are fundamental to its very emergence and formulation.[15] So, for example, to speak of "the woman question" in nationalism is, after a fashion, to miss the point.[16] The ques-tion of woman—and of women, and of men—is the foundation of national-ism. The very basic rhetorical and organizational principles of the nation are tropes for and expressions of gendered power. They familiarly include rhetorical notions of, and sociopolitical organization based on, a homoso-cial community of heterosexual men (who protect women, children, and land from foreign threat); the primary identification and allegiance of indi-vidual (male) citizens who congregate in the public sphere to rally, lobby, and legislate for the continued (often near-fictive) sequestering of a private sphere where women, children, sexuality, and family reside; the genesis of the nation-state as the (masculine) principle that brings regulatory order to the undisciplined and excessive (feminized) masses. When formal citizenship and suffrage for women and other previously excluded peoples are added to this scheme of things, the fundamentally gendered character of the nation and the nation-state still remains substantially unchanged. To borrow the trenchant image of James Joyce's *Portrait of the Artist as a Young Man,* the struggle to sit at the (national) refectory table does not thereby shift the structural or organizational principles that govern at that table or that established that table as the site of power in the first place. It is in this context that the often radical demands of women and minority peoples—and some majority peoples—within an already established or an emerging state are so frequently overwhelmed, devalued, and ultimately foreclosed by a claim to "exigency." This is not at all to suggest that formal demands for equality, recognition of civil rights, and equal citizenship status be relinquished or abandoned. But the simultaneous need for a structural reorganization of the relationship between the state and its citizens and noncitizen residents and between and among those citizens and noncitizen residents is forgotten or ignored at fearful cost.[17]

If this emphasis on gender and culture as fundamental elements of nationalism seems to draw the outlines of nationalism with a broad brush, yet in each specific historical and cultural instance taken up in the chapters that follow, there are no contradictions of this outline by the rhetoric or the grammar of a particular nationalism in crisis or by responses to that crisis. There are particular cultural and historical conditions that inflect the shape and contents of that outline, but it remains recognizably consistent. The three examples that follow of crises of nationalism and of cultural responses to crisis challenge and sometimes retell the dominant boundaries of the nation. Nationalism as narrative and its crisis, which these responses articulate and reconceive, retell in often radically suggestive ways the very definitions and ground rules of the nation and of those who claim to speak for and from the nation. They reconstitute, with a difference that is often ignored in official political discourse, boundaries and the rules for crossing them in ways that are perhaps unimaginable and (arguably) impossible. They insist on alternative visions of the "larger picture" and policy issues in that "larger picture" that are too often ignored in the insistently antiofficial and oppositional objects of much cultural criticism.

There may be numerous variations on the theme, but a general structural pattern in the claims of nationalism(s) is not difficult to distinguish. In the name of a usually "continuous" historical past, a usually linguistically or ethnically "unified" cultural present, and, at least rhetorically, a usually sovereign, democratic, equal, or in any event simply better future, the priority of a particular group of people over a particular geographic space is declared. Allegiance on the part of that particular group of people is directed toward their national community, its national space, its national history, and its national structural organization. Thus, nationalism seeks to define and bound the nation, to construct and maintain the boundaries and internal organization of the national. And, most often, the structural organization of the national community is designated a "nation-state." The always fiercely loaded and often coercive force of the hyphen that professes to link "nation" and "state" notwithstanding, (national) history and (national) culture legitimize—in fact, demand—not only the (national) associations of (national) people but their allegiance to the (national) state. This directive of allegiance claims its own call as superior to all other allegiances. Its boundaries, especially in times of national crisis, are supposed to be impermeable. Any other allegiance is tantamount to treason. (This consuming anxiety of national "structural organization" or the state is distinctly apparent in the most often immediate declaration of sedition, alien, and censorship laws after the "success" of national struggles.)

It is from within this general structural pattern of the claims of nationalism as narrative that each of the three chapters that follow locates predominant concerns and tropes of three distinct cultures and moments in the eastern Mediterranean as responses to nationalism in crisis in the (1922) Greek, (1974) Cypriot, and (1982) Palestinian instances. The workings of nationalism, culture(s), and narrative—and often the implicit critique of the former by specific instances of the latter—are most apparent precisely in moments of crisis rather than in the presumably more expansive and lenient culture of national prosperity and stability. There would seem to be an urgent necessity in a state of siege (whether literal or metaphorical) for reformulating the nation, its narratives, and its interruptions: an urgent necessity for remapping and containing the boundaries of class, gender, and ethnicity. For the perhaps once apparently decisive and incontrovertible boundaries are breached. To the questions of such national and cultural reconfiguration under challenge, there can be no exhaustive answers. But then, exhaustive answers—a representational catalog—are scarcely the point. Rather, it is to look again after what was foreclosed, what was impossible but just barely visible or barely audible, in the cultural configurations of and response to those moments of crisis.

Traces persist of the foreclosed, the impossible, the barely seen or heard in official political and governmental documents and decrees, popular

and elite cultural texts, songs, poetry, newspaper articles, public monu-
ments and buildings at and around each moment of crisis. Testimonials by
and informal interviews with refugees, exiles, and public officials are occasionally included as well. In this process, attention is directed toward
the very contradictions of nationalism and of cultural response to its
crises, the gaps between nationalism's rhetoric and its grammar. For it is
there that we can perhaps dimly make out other imaginings and experiences of the (extra)national, there in the reenactment of the fierce struggles
over the constitution and maintenance of the boundaries of national communities. And it is there that we might consider what is, more properly,
their simultaneous necessity and impossibility. Nationalism—as it attempts to map and contain the constituent elements of the nation—is neither demonic force nor redemptive paradigm. But rather, nationalism's
critical conclusion may well be precisely the impossibility of national
community. Rather than seeking to dispense with or salvage the nationalist project, the chapters that follow seek to articulate a critical commentary
on nationalism in general and on specific attempts at alternatives to nationalism in particular. The three instances of Greek, Cypriot, and Palestinian society are historically specific but not utterly unique; they each
foreground particular critical elements of the national project and of the
pivotal role of culture both popular and literary in that project. And so
chapters 1 through 3 take up in turn the complex formations of notions
and practices of "home," of the (inviolable) woman as (sovereign) nation,
and of the multivalent construction of insides and outsides in the national
project. Although each of the three instances of nationalism in crisis discussed here are at least partially a result of external threat or foreign invasion, the crucial role of intracommunal strife—if not explicitly of civil
war—is an equally important factor and is unquestionably exacerbated by
foreign assault.

Chapter 1 looks at the radical displacement, yet ultimately aggressively
pursued "assimilation," of Asia Minor refugees sent "home" to Greece in a
forced exchange of populations between Greece and the newly established
Republic of Turkey. The previous everyday negotiations of Asia Minor
Greeks (and Armenians and Jews) across borders—whether national, religious, ethnic, class, or racial—are radically challenged, forcibly terminated, and of painful necessity reshaped by the Asia Minor Catastrophe
and its aftermath. The extremes of the displacement of Asia Minor Greeks
(and Armenians and some Jews) at "home" call sharply into question the
notion of "home" itself, as they do the enforcement of the putative ethnic
homogeneity of nations—what we now call "ethnic cleansing."

Chapter 2 takes up the use of the body of woman as figure for the nation in the case of the right-wing Cypriot coup and the Turkish invasion of the island that immediately followed. In that instance, the prevalent trope of the nation raped had a rather grim literal significance. Yet the popular, if not official, representations of the sovereign national (and usually female) body violated suggest rather startling redefinitions of the gendered nation and turn the tables on the analogic construction of national violation (foreign invasion) as bodily violation (rape).

The third chapter takes up the loaded construction of national insides and outsides in the absence of internationally recognized national territory. The Palestinian and PLO expulsion from Beirut after the Israeli invasion in the summer of 1982 necessitated (again) a rethinking of the nation, its ground, and the residents on that ground. Here again the issues of ethnic or cultural or linguistic homogeneity and the gendering of the nation are recast, though differently. And the potential threat and challenge of regendering the nation and of redefining the boundaries of the nation itself are most acutely registered.

Chapter 4 draws from the specifics of the previous chapters in a challenge to the cultural and political notions and practices of "citizenship" and in an attempt to figure the traces of other possibilities suggested by the configurations of Greek, Cypriot, and Palestinian cultural responses to nationalism in crisis.

In certain ways, between the titular markers of this introduction (culture) and chapter 4 (citizenship) are two distinct but related aspects of the question of nationalism. Between them are enclosed three historical moments and instances of nationalism in crisis, each one gathered around different cultural and political tropes but related nonetheless in their mapping of a national terrain for which purity is sovereignty, rape is the violation of sovereignty, and consummation is possession of pure and sovereign land. Between the two poles of culture and citizenship—the one emphasizing the cultural that defines, or at least seeks to define, a sociocultural community of members, the other emphasizing the political rights possessed by members of a political community regardless of their cultural communities—are figured many of the contradictions, possibilities, and silences of nationalism.

1 National Homongeneity and Population Exchanges: Who Belongs Where? —Greece 1922

A meaning only reveals its depths once
it has encountered and come into contact
with another, foreign meaning; they
engage in a kind of dialogue, which
surmounts the closedness and one-sidedness
of these particular meanings,
these particular cultures.
—M. M. Bakhtin, *Speech Genres*

My maimed generation,
. . . we've been erased from the map
"Sakatameni mou genia"

We've endured scorn, injustice and slaughter;
take with you whatever we love
and let's leave for other places,
refugees wherever we go.
"Chronia perifronimena"

The metal poles of the bus stop awning were hot and gritty to the touch, the sunlight on the pavement blinding. The bus bound for the center of Athens worked its laborious way up the incline toward the plaza where a small knot of people stood waiting. It was late; everyone was returning home at midday; the bus would be crowded. The piles of dusty newspapers, books, and pamphlets in the shadowy interior of the archival library spoke of a fierce battle over the meaning and consequences of the "Asia Minor Catastrophe."[1] But for the still noticeable difference in accents and idiomatic expressions in the "refugee district" of Nea Smyrni in Athens, that battle seemed to fade in the bright midday light of late summer as everyone hurried home. Yet, as the alternately heated and resigned discussions of the old men who spent their mornings at the second-floor coffee bar of the Estia Neas Smyrnis (the Nea Smyrna Center) suggested, it was a battle never quite over, never quite forgotten. Nonetheless, official history was to claim for the forced exchange of populations between Greece and Turkey in 1923 that was the end result of the Asia Minor Catastrophe the magnificent achievement of national homogeneity. But for the Greek mainland and for the Asia Minor refugees in the aftermath of the catastrophe, that ethnoreligious cum national homogeneity was still a violently wrought utopian—or dystopian—project. And the conflictual and still potentially unsettling implications of that project are visible not only in the dusty books and pamphlets and the old records of the Estia Neas Smyrnis's archives.

Above and just to the right of the main entrance to the Estia Neas Smyrnis, the figures of two women are fixed in a mural that is almost hidden in the upper reaches of the columned portico. One, in Greek village dress, her head covered with a scarf, clutches a small child in her arms as she looks back at a man who, also in village dress, kneels to load a cannon. A young girl-child clings to the woman's skirts, also looking back at the man. To the right of the woman and two children and with her back to them (and her side to us), is a second and apparently younger woman, with uncovered head, wearing a shapeless shift and clutching her empty (childless) arms to her chest; she sits on a boulder staring out across an expanse of water, the Aegean, at Smyrna in flames.

The Estia Neas Smyrni mural: Smyrna in flames

In this visual account, Greek irredentism—the *megali idea* or "great idea," originating in the aftermath of the fall of the Byzantine Empire in 1453—and its demise are marked, if passively, by and on the figures of these two women. The first woman and her children are witness to the military preparations of the man with his cannon; the second is witness to one of the grim results of such military action: the Asia Minor Catastrophe. In fact, the man loading a cannon and the mounted horseman to his left are a visual gloss on at least two moments of military action in modern Greek history: the 1821 War for Independence against the Ottoman Empire and the 1919–1922 Greco-Turkish War. The figures of the watchful young mother and her children mark the transition from one military action to the other. But, for the mural that runs the extent of the entrance portico of the Estia Neas Smyrnis as for "the great idea" itself, it is the Byzantine Empire that is a privileged, originary moment. That moment is emphasized visually in its location directly above the formal main entrance to the building—and prior to the figures of the two women.[2] Thus, with the Byzantine Empire as a focal point and between its two historically consequent poles—"the great idea" and its denouement in the Asia Minor Catastrophe of 1922—is constructed the national space that is the focus of this chapter, that of the Asia Minor refugees and, retrospectively at least, of post-1922 Greece as a whole.

The Estia Neas Smyrnis itself is generated by the same two moments in diaspora and mainland Greek history, "the great idea" and the Asia Minor Catastrophe. The cultural center was established by (the Onassis family), for, and as a tribute to, the Greeks of Asia Minor, refugees in Greece as a result of the Greco-Turkish War. Not surprisingly, the mural on the building's façade includes the prehistory that generated the building itself as it generated the district in which the Center is situated. For Nea Smyrni

(New Smyrna) is not only a district of Athens, one of many in which the Asia Minor refugees were settled after 1922. It is also a citation of "old Smyrna," the coastal city of Smyrna/Izmir in present-day Turkey. But that old Smyrna, as the mural itself illustrates, is irrevocably distant and beyond reach, consumed in flames under the mournful gaze of the young refugee woman on the opposite shore of mainland Greece.

The mural of the Estia Neas Smyrnis as it renders the cultural configuration of the Asia Minor Catastrophe and of its aftermath for mainland Greece, for its indigenous citizens, and for the refugees who resettled there is a suggestive point of departure for the reconsideration of this particular historical moment of nationalism in crisis and for a more general national concern with assigning the people(s) of the nation to designated spaces and containing them therein. In the mural's ambiguous configuration of the national narrative, the figures of the two women are crucial markers for decisive moments in that narrative. Their figures are positioned as boundary markers in a national project of impossible containment. The situation of their bodies as boundary suggests, even invokes, the bodies of women as precisely that which will be overrun, violated, conquered. It is the literal and metaphoric functions of such gendered figures and the ways they crucially inform the shape and redirection of Greek national narratives on which I focus here. For the workings and aftermath of the Asia Minor Catastrophe are a suggestive elaboration of the problematic configuration of nation, gender, and culture outlined in more general terms in the introduction. That catastrophe and its aftermath exemplify the violence wrought in the name of national "belonging," the simultaneous coercion and persuasion in the redefinition and reassertion of the national project. It is perhaps an understatement to refer to it as the construction of a "fearful symmetry." But it is equally, in the very social and cultural disjunctures of nationalism in crisis, in the fierce contradictions of that fearful symmetry that critical perspectives on and perhaps even alternatives to the national project might be discernible.

The landing of Greek troops in Smyrna on 15 May 1919 that launched the latter-day attempt at coercive military performance of "the great idea" was the occasion of a triumphant proclamation by the prime minister of Greece at the time, Eleftherios Venizelos. Perhaps even then, and certainly in retrospect, that proclamation suggests some of the fierce contradictions and ambiguities that underlie the "Asia Minor expedition" (*e mikrasiatiki ekstratia*) and the nationalist ideological configuration that propelled it. Eyewitness accounts of the reading of Venizelos's proclamation (he himself was not present) tell of flower-strewn streets, rosewater in the air, tearful eyes, waving Greek flags. But, persuasive and powerful as Venizelos's statement was, it equally maps the crucial and ominous problems of official Greek politics of the day.

The opening of Venizelos's proclamation—"The fullness [or, fulfillment] of time has arrived"—resonates with biblical reference. In addition, and more to the immediate political point, Venizelos's opening line invokes "the great idea," itself a notion fraught with largely Byzantine images of Christian resurrection and salvation. The "great idea" was, more exactly, the quasi-mythological proposition that the lands and (Christian or Greek Orthodox) people of the Byzantine Empire, defeated by the Ottomans with the capture of the Byzantine capital of Constantinople in 1453, would one day, in the "fullness of time," be "redeemed." Various associated folk stories and popular prophetic and apocalyptic beliefs told of divine intervention that would liberate the Orthodox/Christian community from Ottoman rule.[3] But if the *megali idea* had been a variously foregrounded element of popular culture from the fifteenth to the nineteenth century, subsequent to the success of the Greek War of Independence against the Ottoman Empire (1821–1828), "the great idea" was reconstructed as state policy of the newly formed Greek kingdom. From a rallying cry for national unity against Ottoman rule,[4] it became the justification for the expansionist claims of the new Greek state. In the Greek National Assembly of 1844, on 15 January, Yiannis Kolletis effectively argued for "the great idea"—the term itself, though not the sentiment, one he purportedly coined—as official Greek government policy.[5] Subsequently, "the great idea" became an increasingly contentious component of Greek political life. It is an irony of sorts[6] that, in the first two decades of the twentieth century, the expansionist aims of "the great idea" became increasingly the policy of the cosmopolitan, "liberal" politician Eleftherios Venizelos, the hero of the Cretan revolution against the Ottoman Empire, and his followers. The conservative royalist opposition insisted on a "small but honorable" Greece.

Apart from the mainland, though the Greeks of Asia Minor presumably consented to the goals of and their own incorporation into "the great idea," that consent was scarcely unambiguous or unremarked upon. The newspapers and journals of the Greek communities under Ottoman rule are full of debates about "the great idea" as (mainland) Greek state policy and its implications for Greeks of Asia Minor. But since at least the first decade of the twentieth century, the calculated and increasingly fierce policies directed against resident minority communities in the Ottoman Empire had their inevitable effect. Newspapers debated the wisdom and implications of "the great idea" for the Greeks, and Christians in general, of Asia Minor. But they also carried accounts of the forced deportations inland and the ethnic killings that were ever more frequent as the Ottoman rulers attempted to ensure their territorial control, their status as a modern state, and to cooperate with the advice, methods, and aims of the Germans in the region. In that context, the rhetorical and policy goal of the "redemption" of the land and (Greek) peoples of Asia Minor cast the Greeks of Asia Minor as the putative object of the irredentist scheme. By September 1922, however, and even earlier for some, for the Greeks of the mainland and the Asia Minor Greeks-become-refugees, the utter failure if not the inherent contradictions of "the great idea" was unavoidable. In the impoverished and constricted mainland Greek state, the Asia Minor Greeks now found themselves the objects of no little hostility and discrimination from those mainland Greeks who were presumably their ethnic and religious brothers. The rhetoric of an expansionist nationalism had ingloriously collapsed in on itself. And the first objects of that collapse were those who, only months earlier, had been the objects of that expansionist "redemption" itself.

It is in this context that the Asia Minor Greeks-turned-refugees in their "homeland" resituated themselves rhetorically and culturally, if not socially, in relation to the hegemony of the mainland Greek state. From within the post-1922 fiasco of "the great idea" and its irredentist scheme, and on the very terrain of that fiasco, the popular and literary culture of the Asia Minor refugees began to formulate a redefinition of the refugee as national—that is, Greek—subject. As the mural of the Estia Neas Smyrnis bears witness, that redefinition circles back around the frozen history of 1453 that is the pretext for "the great idea" to an ancient Ionian past.

In reiterating an ancient rather than a Byzantine or even Christian genealogy, refugee culture constructs a citizen-subject position for its constituents within the mainland Greek state as the "true"—though extraterritorial—historical origins of that state. It asserts itself and the refugees who embody it as the newly restored link with the classical Greek past, not coincidentally the same classical past that was so valorized by the Western European "great powers." To appreciate the implications of that gesture, we might circle back ourselves for a moment to the period before the defeat of the Greek bid for "redemption" of lost lands, to the moment when "the fullness of time" seemed to some at hand.

On 14 May 1919, amidst great nationalist fanfare and heady proclamations about "redeeming" the Byzantine Empire, a Greek army of twenty thousand men landed at the port city of Smyrna in Asia Minor under the protection of Allied warships. Their goal, specified by the Allied Peace Conference, was to "prevent the slaughter of the Christian population of Asia Minor." But of equal if not greater significance, according to Venizelo's proclamation of occupation, the Greek Army was to "ensure order" or, though this is nowhere stated explicitly in Venizelos's proclamation, to contain the rising Turkish national liberation movement and Italian expansionist claims in the region. For their services, the Greek state would be granted interim control of the Smyrna region and, potentially, further permanent territory by the Allies. The unabashed irredentism of Greece's ruling liberal politicians and their fervent desire to be a part, even if only a small part, of the imperial club of Europe appeared to be on the verge of consummation.[7]

The decision to send Greek troops to the west coast of Asia Minor, though debated variously for many months, had been taken in much haste by the Great Powers—England, France, and the United States—and Greece. On 6 May 1919, scarcely two weeks prior to the actual landing of Greek troops, the so-called Council of Four met and reached their agreement. Subsequent to the 6 May decision, England's Lloyd George repeatedly urged Greece to invade immediately, before Italy, excluded from the Council of Four's agreement and with its own interests and claims in the region, discovered exactly what was afoot. But in addition to the Italian threat, there was some unease that France and the United States, suspicious of British plans for dominance in the Middle East, might waver in their support for the Greek invasion. In retrospect, such machinations seem unsurprising; in the first decades of the twentieth century, Greece's maneuver—a small and peripheral country invading another on behalf of the major imperial powers—was unwittingly paradigmatic.

Clearly, the Greco-Turkish War of 1919–1922 and the catastrophe in which it culminated were not simply the result of a small regional war between two minor powers but had distinctly wider causes, implications, and goals.[8] Even before World War I had officially ended in November 1918, France and England signed an agreement dividing between them the vast oil-rich territories of the Ottoman Empire in the Middle East and North Africa. At the same time in Asia Minor itself—in response to the growing misery of the countryside, the increasing political persecution by the Ottoman state of both the urban and the rural populations, and the imperialist schemes that Europe was implementing—a Turkish popular movement arose in opposition both to Ottoman rule and to European designs on the region. Leadership of the movement was quickly assumed by the young, educated, urban bourgeoisie, of whom one of the most able was Mustapha Kemal. Within days after the Greek occupying army landed in Smyrna and began its march inland, Kemal assumed control of the movement and began to organize its resistance to the invasion.

Greece's military adventurism in Asia Minor on behalf of its own irredentism and British imperialism was, in virtually every way, ill-conceived and ill-prepared. The Asia Minor expedition and especially its fateful expansion inland was also rather conspicuously unnecessary. Greece had been fighting since the Balkan Wars of 1912 and had already gained substantial territory as a result of that conflict and of WWI. What were the benefits, then, of an invasion and occupation of Asia Minor: European, particularly British, favor; the liberation of oppressed religious minorities (especially the Greek Orthodox community); still more territory, as the gains of the Treaty of Sèvres (August 1920) confirm; and, most especially, direct access to the substantial wealth of Asia Minor Greeks and what appeared to be a way of solving internal economic (and political) conflicts of mainland Greece through expansion.

Greek (and European) claims in Asia Minor were at least rhetorically based on the rescue of besieged Christian populations. For prior to and during WWI, under the experienced supervision of German military advisors, the Ottoman Empire had forcibly moved inland large numbers of the Christian populations of coastal regions: Bulgarians, Armenians, Greeks, and other Levantines. The brutal massacres of the Bulgarian and especially the Armenian populations of Asia Minor in the late nineteenth and early twentieth centuries were a grisly enough indication of other forms of "demographic control" in which the Ottoman Empire was willing and able to engage. But, by 1919, the Ottoman Empire had been for the most part dismantled and had signed a series of peace treaties with the Allied Powers. Who, then, was protecting whom in 1919? And from what? Though Eleftherios Venizelos's proclamation to the Asia Minor Greeks on the landing of mainland Greek troops in Smyrna does not directly answer these questions, in their context it is a telling document.

Venizelos's proclamation begins with that ringing messianic pronouncement already cited: "The fullness of time has arrived. Greece has been summoned by the Peace Conference to occupy Smyrna so as to ensure order. The Greek community must recognize the decision, because in the consciousness [*suneithisi*] of the leaders of the conference, it is decided that Smyrna should be united with Greece."[9] The implicit irony of an occupying army dispatched by a Peace Conference was no doubt unintentional on Venizelos's part. But the characterization of the agreement among the United States, England, France, and Greece as one emanating from a Peace Conference that "summons" Greece to occupy Asia Minor is hardly coincidental. The entirety of the Greek invasion and occupation of Asia Minor would seem, by Venizelos's own account, to hang on very slender threads.[10] His proclamation justifies the decision taken by the conference as based on their awareness or inner sentiments (*suneithisi*) that Smyrna should be united with Greece. Yet the predication of a military invasion and occupation on an attributed "awareness" seems a rather slight and certainly volatile foundation for such serious action. Even more suggestively, Venizelos bases his narrative authority here on the implicit situation of himself as the reader-interpreter of Great Power intentions or "inner sentiments" and on his own self-appointed role as medium for those intentions. Venizelos presumes to know the "consciousness" of the Peace Conference leaders and the intentions of that consciousness. Only arguably at the time, but certainly in retrospect, the unwitting aptness of Venizelos's characterization of the implicit instability of Great Power intentions foreshadows the denouement of the Asia Minor expedition.

But in the spring of 1919, the possibilities of defeat apparently seemed distant.[11] The nationalist rhetoric of Venizelos's proclamation was paradigmatically sweeping. What I have called the grammar—or order—that his appeal suggested was enticing. And essential to both the constitutive rhetoric and grammar of Venizelos's proclamation is a striking textual reordering of historical time. That which once was (the glory and territory of the Byzantine Empire) will be again: "The fulfillment of time has arrived." But its arrival is marked by a curiously conflated temporal logic. A military invasion based on a contemporary Peace Conference is the means to restore a Byzantine "promise" that cites classical notions in classical language of "equality" (*isotita*) and "justice" (*dikaiosyne*). And this historical conflation will, as the folk legends that flourished after the Ottoman conquest of Constantinople promised, resurrect time.

Venizelos's proclamation explicitly designates this "fullness of time" as for the "homogeneity" (*omogeneis*) of those of Greek descent. And this Greek homogenity is differentially juxtaposed to the "general population" (*plithismos*). There is a curiously repetitive exhortation concerning the appropriate responses on the part of the Greek Asia Minor audience to other audiences for Venizelos's proclamation and the Greek invasion. In fact, this exhortative narrative constitution of audience response dominates the rest of Venizelos's proclamation:

Remaining until the Balkan Wars enslaved by this [same Ottoman] yoke, I well understand the feelings of joy that must today fill the hearts of the Greeks of Asia Minor.

I do not wish to hinder the expression of these feelings. But I am certain that their expression will not include either hostility or contempt towards anyone of the cohabitant population [*ton sunoikon tou plithismou*]. To the contrary, let the expression of this overwhelming joy be accompanied by an expression of brotherly affection towards the cohabitant population. Let them understand that we are not celebrating the overthrow of one yoke to substitute for it another domination of our own to the detriment of others. But that Greek freedom will bring to all, without regard to race or religion, equality and justice [*tin isotita kai tin dikaiosuni*]. Inspiring confidence in all of the cohabitant population concerning this, we not only remain faithful to our own ethnic/national foundation[s] but we also render excellent service to higher ethnic/national interests. Particular care must be shown to the Italian element [*stoixeion*]. Do not ignore [the fact] that Italy agreed to the Greek occupation of Smyrna with the rest of the Allies. I know that my appeal to Greek Asia Minor is not in vain and I hope, as soon as possible, to be able to visit her, [as] the bearer of the Testament/the Good News [*Evangeliou*] of this ethnic/national restoration.

Venizelos's proclamation is, in many ways, a masterpiece of expansive nationalist rhetoric—its language grandly messianic, its focus distinctly myopic. The entire proclamation is framed by religious reference. The "fullness of time" in the opening line culminates in Venizelos's closing assertion of himself as the bearer of the ethnic/national "Good News" of new life (*komistis Evangeliou ethnikis di'autin apokatastaseos*). Allusion to the Old Testament opens the proclamation of occupation; direct reference to the New Testament closes it. And within this messianic biblical frame, the historic time of the classical Greek past, of the Byzantine Empire, of modern Greek nationhood are all implicated and ordered. Historical time is made content for, is bounded by, the frame of messianic time.

Within this messianic frame, two additional markers around which rhetorical meaning coagulates are significant. One is linguistically defined, that is, in the nondifferentiation in Greek between "ethnic" and "national." Both are *ethnikos*. One of the favorite hypotheses of modern European nationalist definitions of the nation was precisely that the "ethnic" *was* the "national." That conflation and the linguistic nondistinction between the two terms in Greek served a particularly useful function in

Greece's irredentist claims in Asia Minor. For the Asia Minor Greeks were claimed by mainland Greece as "ethnic" Greeks and therefore as "national" brothers. The elision of ethnicity into nationality serves to obscure the possibility—in fact, the overwhelming likelihood—of the noncoincidence of the two. The Cypriot and the Palestinian crises discussed in subsequent chapters will reiterate this possibility. For, though the conflation of the two terms is peculiar to the Greek language, the elision of the ethnic and the national most certainly is not.[12]

The second marker in Venizelos's proclamation has less to do with the linguistic structure of Greek than with the rhetoric and (almost ominously in retrospect) the "order" of his appeal itself. Although reference to the "cohabitant population" occurs three times in fewer than a dozen lines and the Italians are mentioned in particular, there is not a single mention of those who made up the vast majority of the cohabitant population of Asia Minor: the Turks. The repeated insistence on "orderly" relations with the cohabitant population is striking. And yet it is the Turkish cohabitant population, as much as if not more than the Italians, who are the crucial challenge to the mainland Greek occupation of Smyrna. And it is they with whom the Asia Minor Greeks had variously cohabited for centuries. This absent reference is even more pronounced in the constant and nervous insistence of the proclamation on the proper behavior of the Asia Minor Greeks. Here, it is not just the rhetoric and grammar of Venizelos's proclamation but also its silence—what is not articulated but compelling in its absence—that is critical.

In fact, however, the nervous exhortations about orderly behavior toward the cohabitant population of Venizelos's proclamation proved more than warranted. The British historian Richard Clogg notes: "In an ominous presentiment of future trouble, the landings [of Greek troops in Smyrna] were marked by Greek atrocities, with some 350 Turks being killed or wounded in fighting with Greek troops. Despite the ruthless punishment of the Greek culprits and the arrival a few days later of the Greek high commissioner, Aristeides Stergiadis, an austere disciplinarian with a genuine commitment to the even-handed treatment of Greeks and Turks, the damage had been done.[13] Nikos Psiroukis, in *The Asia Minor Catastrophe,* is even more adamant about the character and results of the Greek army's occupation of Smyrna: "From the first day of the appearance of Greek troops in Smyrna there were grave disturbances and outbreaks of such seriousness that the very next day extraordinary court martials were convened. The first death sentences were delivered to two Greeks, a soldier and a civilian of Smyrna. The sentences were carried out on the same day.

Both of the executed men were found guilty of serious and violent crimes" (115). The rhetorical benevolence, then, of "Greek freedom," which was to fulfill its "higher ethnonationalist interests" and "foundations" in convincing the "cohabitant residents" of Asia Minor of its widespread applicability, is predicated on silence about the one crucial community against which the order of that putative benevolence will be directed: the Turkish community.

Three years after Venizelos's proclamation and the invasion and occupation of Asia Minor, however, "Greek freedom" was as problematic for the Greeks of Asia Minor as it had been and remained for the Turkish population. For the Greeks of the mainland Greek state, by the elections of 1920 that removed Venizelos and his liberal government from power, the invasion and occupation of Asia Minor had grown too costly. It is not now nearly as clear as some historians of the time maintained that the resounding defeat of Venizelos in those elections was an indication of the backwardness and conservatism of the mainland Greeks in overturning a "liberal" European-style government and returning a conservative monarchy to power. It is equally possible that, after eight years of continuous fighting from the inception of the Balkan Wars in 1912 through the end of WWI, the results of the 1920 elections were also, and perhaps more crucially, a battle-weary refusal of further fighting in general and of the continuation of the war in Asia Minor in particular.[14] For the monarchists ran against Venizelos on a platform of the immediate return of Greek troops from Asia Minor and an end to the war. Once elected, however, and in spite of their election promises, the royalist government continued to follow the same course mapped by Venizelos. They even recklessly exceeded that course in their further (and tremendously overextended) expansion into the mountainous interior of Turkey. The promised withdrawal of Greek troops from Asia Minor would only occur some ten months later with their utter rout by the Turkish popular movement and the fiery destruction of the Greek, Armenian, and European quarters of Smyrna. The Asia Minor Expedition of May 1919 became, without much hyperbole, the Asia Minor Catastrophe of August 1922.

The outcome of this series of events was, on the one hand, the further carving up of the oil-rich Middle Eastern territories of the former Ottoman Empire into protectorates, mandates, and spheres of influence by England, France, the United States, and, nominally, Italy. And the popular Turkish forces, under the leadership of Kemal Ataturk, gained control of what was shortly afterward proclaimed the Republic of Turkey. Further, in January

1923 an agreement that became a convention to the Treaty of Lausanne (in July 1923) mandated something of a test case in modern political history: the forcible exchange of populations, based on religious affiliation, between Greece and the new Turkish state. Thus, the Republic of Turkey was established and the state of Greece redefined with, for the most part, religiously and/or ethnically "homogeneous" populations. One and a half million Christians from Asia Minor, largely ethnic Greeks but including other ethnic minorities as well, were "returned" to Greece.[15] Equally, some eight hundred thousand Muslims were "returned" to either Turkey or one of the Balkan states (particularly Bulgaria).

The Lausanne Treaty and its conventions, then, might seem a high point of sorts for the preferred self-image of the modern nation-state as guardian of national homogeneity and ethnic, religious, and linguistic purity.[16] But in the Greek nationalist scheme of things,[17] that treaty is also and ironically a textual marker of the forcible contraction of an imperial and multiethnic national self-definition to a putatively homogeneous, pure one. That homogeneous purity was certainly the rhetorical basis for the forced exchange of populations. But here too, even in strictly textual terms, there is an additional irony. For it was more religion than ethnic or linguistic affiliation that formed its textual basis.

The opening paragraphs of the Lausanne Convention, with their slippage from one category of identification to another, are an apt reminder of the confusion of ethnic, religious, linguistic, and political citizenship that underlies the attempt to forcibly (construct and) exchange populations of "the same." The initial reference (Article 1 of the Convention) seems definitive: "There shall take place a compulsory exchange of Turkish nationals of the Greek Orthodox religion established in Turkish territory, and of Greek nationals of the Moslem religion established in Greek territory."[18] But five lines later (Article 2), an exemption is made on ethnic rather than religious grounds for "Greek inhabitants of Constantinople." The same exemption for "Moslem inhabitants of Western Thrace," however, maintains the boundaries of religious designation. Thereafter (in Articles 2–6), the treaty makes reference to "Greeks" in Turkey and "Moslems" in Greece. The shift in reference is noteworthy. The religious designations are differentially employed: "Greek Orthodox" quickly becomes "Greek"; "Moslems" remain, for the most part, "Moslems."

The arguably unsurprising intratextual equivocation of the Lausanne Treaty suggests an extratextual ambiguity about the definitive "boundaries" of the peoples being legislated. The depositions and testimonials of refugees in Greece attest to some considerable ambiguity about who "belonged" where and what exactly constituted membership in one or another community. Of course, such literal and textual ambiguity and nuance made no political difference. The Convention and Treaty have absolutely no provision for such ambiguity. Its assumption is of clear and unequivocal distinction between "Turkish nationals of the Greek Orthodox religion" and "Greek nationals of the Moslem religion," or, in the subsequent conflated slippage of the Convention's language, between "Greeks" and "Moslems." And so, Christian nationals of Turkey and Moslem nationals of Greece were given four months to uproot themselves and move "home"—or, although a possibility only infrequently conceded, to realign themselves in religious terms.

But bracketing for the moment claims to or even the desirability of ethnoreligious purity, the enormity of what the signatories to the Lausanne Treaty and its Convention enacted is more apparent if we recall that the population of the Greek mainland in the fall of 1922, before the influx of refugees and including the expanded territories of Macedonia and Thrace in the north, was scarcely four and a half million people. Virtually overnight, with the arrival of the Asia Minor refugees, that population was increased by more than 25 percent. And, impoverished and déclassé, the refugees appeared to mainland Greeks to bear many of the markers that, only months before, designated "the enemy." Many of the refugees spoke only Turkish. Or, when they did speak Greek, it was often a dialect (such as Pontian) or a schoolbook Greek barely comprehensible to the mainland population. And, in spite of putative religious or ethnic sameness, much of the social and political culture of the refugees (*prosfuges*) was distinctly foreign to that of the mainland Greeks (*palioelladites* or *ndopioi*). In fact, the distinction marked by these terms, *prosfuges* and *palioelladites* or *ndopioi,* is still common in everyday speech.[19] The latter's perception of the Asia Minor refugees as dangerously "foreign" was aggravated by the defining characteristics of the refugee population: their déclassé poverty; their generally higher literacy rate, especially among women; their often more visible cultural sophistication, especially among the substantial number of refugees who came from the cosmopolitan urban regions of coastal Asia Minor; and their "liberal" social and political positions—the refugees were by and large supporters of Venizelos, whose government had been ousted by the mainland Greeks in the 1920 elections that returned the monarchy to power. They subsequently affiliated for the most part with even more liberal to leftist politics in Greece.

The differences between the now compatriot populations of Asia Minor refugees and mainland Greeks were further exacerbated by the initial de facto forced agroticization, and hence effective isolation, of nearly 70 percent of the refugees.[20] This was in spite of frequent citation of the official Greek government goal of their *afomoiosis* or "assimilation." The refugees were settled on territories acquired by Greece in the Balkan Wars and on large fallow estates expropriated by the state and broken up to provide small agricultural land holdings for the refugees. In addition to affording land for the newly arrived population, this settlement policy also served the purpose of creating a dense, ethnically "Greek" buffer zone at the northern boundaries of the Greek state. The remaining 30 percent of the refugees settled on the fringes of large towns and cities where, for the most part, they struggled to survive as day workers in an already depressed labor market. The urban refugee population grew even more in subsequent years as refugees originally settled in rural areas were unable to survive and moved to cities or towns. And, as is most often the case with refugee populations, the majority, more than 55 percent in this instance, were women; another 25 percent were under fifteen and over fifty-five or sixty.

The founding documents, but even more explicitly the reports and recommendations of the Refugee Settlement Commission (RSC), established in 1923 with the cooperation of both the League of Nations and the Greek state, suggest both predominant Greek and international notions of "native" and "refugee" and of the "proper place" of each. The documents establishing the RSC[21] are striking for their overwhelming focus not on the settling of refugees per se but on the relationship of the RSC to the Greek government, seeking to insulate the workings of the RSC from any direct interference by the government. Direct reference to the settlement of refugees in those documents is limited to a specification, in the Protocol Agreement, of the function of the RSC as "the settlement in Greece of refugees upon lands to be assigned to the Commission or otherwise in productive work." The stipulation of "productive work" was a crucial one for the immediate condition of refugees. For the RSC was, in Article 15 of the appendix attached to the Protocol, explicitly precluded from using any of its resources for providing "relief of distress or other charitable purposes. . . . All assistance given shall be given on terms of ultimate repayment." In addition, the reference to "lands to be assigned to the Commission" points to what became a fierce point of contention between the settlement of the refugees "upon lands" and the expectations of land reform of the indigenous Greek peasants.

The issue of land reform had been a crucial and vexed one in Greece since the beginning of the century.[22] But until the massive influx of Asia Minor refugees, the promises of land reform by various political regimes in

Greece far exceeded their actuality. What was perceived by the Greek urban bourgeoisie in the early decades of the twentieth century as a means to gain popular support in its battle for political power against the conservative landed gentry had shifted by the end of WWI to a means to counter the radicalization of the peasantry and their potential alliance with workers in the cities. This threat of popular radicalization was increased exponentially with the massive influx of refugees from Asia Minor. So it was that the majority of land expropriations in Greece took place between 1923 and 1925. The refugees were to be located on lands left behind by "exchanged" Muslims and, when those lands were settled, on large estates expropriated by the Greek state. But the tension and antagonisms were considerable between the indigenous peasants who had struggled for at least a decade for agrarian reform and the refugees who were presumably the designated primary recipients of land reform in Greece.[23] Willingly or unwillingly, the RSC thus played a primary role in what Mark Mazower characterizes as a land reform that was "the most radical in post-1918 Europe" and that "turned Greece into a nation of smallholders" (78).

Of less economic significance than the RSC's role in land reform but of greater social and cultural significance for the refugees and for the indigenous residents of Greece were the RSC's assessments of the "character, temperament, and mentality" of the refugees, which assessments at least implicitly underlay the directions of their refugee settlement policies. In the League of Nations's publication of the RSC's account of the first two years of their efforts, *Greek Refugee Settlement,* the Commission insists that the refugees are "brothers by race" with "a complete identity of feeling, aspirations, and national and religious tradition." But, the report continues, "having lived in different countries and districts, they differ in character, temperament, and mentality and show striking individuality." In the pages immediately following the assertion of a complete identity of racial brotherhood, the RSC details its perceptions of the psychosociological characteristics of refugees from different regions of Asia Minor. Those from inner Anatolia, for example, are "backward, submissive, and timid." This passage, cited in Dimitri Pentzopoulos's *The Balkan Exchange of Minorities and Its Impact on Greece,* is further specified in a chauvinist flourish of that author as the result of "living in the midst of Turks and Kurds." Hence the Greek Anatolians display the "characteristics of Asiatic peoples" (101). The refugees from Cappadocia are "a serious and reflective type, hard working and energetic, enterprising and practical." The Smyrniots are "true Ionians in their individualism." The refugees from Pontus—still the butt of ethnic jokes in Greece though more recently superseded by Albanians—the report averred, ran the gamut from "the rough, heavy and dull-witted type to the subtlest of Greeks." But the "truest of the Hellenes" are those linguistically distinguished by their use of a Greek language "rich in classical expressions and Homeric phrases." (Here, already in the period immediately following 1922, are traces of the claim that the refugees, from various parts of Asia Minor, made about their relation to a classical Greek past, regardless of the language they spoke; 20–22.) The rather crude characterizations of the RSC's report are far less noteworthy, though, than that report's demonstration of the profound contradiction between putative national brotherhood on the one hand and the social and cultural organization of arguably non- or metanational communities on the other, between an at least arguable "complete identity of feeling, aspirations and national and religious traditions" and the in fact *non*identity of community and interests among refugees and between refugees and native Greeks. Of course, the refugees themselves were not necessarily consulted on the terms of this enterprise; they were to be administered and "settled."[24]

In spite of the RSC's relative accomplishment of the tremendous and even onerous task of refugee settlement, its reports are nonetheless almost poignant testimony to the contradictions of its enterprise. The immediate relief of the "distress" of the refugees was not the Commission's task; theirs was a longer-term goal of the successful settlement and assimilation of the refugees. This latter long-term goal was, therefore, not predominantly a philanthropic or humanitarian one; it was a political one. The major concern of the RSC designated by its founding documents—and in spite of the sometimes principled reinterpretation of those documents by RSC workers—was no less the daily misery of more than a million refugees than it was the sustenance of the cultural, linguistic, and even religious diversity among them. It was the promotion of precisely a national "brotherhood of race" over other, less desirable possibilities: the likelihood of the Greek state's mishandling of the situation; the radicalization of the refugees and the broader Greek population and the possible destabilization of the Greek state; the fears of that state and establishment and of others in Western Europe in general of revolution and of the influence of the newly established Soviet Union. Apprehension over such possibilities and a fervent resolve to effect a national "brotherhood" perhaps inform the RSC's studied ignorance of the refugee's prior occupations and places of origin. So, in spite of the Commission's acknowledgment that "the notable feature in this community [of refugees] was the large proportion of the urban element compared with the purely agricultural element," the number of refugees settled "upon lands assigned to the Commission" (i.e., in rural, agricultural areas) was initially around 70 percent. This policy of rural settlement was, to some extent, at least originally dictated by necessity. The majority of land and houses vacated by Greek Muslims forced to "return" to Turkey (or Bulgaria) were in the rural north of Greece. But the Commission, ever cognizant of international politics and of the potential political effect of the refugees on internal Greek politics, was wary of allowing too many refugees to settle in the urban areas. Not only were there few jobs and even less housing available there, but there were far more opportunities for organized political action and for potential political coalitions between different groups. The RSC but also more than one foreign observer noted the potential for "a Bolshevik threat" in Greece if the refugee settlement issue were not handled "successfully."[25] The issue of refugee settlement was a complex and loaded one. While the succession of governments in Greece held nervous if never quite effective reign over the refugees and the RSC attempted to administer the refugees so as to underwrite the stability of the Greek state and the construction of a "complete identity of feeling, aspirations, and national and religious tradition," their task vastly exceeded them.

In addition to state and organizational difficulties in administering the refugees and reconstructing them as national subjects, the initial popular responses of indigenous Greeks to the refugee population were vexed and perhaps not surprisingly equivocal. Even with the best of individual intentions, the magnitude of the catastrophe was overwhelming for an impoverished and defeated country that had been at war since Greece's entry into the Balkan Wars in 1912. And, as noted earlier, the differences among people who were rhetorically cast as national compatriots were often immense.[26] In the aftermath of the destruction of Smyrna and Greece's utter rout from Asia Minor, the difficult consequences of the compulsory "ingathering" of Asia Minor refugees is bluntly suggested in the accounts by the refugees themselves of their arrival in Greece:

> And later we reached Greece. We said now our troubles are over. We'll rest and live [*tha xekourastoume kai tha zisoume*]. But we were mistaken because from the first day worse troubles began [for us]. (Katina Georgiadou)

> We, we drew courage from hope. Widows, most of us, with babies in our arms, we hoped that we'd find help and live our lives better.
> At Ai-Giorgi though we were placed in quarantine and things were awful. They shaved our heads; they treated us badly; they cursed at us. We were overcome with despair. Then dysentery began to spread;

10 people died. They took them away—where they took them, where they buried them, we didn't know. Eh, later this too passed; we forgot it more or less; and we stayed in this new place and raised our children that we brought here as infants; but still our life was miserable. (Katina Kasnakidou)[27]

Refugee and nonrefugee newspapers published in the first months and years after the catastrophe abundantly document the contradictory situations in which the new refugees and "old" Greeks (*palioelladites*) found themselves. Letters to the editor in refugee newspapers complain of bread sold at one price for "Greeks" and another (and higher) price for refugees; of the police who chase off refugee vendors and peddlers "for the protection of Greek neighborhoods"; of refugee camp structures so poorly built that roofs collapse or slide off and walls crack open, and of the camps themselves without running water or functional outhouses.[28] Such accounts of the miseries of refugee life are juxtaposed with poems of nostalgic longing for a life left behind in Asia Minor; serialized novels offered fictionalized versions of, most often, the flight from Asia Minor or life before the Greco-Turkish War.[29] And, in a patently racial and often sexual vein, popular in both refugee and nonrefugee newspapers, serialized novels told of Christian (usually Greek or Armenian) and Muslim (almost always Turkish) confrontation, as in the stories of Greek women in Asia Minor held captive in Turkish harems.[30] But of equal significance, a counterpoint of sorts to the fictional economy of desire circulating in such newspaper novels can be found in the testimonial accounts of (Greek, Christian) women who remained in Turkey, married Turkish men, lived their lives and raised their families not as "sex slaves" in a Turkish harem but as wives, mothers, sisters-in-law, coworkers, and coresidents of the Turkish people.

The story "Antigone" in Isabella Sikiaridi Malovrouva's *Mikrasia E Megali Ellada* (Asia Minor, Greater Greece) is a suggestive example of such accounts and their implicit contradictions Malovrouva records a testimonial of a young Greek girl hidden by her mother in an empty grave during the expulsion of the Greeks from Mersina. The young girl and her mother, the latter with a younger boy-child in her arms, are discovered by a Turkish officer who apparently knows them for he speaks of the young girl by name. He proposes to marry Antigone and save the rest of her family, an offer the mother initially refuses as "unheard of." But in a footnote to the testimonial proper, Malovrouva offers further information in her own voice: "Antigone lives today in Mersina. She is very wealthy; she married the Turkish officer and they had three sons, [who all became] professionals, and a daughter. Her husband had died. She was not in the least sorry for making this sacrifice and saving her entire family. And as her sister told me, Antigone lived all of her years happily with her Turkish husband who absolutely adored her." Malovrouva then adds in apparent approval: "Her family remained in their homeland and returned to their own household. There are many such families in Asia Minor. When I was there in 1972, I visited many of them and was impressed" (74–75). The almost fairytale happy ending of this particular story notwithstanding, Malovrouva's book is subtitled *True Accounts Related by the Witnesses Themselves of the Greatest Tragedy of Our Century.*

The tension between Antigone's testimonial and the subtitle of Malovrouva's book is apparent in the stark contrast of Antigone's story to other testimonial accounts of the interaction between the Turkish regular and irregular soldiers and the civilian population. The latter accounts of atrocity still circulate in Greek journals, newspapers, and books with tremendous inflammatory power. Yiannis Kapsis's recent *1922 E Mavri Biblos* (1922, The black book) is provocatively (and obsessively) enframed by the deposition of a refugee from Ivrindi, Sophia Nikolaou, on both the outside back cover and on a dedication page entitled "The Victims." Nikolaou describes her escape with her husband and eight-year-old son from her home to a nearby flour mill. They are discovered there by Turkish villagers (*Tourkoi horiates*) who surround the mill, break down the door, and seize the family, gang raping the woman in front of her husband and son. They then kill her son and her husband, cutting out the latter's intestines and forcing his wife to eat them: "They shouted at me that if I didn't eat my husband's flesh they would kill me as well" (9). At the fortuitous approach of the Greek army, the Turkish villagers flee and Sophia Nikolaou is saved: "The officers and soldiers saw what had befallen me and took me with them." As foil (intentional or not) to Nikolaou's statement, the front cover of Kapsis's book is a photograph of a woman standing in front of a hovel with a baby in her arms and three children gathered around her. That photograph is a stark visual marker for the woman/family violated and without male protection or supervision. The potent charge of the woman/family and, by extension, the nation violated is scarcely subtle.

Yet, as the testimonials of Antigone and others would suggest, the "unheard of" relationship between Turk and Greek, Orthodox Christian and Muslim, is a familiar story both before and during the Asia Minor Catastrophe. Of course, those testimonials do not arouse quite the same fervor as that of Sophia Nikolaou. What is "unheard of" in this context is perhaps

Front cover, Yiannis
Kapsis's *1922, The
Black Book*

less the actual lived experience of intercommunal relation, which seems
to have been common enough, than the implication of those relations: that
the very notion of the necessity of "ethnic homogeneity" is utterly disput-
able. And the definition of what constitutes such "ethnic homogenity" is
virtually impossible. For the boundaries between Orthodox Greek and
Turkish Muslim were often tractable, and such tractability was engaged in
mutually. Cross-boundary relations, before and even during the Greco-
Turkish War, are resolutely recounted in numerous refugee testimonials.

The insistence on tractable borders is both deliberate and unintentional,
or at least coincidental. Two women refugees from the mixed (Muslim and
Christian) village of Halvaderé, recounting in the late 1940s and early
1950s their compulsory participation in early 1924 in the "exchange of
populations," each refer to Greek Orthodox women from the village who
married into Turkish Muslim families. The account of Barbara Manaeloglou suggests that she is retelling a story she heard from others; she
consistently uses the third person to account for the story she tells. It is not

a story of herself, then, but of a Turkish man who, married to a Greek widow with two children, was compelled to turn his wife over to the authorities for return to her "homeland," "because they [the authorities overseeing the forced exchange] said that whoever had become Turkish [*tourkepsan*] must also leave" in the exchange.[31] The attempt, at least as the exchange of populations mandate was carried out in this village, was to quasi-biologically define the populations subject to exchange. A woman married to a Muslim Turk but born of Orthodox Greek parents is still Orthodox Greek and hence subject to "return" to her "homeland." This definition of ethnic/religious identity was not uniformly enforced, as it *could not* effectively be. For there are equally accounts of Orthodox Greeks who chose to stay in Turkey, as, for example, Malovrouva's story of Antigone and her family makes clear.

Evlambia Moumtzoglou, Manaeloglou's covillager, provides a first-person account of her experience of the exchange. She begins with an explanation of what the exchange of populations meant—she refers to it as *mouvadelé*—and how her village learned of it. There were multiple sources for the news, her account of which gives, en passant, some sense of life in her village: "Alexandros the teacher, who read political newspapers, told us [presumably the women] about it. But also our husbands, who went to the markets at Akserai and Gelveri where they sold wooden farm implements, heard talk of the exchange. And the Turks in the village knew of it as well and told us, 'You're to go to your grandfather in Greece'" (1:I.1.6a, 30). This last statement Moumtzoglou recounts in Turkish, clearly identifying herself to her interlocutor as bilingual (as were most of her covillagers). She then relates the arrival in her village of Turks from Kozani (in mainland Greece) who knew Greek but were "bad people." They "were always singing the praises of their region" of Kozani but fought fiercely with the Greeks in Halvaderé. The Turkish residents of the village intervened with the recent refugees from Greece to protect the local Greek residents. Moumtzoglou then, more deliberately then Manaeloglou, speaks of the generally close and affectionate intercommunal ties among the village residents: "I mean that as we left, the Turks brought us gifts:*bligouri*, honey, and *kaimaki*. They embraced us and cried a great deal. 'Don't go there,' they said. 'Here we live like brothers. We're brothers of the same earth.'" That "brotherhood," however, had its contradictions, even in Moumtzoglou's generally affirmative account. For immediately after this description of mutual intercommunal affection, she states: "The daughter of [the local Orthodox] priest who had become Turkish wanted to come with us. She was a widow now and didn't have anyone in the world." Moumtzoglou's reference to the daughter of an Orthodox priest "become Turkish" is noncommital, without judgment or comment. Perhaps more than any other woman, that the daughter of an Orthodox clergyman would "become Turkish" is a striking comment on the likelihood of such ethnic antihomogeneity. But the woman's brothers do not share Moumtzoglou's acceptance: "Her brothers though didn't want her. 'You've humiliated us,' they said. 'How can we take you to Greece?'" Presumably, the woman's marriage into a Turkish Muslim family is less of a "humiliation" in their own village in Turkey, but in Greece such intermarriage, even if in the past, is unacceptable. There is no further comment on the widow. Immediately thereafter, however, Moumtzoglou refers to another Greek-woman-become-Turkish—"Barbara, the sister of Ananía"—who warns her Greek covillagers of a plot against them by the recently arrived Turkish refugees from Greece. In a footnote to her account, Moumtzoglou notes, "This woman still lives in Halvaderé; she is called Sampiyié and I saw her on my two trips [to the village] in 1951 and 1952." (Moumtzoglou's testimonial was recorded in January 1954.)

In fact, the collection of testimonials from the province of Cappodocia, Akseraï-Gleveri region in which Moumtzoglou's story is included, titled *E Exodos* (The exodus), reproduces an undated photograph of a clearly older Sampiyié with her granddaughter standing by her side in the village of Halvaderé. Even, or especially, in 1980, when the collection of refugee testimonials was published, the visual image of the Greek-woman-become-Turkish is still powerful documentation of intercommunal relations. The picture of Sampiyié and her granddaughter is included among photographs that are predominantly of the Greek and Orthodox cultural presence in Asia Minor/Turkey: the Greek quarters of numerous cities, the Orthodox churches throughout the countryside, the schools, the fertile fields, the cultural institutions. There are far fewer photographs of individuals, half a dozen in the thousand or so pages of the two-volume collection, and these are most often of (male) village elders or of Greek Orthodox religious men. The persistent figure of Sampiyié stands as a visual reminder of the difficulty of fixing and maintaining ethnic boundaries, a curious yet crucial marker of what was and is. It is equally, if more implicitly, a suggestion of what might be.

The agreement for the exchange of populations, attempting to neatly distinguish and separate Greek from Turk—or, more accurately, given the linguistic slippage of the agreement itself, Greek from Muslim—encounters countless ambiguities in such distinctions that tremendously and often poignantly complicate the task. One of the trenchant ironies of reading through the almost one thousand pages of testimonials collected in the

Sampiyié with her grand-
daughter. From *E Exodos*
(The exodus), Center for
Asia Minor Studies

two volumes of *E Exodos* is the frequent refrain of exceptionalism, such as
that of Socrates Loukidis, who concludes his account by noting: "For us
Gelveriotes the exchange of populations was a disaster; we came to Greece
and were miserable. In our homeland, we lived well with the Turks; they
were good people. But in other parts of Asia Minor the Turks oppressed the
Greeks; for those Greeks the exchange was good because they escaped
from the hands of the Turks" (2:I.1.2b, 14). In spite of the horrors of the
Greek invasion and occupation of Asia Minor, in spite of the horrors of the
Turkish persecution and expulsion of Greeks and Armenians from Turkey,
Loukidis insists that *his* town's intercommunal relationships were excep-
tional. In *his* town, "we lived well with the Turks."

To draw attention to such moments and the ambiguity of their ethnoreligious distinctions is not to deny the historical fact of hostile and
brutal relations between ethnoreligious armies, regular and irregular. The
violence, death, and misery of the Greco-Turkish War and its aftermath are
everywhere apparent in the documents, memoirs, and cultural texts of the
time. But, contrary to feverish official rhetoric both Greek and Turkish, it

was not, even at that time, a simple either/or situation, enemy or cohort, brutality or compassion. There was tremendous and fearful brutality: by the Greek occupying army and some of the local resident Greeks and by the Turkish regular and irregular military forces and some of the local resident Turks. *And* there was a reiteration of the complex, interdependent, and often intimate relations between communities. An occupying army is first of all an occupying army; its ethnic composition is of a significance at least secondary to its coercive military presence. Even at moments of intense conflict, the boundaries of ethnoreligious communities are more permeable than we might allow. Such careful distinctions, of course, do not always hold. People are rounded up and executed, discriminated against, and persecuted for the way they look, the language they speak, the religion of which they are a member. But the refugee insistence in retrospect on such careful distinctions is not only a comment on an after-the-fact moment of historical recollection; it is as much a comment on the lived relations of life in a multiethnic society as are the official proclamations of the necessity of an internationally mandated "ethnic homogeneity."

The refugee testimonial of Kalliope Mouratoglou is situated in this same contested context. She insists to her mainland Greek interlocutor with no little pride that intercommunal relations in her village of Vekse were exceptionally close:

> In Turkey, my dear madame, we lived well. With the Turks, we lived as dear friends. And let me tell you something else.
>
> Can you go and find the letter, daughter? [The old woman addresses her daughter-in-law.] I just received a letter. My brother went back to our place [in Turkey] and two Turks that I'd wet-nursed got my address [from him] and wrote to me. They call me "Sitt Anné" [milk-mother]. And I wrote back to them but I haven't gotten a response yet. (2:I.2.4b, 54)

She continues her story of flight from her inland village to the coast with praise for the efforts of her (Turkish) covillager "Havouz effendi," who cleverly sought (and for the most part secured) safe passage and transport for the fleeing Greek villagers. The Turkish soldiers who terrorize them on their journey or the Turkish refugees from Greece who taunt them as they travel are not remarkable because they are Turkish but because they are cruel and strangers. There is, however, no effort on her part to assert either hostility and brutality or intimacy and "dear friend[ship]" based on the homogeneity of her village or beyond it. She is very clear in her identification: Greeks are Greeks and Turks Turks. But what constitutes "Greekness" or "Turkishness" is for her a functional matter. And in an understated, almost wry tone, she tells of the mundane interactions of daily life and of the extraordinary events through which she and her covillagers, Greek and Turkish, lived. But she is resolute in her noncondemnation of Turks as Turks. She is equally resolute in her insistence on the frequent closeness of Greek and Turk in her village, even, as in her own case, to the extent of nursing two children of her Turkish covillagers. This latter relationship is one that is especially marked for there is a cultural assumption of a special bond between the child and the woman who nursed him. In Greek she is a *paramana* (in place of/next to the mother) or in Turkish a *sittannu* (milk-mother), a relation the functionalist English term "wet nurse" can scarcely encompass.[32]

Similarly close intercommunal relations are accounted for by Theologos Hatziparaskevas, who identifies his village of Nigdi as his "homeland," *e patrida mas*. The homeland, in his account, is conspicuously not in Greece:

A year later the Committee came to Nigdi and most of the villagers left. I and about 15 other families didn't want to leave yet. "We'll harvest the crops," we said, "and leave later." I'd planted a watermelon field with a Turkish man and I didn't want to abandon it. (2:I.4.7b, 221)

After recounting the further orders of the *wali* (or, *vali:* a civil governor of an Ottoman province) that the Christians must leave, Hatziparaskevas continues:

What should we do? We didn't want to leave because our homeland [*e patrida mas*] was good. Where else could you work 6 months and the rest of the year relax and live well? Our houses were full of whatever we needed. Finally we decided. We left the fields unharvested. My watermelon [field] stayed the way it was. We sold some small things and farm animals to the Turks. We loaded our bedding and some food onto the donkeys and set out for Nigdi. We all cried that we were leaving everything behind, our houses, everything. The Turks cried with us.

Not the Turkish refugees who came from Greece, our Turkish co-villagers. They were very fond of us. We lived affectionately with them. In the neighborhood we had excellent relations with the Turks. When a Turkish woman who was our neighbor would go away, she'd leave the key to her house with my wife. And we'd do the same when we were away from home. That's how much we loved one another.

. . . They went with us to the edge of the village and called after us: Be well, be well. (2:I.4.7b, 222)

As Maria Soteriou recounts her departure from her village of Sivrihisar, the implications of the close intercommunal relations to which she and Hatziparaskevas bear witness are carried a step farther. Soteriou's testimony is a striking indication of the subsequent complexification of ethnoreligious boundaries:

> Later Turkish refugees from Greece arrived, from Akpounar and Kozani, they said. Most of them were good people. "Don't leave, stay here and we'll live together," they told us. When the time drew near for us to leave, Turks from Melendiz, Azatala, and Sorsobou came to our village. We traded with them; we sold them cloth that we wove on our looms. They pleaded with us, "Don't go to 'Yunanistan'; you'll suffer. There's only a lot of work and little food there. The only good thing about that place is that a widow can [re]marry three times. If there are no Turks there, there's no *bereketi* [wealth]." Some of them had fought against Greeks and knew them.
>
> . . . We sold them whatever we couldn't take with us and they paid us a good price. "*Xelal olsoun*" ["It's all yours"], they said to us. (2:I.1.4a, 19).[33]

There is a fascinating and suggestive reference to the gap between ethnoreligious and regional identity in Soteriou's distinction between "Greeks" and herself. On the one hand, she is "Greek," that is, a member of the Orthodox Church and presumably born of ethnic "Greek" parents. Yet her first response to news of the exchange of populations is not joy that she is going to Greece-as-ethnic-"homeland." Rather, "we rejoiced when we first heard the news [because] we would go to *a Christian place*" (emphasis added). It is, however, not Soteriou and her 465 Turkish-speaking "Greek" covillagers who "know the Greeks"; it is the Turks from the surrounding villages who "had fought against the Greeks and knew them." The content of the ethnoreligious nationalist category, which would postulate elemental national membership on a common language, culture, and history, is made more than a little problematic in Soteriou's testimonial. "Knowing" Greeks is more accessible to Soteriou's Turkish compatriots through fighting against them (probably in the Balkan Wars) than it is for Soteriou through her putative biological, ethnic, religious filiation. The testimony of Soteriou and others makes clear that there were not simply two ethnoreligious or national categories, Orthodox Greek and

Muslim Turk, as the Treaty of Lausanne asserted. There were far more, and more complex, gradations of communal belonging and intercommunal relationship than the signatories or the writers of the Treaty could even begin to articulate.

In general and perhaps unsurprisingly then, the Asia Minor refugees speak of generally cordial and sometimes quite intimate relations with their covillagers or, in the case of a village, town, or city that was predominantly Greek, of their relations with the Turkish Muslim communities nearby. But it would be a mistake to forget the fiercely charged context in which the insistence of refugees like Mouratoglou or Soteriou or Hatziparaskevas on viable intercommunal relations between Greek and Turk is located. Even some thirty years after the event, it is not in a general milieu of fondness for or tolerance toward Turks that these refugees retell their stories of coexistence and mutual relation. Quite the contrary. In the mid- to late 1950s, when most of their accounts were recorded, the recent and destructive violence in Istanbul (in September 1955) was a fresh reminder of the potential for fierce confrontation along ethnoreligious lines.

The ferocity and violence occasioning and accompanying the flight of Asia Minor refugees is clearly figured in the depositions taken by various Greek ministry clerks and officials as the refugees reached Greece in 1922–1924. The eyewitness accounts of the slaughter of men and boys, the rape and disfigurement of women and girls are short, blunt, graphic. "I saw with my own eyes" (*eida me ta matia mou*) or "right in front of my eyes" (*brosta ap 'ta matia mou*) is a frequent and plaintive refrain in the refugee depositions.[34] It is precisely in the context of eyewitness accounts and reports of rape, slaughter, and brutality and the reference to and reiteration of those accounts and reports in the popular press and in official government proclamations that refugees such as Soteriou and Hatziparaskevas and Mouratogolou tell their stories of coexistence and cooperation. It is in that context that their stories are most comprehensible, as small but insistent counternarratives to the dominant (and official) story. This jagged disjuncture between official and popular accounts of fierce ethnoreligious hatred and the daily lived experience of intercommunal cooperation and often intimacy is evident in the account of the Greco-Turkish War by Maria Iordanidou, a novelist from Constantinople/Istanbul: "The newspapers and our local leaders all cried out: 'The Turks are coming. The Turks are coming.' We were terrified. It was [as if the Turks were] a tremendous wave ready to wash over us and sweep us away. But who were 'the Turks'? It wasn't Mehmet who lived next door to me or Fatima who I'd played with since I was a girl or Sultana who nursed my mother when she was sick."[35]

But for the most part, for the Greeks of the mainland and for their government, the Turks were a singular and identifiable enemy. And the "proper place" for Greeks, however they were defined and from wherever they came, was now definitively in Greece, far from Turks. The ferocity with which the enforcement of these "proper places" was exercised is, however, not mitigated by popular or state certainty about the necessity of that separation.

There is a small if telling suggestion of the disjuncture in perception between mainland Greeks and Asia Minor Greeks in the interjection of a Greek government interviewer as he records the deposition of a refugee, Ioannis Koumoglou. When the old man gives his home address as the village of Tomazi in the district of Smyrna, the interviewer remarks in the text of the interview: "It is moving that all of them that are interviewed give as their place of residence their cities and villages in Asia Minor. And they refer to their current addresses in Greece as temporary. They still believe, then, that they will return to their beloved homeland."[36] Koumoglou's deposition with the interviewer's parenthetical remark is dated 4 November 1922. Barely three months after the rout from Smyrna and three months before the agreement on the mandatory exchange of populations signed by Ataturk and Venizelos, the mainland Greek interviewer already regards refugee insistence on addresses in Turkey as futile.

As the disjuncture between public and official discourse on the one hand and refugee stories, on the other, already suggest, there is a further displacement that occurs when all "Greeks" are safely ingathered to the "homeland." In the context of accounts of slaughter and rape in Asia Minor, of the titillating racialism and sexual fantasy of newspaper novels, of the official historical narratives and refugee counternarratives and testimonials, there is a further and telling document of displacement and subjugation, a newspaper "report" of another kind, that is compelling.[37] But this story is not exactly of the Asia Minor Catastrophe itself. Nor is it the story of Greco-Turkish military confrontation. Rather, it is a story of an elderly Greek Christian woman overpowered and displaced—not by the Muslim Turks but by her younger and militarized Greek Christian male compatriots. The feature column, entitled "Instead of the Grandmother" and signed by Anatolitis (an "Easterner" or "Oriental"), opens with a depiction of a cozy domestic scene of children gathered around a fireplace in the winter listening eagerly to their grandmother tell them stories. This "most beautiful and most Greek" scene is interrupted by an exchange of questions and answers between two men as the first man tells the second that a "dangerous rival" has appeared to "definitively take over the position of the grandmother." This disruption of the old grandmother's place evokes mock horror on the part of the interlocutor, who questions the first man insistently about the identity and purpose of the grandmother's rival. That rival is a young Greek man. This compels the second man's exclamation of "Scandalous!" He continues: "It is normally the elderly who love and caress small children, who take them on their laps and tell them stories, who carry the small children to their beds and put them to sleep. It's the attraction of opposites: the old and the child, spring and winter, shining eyes and closed eyelids, loving companionship and wrinkled brow, the East and the West." Situated as an idyllically natural part of the "attraction of opposites," the role of the grandmother and of her stories are nonetheless both displaced by soldiers returning from the Asia Minor war. It is their military adventures—the accounts of their tour of duty in Asia Minor, the battles of the Greco-Turkish War, the exodus from the city of Smyrna as "she [i.e., the city of Smyrna] trembles in agony"—that vanquish the old grandmother and her stories. The article concludes, in a continuation of the exchange between the two gentlemen, with the verdict of the second and formerly scandalized interlocutor: "The children did well to abandon their grandmother. All of this [the soldiers' stories of war] will be our fairytales in the future, in all of the houses, by the side of all fireplaces in the winter, and for all Greek children."

The militarization of the domestic setting in this small newspaper story is not only that of the young soldier who supplants the old woman and her stories; it is also the "martial" dialogue of the two gentlemen who offer their verdict on the propriety of the situation. It is not only or necessarily an "attraction of opposites" that is at textual work here. Nor are those putatively mutually attracting "opposites" only between "old and young" or "East and West." There is clearly a gendered opposition between home and war, private "peace" and public strife. Here, the "most Greek" of domestic scenes is transformed precisely by national military defeat. The (domestic, national) private sphere of the grandmother is "invaded" by that of the (militarized, national) public soldier. The old woman is not taken hostage in a harem, as in the serialized novel mentioned earlier; she is not brutalized through rape. She is usurped and displaced in the name of nationalism, in the name of the even-more-Greek. The vanquished Greek Christian woman taken captive by the conquering Muslim Turkish man is transformed here into the arrogant propriety of the simultaneously vanquished and vanquishing young Greek Christian soldier who subjugates and vanquishes in turn the (Greek Christian) grandmother. Only with considerable difficulty and rhetorical violence can the fierce conflict to

Front page, *Amaltheia's* 1923 New Year's edition

which "Instead of the Grandmother" points be subsumed under "the attraction of opposites." It is instead an indication of the intense struggle over the gendered narrative perspective from which the story of the nation will be told. Clearly, for this newspaper article, the story of the nation will no longer be told by the grandmother.

A related turn in the militant gendering of the national is visible in the front-page illustration of *Amaltheia (Smyrnis)*'s New Year's Eve 1923 edition. The text to the left of the illustration reads: "Finally!" And on the right: "With the dawning of a new year the olive [branch] of peace emerges from [what was] until now the immobilized [literally, "the nailed down"] postwar situation." The text is, on the one hand, visually sustained in the image of an almost bare-breasted woman holding, thrust out in front of her, a cannon with an olive branch emerging from its mouth. In Greek, the new year, *o kainourgios xronos*, is grammatically masculine, here signaled only by the Arabic numerals 1923 on the horizon. The other patently "masculine" marker is of course the cannon itself. But that reference is here perhaps as notable for its dismemberment as for anything else. The foregrounded figure is the familiar representation of the female embodiment of peace—in Greek, *e eirini*, in the feminine. Behind her is the devastation and rubble of the war from which she attempts to stride forward while her dress, held down with three large nails, holds her firmly in place. But strangely enough, there is no visual representation of what the text proposes for the new year. As 1923 dawns on the horizon, the olive branch emerging from a dislocated cannon is held out in the hands of a woman/peace still immobilized. She could, of course, abandon her clothes and move forward. In fact, she would seem to be struggling to do just that, whence her virtually bared breasts. But the still martial "postwar situation" dominates, fixing her place, as it does the old woman in "Instead of the Grandmother."

It seems unremarkable that war, or crisis of any sort, fixes the symbolic and literal places of men and women to greater or lesser degrees. In fact, it might even seem relatively unavoidable that this would be the case. But though, in general, crisis or war (or nationalism in general) interpellates its constituents in gendered places, the representations in these two instances of response to national crisis—the newspaper article and the front-page newspaper illustration—represent a masculinized privilege and mobility either framing that feminized fixedness (after its displacement) or occasioning it. The nationalist question Who belongs where? is not, then, only a proposition about those who do and do not belong to and thus within the nation. It is also a proposition about where and how the constituent members of the nation are situated from within.

The dialogue between the two gentlemanly figures in "Instead of the Grandmother" is not, for example, joined by the grandmother herself. Her proper place in the scheme of things is delineated by the two men's ultimately mutual agreement about the priority of the young Greek soldier's martial stories as appropriate tales of the nation. So too, against a backdrop of war and the progression of time, the female figure of peace is forcefully nailed in place, carrying a weapon of war. The liberation toward which the text accompanying the illustration points is *visually* only possible if the female figure relinquishes her dress. But a stark naked female figure of peace is clearly not the story that the text wants to tell; it is a socially unacceptable if visually possible alternative. For the female figure of peace would be a substantially different visual marker if she escaped her clothed place. Actually, prurient titillation aside, the naked or barely clothed figure of a woman here would resemble nothing quite so much as the eyewitness accounts and photographs of the Asia Minor refugee women themselves. On the eve of the new year that would see, within the month, the signing of an agreement for the mandatory and permanent exchange of populations between Greece and Turkey, the graphic struggle to free herself by this immobilized female figure of peace is almost prophetic. Her face, presumably hopeful and looking up and away toward a better future, nonetheless and perhaps ominously avoids the weapon she carries, the protruding olive branch notwithstanding. In a similar fashion, her up-turned face ironically avoids the very ground to which she is so securely fastened. And in a further irony, the female figure of peace is additionally circumscribed by the symbol of that which has metaphorically fastened her gown to the ground in the first place: the crowned two-headed eagle of the Byzantine Empire with wings outspread, perched just outside and above the frame of the illustration itself. The iconic marker for the *megali idea* and its expansionist dream of uniting the eastern and western shores of the Aegean, the two-headed eagle frames the figure of peace from above as the monthly religious calendars cataloging the feast days of the Ortho-dox saints frame her from below. Caught between political aspirations of empire and religious marking of time, she is indeed "fixed." To break free of her bonds, to move away from the political space and religious time that enclose her, would also necessarily be to shift those very boundaries.

Yet the possibility of something like this reconfiguration of boundaries is the suggestion of the mural on the walls of the Estia Neas Smyrnis, with its silent watchful women and children who, there too, bear witness to war and a militant nationalism. There too the boundaries of political space and of a quasi-religious time enclose the figures. But if we trace the mural to the right, beyond the young woman and her children watching the Greek man load a cannon (later to find itself thrust out stiffly in the hands of a post-1922 "peace" in the visual marker from another source), beyond the young woman sitting with empty arms clasped to her chest watching the burning of Smyrna on the opposite shore, we arrive at a marker of sorts for the possibility of boundaries reconfigured. Standing on the western shores of the Aegean, on the far side of Smyrna in flames, is a small group of men, women, and children. One woman, standing at the back of the small band of people with a young child in her arms, looks back over her shoulder at Smyrna. The others—a man holding a bouzouki and grasping a girl-child by the hand, a woman and a priest with a religious icon, a bare-chested man holding the headless and limbless torso of a marble statue—look vari-ously away from Asia Minor and apparently toward Greece. Carrying with them from Asia Minor symbols of the Orthodox Church (the icon), popular culture (the bouzouki), and the classical past (the marble statue), this seg-ment of the mural constructs and registers the potential for the cultural, historical, and religious wealth that the refugees bring to their new "home-land." With knees bent, shoulders slumped forward, feet arrested in mid-step, or bodies turned back toward the eastern shore of the Aegean, the

The Estia Neas Smyrni mural: contributions of the Asia Minor refugees (on the left of the grieving woman in black)

figures of the men, women, and children are disheveled, angular, apprehensive. Their apprehension both precedes and stands behind them in the mural. They are caught *between* "homelands." They are caught between positions in the national story; they are the liberated subjects of "the great idea," refugees from a country no longer their own, and they are refugees by virtue of the very same "great idea," immigrants to a "homeland" not (yet) their own. Richard Clogg, in a suggestive article on the Turkish-speaking Greeks of Asia Minor in Greece, gently notes in conclusion: "Their reception at the hands of the indigenous population was not always a happy one. Among other epithets they were derisively referred to as *yiaourtobaptismenoi* ('baptised in yoghurt') and there were complaints of *ogloukratia* ('the predominance of those with names ending in the Turkish suffix *oglu*')."[38]

It may be in response to the tensions of their literal and metaphoric border positions, to both such reception as Clogg notes above and their expulsion from Asia Minor itself, that the transition between the group of refugees arriving from Asia Minor and another and presumably subsequent generation of young men and women is marked by a grieving female figure sitting, legs outstretched, on the ground between the two clusters of people. She is dressed in black, her head covered with a black scarf, one hand on the ground supporting her weight, the other mournfully held up to her face. As in the two women figured earlier in the mural, here too a

The Estia Neas Smyrni mural: the refugees in the next generation (on the right of the grieving women in black)

critical transition in the mural's performance of the national narrative is marked with an apparently passive female figure; it is the site of ponderous loss, silence, and not too implicit violation. The black-clad figure of lamentation is made to bridge the movement to and from loss; at least in the narrative of this mural, her figure has an implicit conjunctive function. With little room for lyric hesitation, the female figure is the understood, if mute, narrative marker of change, of passage from one narrative moment to the next. On the far side of her grieving figure, the second group of men and women stand as the consummated product of her grief; her figure serves as the conjunction linking these two groups of narrative characters, these two narrative moments. In contrast to the earlier moment and group, the second group of men and women stand uniformly upright, their bodies tidily composed and dressed, facing the mural's implied viewer directly. Rather than icons, musical instruments, or classical statues, they carry objects that betoken the fruits of their labors, of plenitude and abundance. So too, their bodies speak neither the language of disruption nor of despair but of health and vigor. In this mural, it is the black-clad, mournful female figure on the ground that marks the reception and transformation of the Asia Minor refugees in Greece. But shrouded in black, with covered face, her rhetorical figure is silence, a grammatical marker of interruption and silent conjunction. She marks a transition that can only arguably be represented at all, visually or linguistically.

In a similar fashion, the old grandmother and her stories in "Instead of the Grandmother" mark a (silenced) transition from prewar irredentism to postwar defeat, from the "traditionalization" of the domestic sphere to its militarization. In that newspaper account of the national narrative, the war and its combatants take over the national hearth and the task of (nationalized) domestic education that is to take place there. So too, the sanguinely rendered female figure of (an immobilized) peace struggling to stride forward against a backdrop of war and the progression of time, marks an attempted transition from the smoldering militarism of "the postwar situation" to the "dawn" of the new year (see *Amaltheia* illustration).

Figures such as these are rendered with some difference in the literary narratives that tell and link the stories of violent displacement, of becoming-refugees, of "return" to an alien homeland. Although the literary configurations make clearer in comparison how distinct narrative modes articulate similar questions differently and respond to them variously, the basic problematic remains. It is one of the rhetoric of redeemed national community, the "grammar" of displacement and belonging, and the silences that neither can compel to speech.

The "impact" of the Asia Minor Catastrophe on modern Greek letters has been singularly and admirably addressed in Thomas Doulis's *Disaster and Fiction.* Doulis's careful survey of immediate and longer-term consequences of the 1922 debacle for Greek literature includes in its purview a wide and diverse array of texts. But I would draw attention to several fictional texts that render the question of the gendered nation and the proper place of its constituent members rather differently from that "impact" for which Doulis accounts. As Doulis notes, the first Greek narratives of the postwar period were nonfiction accounts of men taken hostage in Turkish forced labor battalions; these were subsequently subsumed by fictional accounts of the same phenomenon. Stratis Doukas's *Istoria enos aixmalotou* (Story of a prisoner of war; 1929) and Ilias Venezis's *To noumero 31,328* (The number 31,328; 1931) are well-known versions of the latter narratives. They chronicle, with varying degrees of fictionality, the struggle to survive and maintain some sense of humanity in the face of intercommunal and intracommunal brutality. But the extent to which even such captivity narratives attest to interethnic or interreligious community between Greeks and Turks against their overseers and commanders is striking given the historical experiences the narratives document. If the captivity narratives must ultimately reiterate the "safety" and "inevitability" of a homogeneous national community and its narrative/s, they also make clear the violence wrought in the name of that "inevitable safety" of putative sameness. That necessary ending, the inevitable strategy of narrative containment that makes an always fictive ending possible at all, is even more forcibly marked in literary narratives.

In literary narratives, the conclusion of the Asia Minor Catastrophe is, not surprisingly, always already there. But the period that precedes the catastrophe presents itself as an insistent preoccupation of literary narratives as well. In fact, the fiction of one of the most accomplished and important chroniclers of the Asia Minor Greeks, Dido Soteriou, suggests that the fierce upheavals of the catastrophe were already present, if better camouflaged, *before* that crisis and its aftermath. Soteriou's first novel, *Oi Nekroi perimenoun* (The dead are waiting),[39] is a powerful fictive elaboration of precisely this suggestion. Putative precrisis safety and stability are, in retrospect at least but not only then, already marked by the *absence* of safety and stability. The first-person narrator of *Oi Nekroi perimenoun,* Aliki, is a young girl from Smyrna; she is already a "refugee" of sorts in that coastal city, having fled there with her family from the strife in Aidini. But it is only in the opening pages of the second half of the novel that Aliki tells her story of becoming-a-refugee, that being her departure from Asia Minor for Greece. Ironically, when she leaves Smyrna with her wealthy aunt only a few days before that city's fiery demise, it is not (yet) quite in flight from disaster but for a "vacation" in Greece. The "vacationers," however, are overtaken by historical events; they find themselves situated, and narrated, otherwise: "As soon as we landed in Piraeus, full of smiles and plans for tourist excursions [in Greece], we found ourselves in front of a strange sight: a large crowd was gathered, [standing] here and there, [looking] gloomy and dazed. Young and old women, their heads covered with scarves, shouted and gestured nervously" (131). There is a subtle if striking differentiation asserted here between women of the mainland and women from Asia Minor in the young girl's attention to the scarf-covered heads of the mainland Greek women. That their heads are "covered with scarves" would be unremarkable, not even worth mentioning, if all women wore scarves. Language further underscores this differentiation of the two groups of women:

> But it was impossible to make out exactly what they were saying and why the police were pushing them back. Later some sailors jumped into their midst, battered [looking and] glaring fiercely. They began to shout [at the police].
> —Why are you hitting the women, eh? What are you hitting them

for? Who did they hurt? Are you afraid that they'll disturb the peace?
The peace, eh? They're asking about their children; they don't know
what's become of them in the massacre [in Asia Minor].

As we were trying to listen and understand what was happening, a
sailor pointed to us and said:

—There, the first refugees have [already] come from Smyrna.

My Aunt Ermione turned and looked at us, as if expecting a denial.

—Are they talking about us? Just listen to the way rumors are
started. (131)

For the women from Asia Minor, their story of becoming refugees is one
they hear first from others. Before they themselves are aware of the refugee
story in which they are cast, they are narrated as such by others. And for
the mainland Greek women and the sailors at the dock, and by extension
for society at large, the rupture between official rhetoric—of the glorious
recapture of Byzantium—and reality is already painfully evident. As the
young girl and her aunt search for a room in Piraeus, they are repeatedly
turned away because they are refugees. They, too, are forced to a realization of the gap between official rhetoric and personal stories. For at some
unidentifiable point in that process of being identified by others as refugees, they in fact *become* refugees. They finally find "a dark, dismal room
with six beds" and Aliki admits, "When we became real refugees, we
didn't understand. Within a few days, the whole world had turned upside
down" (133).

Yet, it is actually in the first half of *Oi Nekroi perimenoun,* which recounts life in Asia Minor *before* the 1922 catastrophe, that the putative
certainty and coherence of things have already begun to collapse. Other
disasters are already in the making. In fact, upheaval and disjuncture are
conspicuous from the very first lines of the novel that recall the narrator as
a young girl:

A small girl sets out on the uneven cobblestone path of Aidini, a
provincial city in Asia Minor. Her dark face and black eyes are framed
by blond curls elegantly covered by a light, pink hat—a cheerful sign
of a rosy, carefree life. Those childish curls, that were as soft as silk
and shone like gold in the sunlight, gave to the pallid girlish little face
a strange joy, a promise, a hope. . . .

But they weren't real. They had bought them for her and sewn them
to the child's hat to cover, to camouflage (*exoraisoune*/εξοραΐσουνε),
an ugliness, a stubborn case of scabies that had forced her parents to
shave her head. . . .

Because of this, one of the first lessons that that little girl learned was how even the ugliest things in life can be whitewashed (εξορᾴζονται) as long as you didn't hesitate to hide reality with a beautiful, gold-plated lie. (9)

The young girl now grown urgently evokes the potentially treacherous contradictions of what seem to be "cheerful signs" of "rosy, carefree" narratives—of family, of religious community, of nation. Although the narrator acknowledges that to begin her story by recalling "a pink hat with a few fake blond curls" will seem strange to many, she insists that "this insignificant detail preoccupies me, it almost challenges me." And if the apparent insignificance of fake blond curls distinguishes the story's point of departure, the threat of imminent and premature closure is also signaled from the opening page by the sound of "volleys of gunfire from Nazi firing squads in Athens." And so the narrator is "in a hurry, in a hurry to say those things that consume me before what might be my turn [in front of the firing squad]." The story that begins with the "lie" of a little girl's fake curls is, in the narrative present, threatened with occlusion by the Nazi occupation of Greece during WWII. This fictional pretext of urgency in the narrative present is equally a rhetorical strategy that implies the story of the little pink hat and fake curls retold with a difference; its symbols, signs, and road markers read otherwise. Faced with the possibility of death before a firing squad, the narrator hastens to tell her story and, from the beginning—as she "sets out"—to disavow her readers/listeners of uncritical faith in what might appear to be the case. Aliki's implied audience is enjoined to recognize, as she herself was as a young girl, that apparently "cheerful symbol[s] of a rosy, carefree life" are other than what they seem.

Perhaps it is not surprising that the story of refugee uprooting would implicitly, even explicitly, assert the apparent scheme of things as unstable, as not what it seems. For life as a refugee is predicated on the violent overturning of things as they appear(ed). Ostensible sureties of state governance and protection, of regional and local communities, of family, of national or ethnic or religious definitions are brutally exposed as inadequate, as not sureties at all. It is in such a context that refugee narratives, fictional and nonfictional, can be read as a critique of business as usual, whether that business as usual is the business of relations to and workings of the state, of communal self-definitions, of sexual and gender roles, or of the family. The operative circumstances of becoming-refugee are precisely those of a radical transformation of daily life, the disrupture of established definition and place. In fact, Bertolt Brecht (in reference to refugees from

Hitler's Germany) identifies refugees as "the keenest dialecticians . . . refugees as a result of changes, their sole object of study is change (*Arbeits-
journal*)."[39]

And yet, of course, the young girl Aliki continues down the road and
through the rest of the novel. Her becoming-a-refugee is narrated by her as
unavoidable, as beyond her control. And it is. But the narrator as young
girl already knows that the dominant stories that govern her prerefugee life
are dubious, precariously held together, not altogether credible. In the retrospective moment of the narrative present—and with the threat of death,
the absolute end of re-membering and narrating, looming for the woman/
girl—the retelling of her story is simultaneously an indictment of uncritical confidence or belief in things as they appear. And this indictment is
equally an implicit suggestion of the need for critical community. That
critical community, refugee and nonrefugee, would recognize refugee
memory as not simply plaintive stories about a lost past. For memory is
also, and perhaps more crucially, about the present. And about possible
futures. This is as clear in Soteriou's literary account of the Asia Minor
Catastrophe and its aftermath for one young woman/child as it is in nonliterary refugee testimonials and popular cultural documents. Those various documents record a struggle over the content of memory that seeks to
"forecast" the character of the future as it seeks to comment on the present.
For Soteriou's *Oi Nekroi perimenoun,* it is a struggle for the outcome of
which "the dead are waiting." Their anticipation is literally the end of
her novel.

Soteriou's later and literarily perhaps more accomplished novel, *Matomena xomata* (Bloodied Earth; 1962), extends this function of memory
and its stories as it does the critique of things-as-they-appear. And it articulates some of the implications of understanding and rethinking the massive "change" with which Brecht characterizes refugee displacement and
the struggle over the construction of new places. *Matomena xomata* is also
a variation of sorts on the captivity narratives—circumscribed places—that
registered in Greek letters the initial impact of the Asia Minor Catastrophe.
The main character and first-person narrator is a young Anatolian peasant,
Manolis Axiotis, from the village of Kirgidzes in Aidiniou. Axiotis's captivity narrative begins, not with his being taken prisoner of war by Kemal's
soldiers after the disaster of August 1922; that story is (briefly) told in the
fourth and final section of the novel, "The Catastrophe." Rather, Axiotis's
first "captivity" is within his family, at the hands of a harsh and demanding father, whose "sole concern was to accumulate as many fields and
olive and fig trees as possible" (11). The barely contained violence of the

father toward his children emerges from the beginning of Axiotis's recollections of his childhood. He recalls confronting his father's rage as "my first encounter with the blindness of power and I was distraught. How was I to know then that I would struggle against such blind power for my entire life" (12–13). But his mother's tenderness and the affectionate companionship of his siblings and covillagers counter the boy's patriarchal circumscription. The violence of Axiotis's father, restrictive as it is, is the exception rather than the norm in the "Peaceful Life" (*Eiriniki zoi*) of the first section of the novel.

From the circle of his family and rural village, Axiotis is sent by his father to work as an accountant on an estate and subsequently to Smyrna. There he is confronted with the dishonesty and greed and, alternately, the good-natured fairness, of those in whose employ he is placed. Greeks, Turks, Jews, and Armenians—what distinguishes people for the young peasant is less race and ethnicity or religion, any more than it is language, as they all speak Turkish. Axiotis sees corruption and brutality among his own as much as among other communities. Even the functionaries of the ruling Ottoman authority are differentiated from one another by their character rather than by their official roles or their ethnicity. Some are fair and reasonable, others greedy or brutal.

But, by 1915, Axiotis is forcibly inducted elsewhere; he is drafted by the Ottoman state into a labor battalion.[40] After months of grueling labor, brutalization, and near starvation, but more decisively after hearing Stephan, a young Armenian boy, recount the agonizing story of the slaughter of his family and village, Axiotis decides to desert. It is clearly not just his own miserable condition or the plight of his coethnic and coreligious fellows that impels him; it was "the things that I heard from Stephan [that] made me decide to leave as soon as I could" (149). Axiotis joins the countless deserters from the Ottoman army roaming the countryside of eastern Anatolia—Kurds, Greeks, Turks—a massive, multiethnic group of fugitives. He makes his tortuous way back to his village, traveling at night over the mountains. Assisted in his flight by Muslims and Christians, by Greeks, Turks, and Armenians, he narrowly escapes capture by Ottoman authorities or their sympathizers of various ethnic and religious identifications. Finally he and his cohort fugitives are saved by the end of the war and a general armistice.

Thus, in the third section of the novel, "The Greeks Came," Axiotis reenters his village one March afternoon in 1918 full of plans for the future: of the house he's just finished building, of marrying the young woman from a nearby village with whom he's in love. But gathered in the

central square as he approaches are the men of the village, and Manolis
wonders anxiously why they've abandoned the fields so early. The newspapers have just arrived with a call for all "those in Asia Minor who are
Greek citizens/nationals [*upikoous*]" to report to the occupying Greek
army for mandatory military duty. In an extraordinary moment in the
novel (or out of it), Axiotis protests the obvious but unspeakable to his
fellow villagers. They are Ottoman and not Greek nationals and therefore
should not have to serve in the Greek army.[41] However fictional here, this
passage echoes the sentiment of a number of the testimonials of the Asia
Minor refugees cited earlier, that is, that the Greeks in Asia Minor are
Christians and ethnic Greeks but residents and subjects of the Ottoman
state (later of Turkey). The mainland Greeks are brothers but foreigners;
the mainland Greek state is not theirs. But in both the historical and the
fictional instances, this sentiment was derided and ultimately overruled—
in the novel, by the hierarchy of village elders and clergy. The following
morning, Manolis and all the other young men of the village between
twenty-one and thirty-five are forced to depart to Smyrna for military
service in the mainland Greek army.

While in this coercive community, Axiotis is befriended by Nikitis Drosakis, a Cretan student serving in the Greek military. Drosakis comments
in exasperation to Axiotis on an argument among his fellow soldiers about
who is to blame for the imminent failure of the Greek occupation of Turkey: "Did you hear them? Worthless, cheap chatter! They don't look for the
root of the problem, the fools. It's the same old story: Venizelos, King
Constantine.[42] These guys, at least, have an excuse; they don't know
what's happening to them. But those in power? The leaders? None of them
wants to see that what we're doing is suicidal" (217).[43] Here again, for the
benefit of his narratee, Axiotis—and by extension for the benefit of the
implied audience for Axiotis's own reminiscences—Drosakis indicts facile
acceptance of things as they appear. Such uncritical acceptance is deadly.
For both the troops in the field and the civilians at home, it leads to (and
over) the edge of a precipice. The choice between Venizelos and King
Constantine is no choice at all; the quarreling soldiers will literally die for
failing to locate "the root of the problem" and instead entrusting their fate
to either Venizelos or Constantine. Even Drosakis's critical acumen will
not save him; he dies at the front. And Axiotis's story culminates in still
another captivity narrative as a member of the infamous prisoner of war
battalions into which Anatolian Greeks and mainland Greek soldiers were
forced at the end of the war. But novels must necessarily have endings that
(appear to) accommodate and conclude the stories told in the preceding

pages. Axiotis escapes with a friend. They are picked up by two fishermen from the Greek island of Samos and subsequently find themselves on a ship full of refugees seeking a less crowded Greek port. *Matomena xomata* ends with Axiotis's invocation of the Greek and Turkish dead and of their lost homeland, "of the land that bore us all . . . may it not bear us malice for the blood in which we drenched it." And, finally, Axiotis concludes with "a curse on those responsible" (313).

What is the literary function of this insistent fictional remembering and retelling of stories from the past? It is not, at first, an abstract question of the efficacy of stories in general. Rather, it is a smaller question of the role of such stories within the context of Soteriou's novels, or in any of the other numerous fictional renderings of a prelapsarian past in Asia Minor. For the first-person narrators of both *Matomena xomata* and *Oi Nekroi perimenoun,* at least, retelling the past is undoubtedly a counsel of sorts to those who would not critically consider things as they appear in the present *or* in the past. For the imminent betrayal of uncritical faith in appearances is, figuratively at least, as close as the story read on the page in front of your eyes or heard in your ear. For these two narrators and for the novels in which they are figured, remembrance and retelling are means to keep from the precipice of oblivion other stories of coexistence, of brutality, of love that have been foreclosed—drenched in blood, dead. But another foreclosure threatens such stories. For Aliki it is, of course, the threat of her own death in front of a firing squad—the unequivocal end of remembering and retelling stories. But also, and as important, it is the threat of fascism, foreign or indigenous, and, not least of all, its attempt at the absolute ordering of all stories in a master narrative of coercive unity, homogeneity, and absolute propriety of place. In fact, the refugee displacement that fascism causes in Europe is rationalized in the name of "exchanging populations" and national and ethnic "homogeneity" that underlie the Asia Minor Expedition and Catastrophe. Fascism answers the titular question of "who belongs where" with resoundingly brutal certitude.

But for Aliki's male counterpart, Manolis Axiotis, the threat of foreclosure on the stories he must tell is not (yet) fascism. The novel ends in the mid-1920s. For Axiotis, the foreclosure on his stories is that *"tuflosi tis exousias"* (blindness of power), which would shut out and silence opposition to the dominant (patriarchal) scheme of things. He narrates himself as an opponent, even as a child, of such blind power. And at the end of his narration, he acknowledges the power of stories that overwhelm the teller and the audience. On a ship loaded with refugees seeking a friendly port,

"The stories begin. Wherever you stop, wherever you go, they hound you. They burrow into your ears, like fantastic voices in the mind of a lunatic" (311). The stories overtake the listener who, in his turn, becomes a teller—whence the fictional pretext of the novel.

What is perhaps most suggestive in these fictional and nonfictional stories of refugee displacement is not simply their accounts of violence and rupture. It is a simultaneous suggestion of a kind of narrative skepticism to which the narrators lay claim even in the prerefugee past and with which they counsel their narratees and, by extension, the implied audience. This often emphatic assertion of skepticism is made precisely in the narrative *present* of retelling the story *past*. Retelling the story of refugee uprooting and displacement makes possible (but not inevitable) a critical configuration in which the narrator recounts—but not only—the trajectory of a violently uprooted past leading inexorably to the misery of the narrative present as refugees. That trajectory is certainly omnipresent in literary and historical accounts of refugee experiences. But implicitly and sometimes explicitly, the very narrative organization of meaning in the prerefugee past—the dominant stories of family, home, village, ethnos, religious community—is narrated as questionable and unstable, as not what it appears. The apparently self-evident narrative organization of the story past is retold analytically, critically. The implicit and sometimes explicit question underlying those stories is something like: What is it in the way we organized social and political meaning, community, family in the past that could have contributed to the massive displacement in which we find ourselves now? For some, of course, the answer is simply a resoundingly defensive "nothing. "Those responsible," in Axiotis's closing curse, are someone and somewhere else. But, for others, the answer is more complicated, ambiguous, and ultimately, more incisive. "Those responsible" are both far away and near. Their rethinking and retelling of the dubious organization of meaning in the past at least implicitly suggests the possibility of alternative organizations of meaning. Not in the past, of course, for that is beyond reach. But in the present and in the future. So, for example, Axiotis's assertion about citizenship that does not necessarily correspond to ethnic or religious affiliation is not just a singular and even shocking moment in Soteriou's novel (although it is that, especially in its Greek context). But it also and more importantly points to other ways of thinking communal and state affiliation, scandalous, unspeakable, and fictional as they may be.

To postulate prior suspicion of dominant narratives in a present in which those narratives have been brutally exposed as inadequate is scarcely surprising or inexplicable. The retrospective skeptical qualification of past acceptance of dominant narratives is a way of ameliorating the grimness of the present. To tell the story of becoming-refugee is to attempt to reconcile the teller of the story with the seemingly unresolvable conflicts that cast her or him in the role of refugee narrator in the first place. Perhaps with Soteriou's novels as fictional pretext, we can return to the issue of remembering and retelling stories from the past and even, though implicitly, of the efficacy of stories in general. For dominant narratives of family, nation, state, community, and selves can be considered dubious *even as* they exert their persuasive and coercive power over their tellers and audiences. There is no necessary space outside of those dominant narratives from which participants and narrators could construct other, less dubious narratives. Based on literary and testimonial accounts of the massive upheaval of the refugee experience, that space is often imperceptible, if not, for all practical purposes, nonexistent. To question, to mistrust, or even to refuse existing narrative configurations is not thereby to accede to the possibility of some leveraged Archimedean point outside of them. Participation in dominant narratives is not necessarily unequivocal belief in them; it is not necessarily the *non*recognition of their contradiction by lived experience. What seems far more often the case is, rather, that narrators of and characters in dominant narratives attempt to redefine their positions both individually and collectively. To shift their place(s) within the narrative. To suggest an alternative telos and/or a different informing rationale for the narrative. And, sometimes at least, to propose another story and another way of telling that story. The alternatives, then, are not simply between utter determinism on the one hand and unlimited possibility on the other: between total belief in narrative(s) and absolute skepticism of them, between a prerefugee moment of trust and a refugee experience of mis- or distrust. If the story of trust betrayed is a touchstone of the refugee experience,[44] so is the story of the resolute unavailability of any handy exit from the exigencies *and* contingencies of a specific historical moment. The extent to which the massive forces that cause their becoming-refugees neither originated with nor were simply controllable by them is apparent in virtually all refugee stories. Nonetheless, one of the overwhelming concerns of telling the refugee experience, literarily or autobiographically, is to understand, to come to terms with, those forces. And no less significantly, it is also a way of attempting to tell-with-a-difference, to reconfigure possible futures. For, finally, if the focus thus far has been on notions of the story (past) and narration (present) of the refugee experience, there is also a crucial figuring of the future in this rhetorical economy.

It is here that I would like to reinsert the notion of critical community as one underlying the question of refugee narratives about "who belongs where" or proper place. First, it is a question of proper place for both the tellers *and* the audiences of those stories. The assertion in the narrative present of a past betrayed is the assertion, at least implicitly, of a claim for what *should have been* (in the past of the story), for the necessity of a critical community "then." But equally, it is a claim for what *should be* in the present. It is a moral or ethical claim, an assertion of different value or meaning or narrative order. And it prefigures possible futures and what might or perhaps would be if the story (and its telling of the past) were different, if critical communities could establish and maintain themselves. This is both the threat and promise of (stories of) the refugee experience. And so, we listen to or read and respond to or retell refugee stories obviously heeding their immediate distress and urgent needs. But there is something more to address in refugee stories than their sorrows, loss, and needs. For there can also be an incisive critical edge to refugee stories, a persuasive argument for calculated critical understandings of dominant narratives, a skeptical recounting of failed critical communities, an urgent appeal for new critical communities. And those elements of "the refugee experience" decisively implicate nonrefugee communities as well. The keen assessment of the Greek Smyrniot writer Kosmas Politis is a particularly germane comment on such implication. An interview with the Greek literary critic George Savvides is the introduction to Politis's 1962 novel, *Stou Hatzifrangou: Ta sarandakhronia mias khamenis politeias* (At Hatzifrangou: The forty years of a lost city), set in a working-class district of Smyrna at the turn of the century. In that interview-as-introduction, Politis responds with no little irony to Savvides's final question about the significance of the dedicatory motto of the novel—"They've managed to make me feel like a slave [*rayia*] in my homeland"—and whether "the sentiment" of that motto is "shared by many other refugees":

> First concerning the freedom that we felt when we lived in Smyrna: we had absolutely no trouble with the Turks at least until 1914; [our] sense of comfort, of affluence—this was dependent, of course, on the concessions of the [Ottoman] regime. But also in the interior of Asia Minor there was, for the most part, harmony between Turks and Greeks. And as for Smyrna, I can say that we lived unaware of the Turkish element. On the other hand, when the Greek High Commis-

sion [i.e., the occupying authority] was established in Smyrna, there came moments when we, the native population, felt that we lived under a foreign—I'm not saying "enemy"—occupation. Now as for the feeling of [being] a slave that I've said they managed to make me feel in my homeland, I don't know how many other refugees feel this—what I do know is that certainly many native Greeks have it.

In the struggles between official rhetoric and popular sentiment and between popular action and official machinations and maneuvering, cultural interpretations of refugee experiences, of the reconstitution of national (if not state) identities, do not play a minor role. And in these contexts, the fierce negotiations and re-formations of gender roles, of "the family," of sexuality, critically inflect and often indelibly shape those national definitions, those social imaginaries and their lived experiences. And these negotiations are, not surprisingly, the site of violent contestation for representation, meaning, and organization.

For certainly the forcible recasting of a group of people as refugees is grounded in violence and in a violent rupture of life as it was conceived *and* as it was lived. The 1922 forcible exchange of populations between Greece and Turkey radically challenged, forcibly terminated, and of painful necessity reshaped prior everyday negotiations across borders, be they national, religious, ethnic, class, racial, or gendered. But, based on cultural representations of the refugee experience and on oral narratives and histories both of refugee life and of sociocultural life before the refugee uprooting, it is not only in times of peace (so-called) or in pre- and postcrisis moments—in other words, not only in times when "stability" is (re)established—that these renegotiations take place. It is also, and most suggestively, during and subsequent to the ruptures to which the very designation "refugee experience" or "nationalism in crisis" points.

The refugee experience of the community or nation in crisis as it is represented in cultural and oral narratives potentially challenges established boundaries of community and nation. For it is precisely those inviolable boundaries that the refugee knows only too well to be violable. Thus, the telling of refugee stories is at least sometimes also a radical reconceptualization of the very definitions and ground rules of community or nation and of the roles of those who claim to speak for and from them. Refugee stories reconstitute, with a difference that is often ignored in official political discourse, boundaries and official and unofficial rules for crossing over them in ways that are only arguably unimaginable or impossible. As Bertolt Brecht insists, it is change for which they seek to account and because of which the respectable boundaries of the normal and everyday are no longer respectable or respected. Refugee stories of critical skepticism and community are crucial to our understanding of their predicaments and also of our own predicaments. Not only for that reason, we would do well to attend to them.

2   The Gendered Purity of the Nation: Sovereignty and Its Violation, or, Rape by Any Other Name —Cyprus 1974

Running in place at the speed of
light, we defensively cling to categories, our
dilapidated signposts in a bleak landscape. . . .
Reflections of control, they reassure us that
there's a time and a place for everything.
Declaring what's right and what's wrong. . . .
Use them but doubt them.
They are the rules of the game, but perhaps
no longer the one being played.
—Barbara Kruger,
"What's High, What's Low—
and Who Cares?"[1]

In midsummer of 1974, after months (and years) of machinations and failed efforts for control of the island, the extreme right-wing paramilitary group Ethniki Organosis Kypriakon Agoniston (National Organization of Cypriot Fighters; EOKA-B),[2] in conjunction with the military junta then in power in Greece, successfully overthrew the elected president of Cyprus, Archbishop Makarios.[3] Amidst their claims of defending the island from "foreign" threats and their brutal violence against the Cypriots who opposed them, they installed a regime headed by Nikos Sampson, an EOKA member and the infamous terrorist of the Omorphita massacres,[4] a parliamentary deputy, and publisher of the sensationalist right-wing newspaper, *Maxi* (Battle). Within the hour of an early morning attack on the presidential palace, the coup's supporters occupied the Cyprus Broadcasting Corporation (or RIK, the state-run radio station) and began broadcasting the first official announcement from the leaders of the coup. A female voice read in monotone the proclamation that was repeated continuously throughout the day: "It is emphasized once again that the problem is strictly an internal one between Greeks. And Makarios is dead. Those who have arms are ordered to surrender them to the nearest military group. And we remind you that any movement in the streets is forbidden, the movement of pedestrians and vehicles. Resistance will be met with execution. And Makarios is dead . . ."

The claims of the coup's leaders notwithstanding and however bloodily forceful their initial efforts at eliminating opposition, they did not quite succeed in their aims. Makarios managed to escape to Paphos, where the fierce battles between his supporters and other members of the Cypriot opposition raged for days. It took two days of intense fighting before the National Guard and EOKA irregulars could decisively capture and control the presidential palace. In the meantime, from an improvised radio station in Paphos, Makarios broadcast news of his escape. Poignant as that announcement is, it is also indelibly marked from its opening address by the ethnonational contradictions of the time: "Greek Cypriots, this voice is familiar to you; you know who is speaking. I am Makarios; I am he who you elected as your leader.[5] I am not dead as the junta in Athens and her representatives here wanted. I am alive and with you, standard bearer and fellow fighter with you. . . . The junta's coup failed. I was the object of that coup. And as long as I live the junta in Cyprus will not succeed. The resistance of the men of the Presidential guard, the resistance of our people, stopped the armored vehicles, stopped the tanks. . . . The junta must not succeed. Now more than ever the struggle."

This last phrase, "*Nun uper pandon agon*," is an elegant but loaded call to arms in classical Greek. But Makarios's exclusive address to Greek Cypriots, though clearly a reassurance and exhortation to his own ethnoreligious community, is made by the endangered president of *all* of Cyprus, at least nominally. Makarios's reiteration of communal distinctions and divisions at such a moment, apparently following on the communal divisions insisted on by the right-wing junta itself, is a revealing comment on the conception of Cypriot society prevalent at the time.[6] Those communal distinctions and divisions were, to be sure, established and codified by the Cypriot Constitution generated at the behest of the British colonial power. And in the years leading up to and following "independence," they were unevenly enacted by both Greek Cypriot and Turkish Cypriot communities and by the mainland powers—England, Greece, and Turkey—that laid claim to the former's representation and "guarantee." Yet Makarios might well have addressed all Cypriots, not just Greek Cypriots. For the events of 15 July surely struck fear in the hearts of Turkish Cypriots as much as it did in those of Greek Cypriots. If Greeks and Greek Cypriots were willing to massacre "their own" with such vengeance, what would they do to Turkish Cypriots?[7] By the evening of 15 July, Nikos Sampson was sworn in as the new president of Cyprus. That very fact and the memories of his fanatical assaults on Turkish Cypriots (not to mention his equally frenzied hatred for and violence against Cypriot "communists" of whatever ethnic derivation) certainly generated transcommunal terror among Cypriots. The claim that the coup was "a strictly internal Greek affair" was so minimally credible that Makarios's implicit reiteration of it in his call to resistance against it is noteworthy. On the other hand, Sampson's own account of that day would be comical if it was not so ominous in its obfuscating claim to "unity" and "democracy": "I accepted the leadership of the democracy of Cyprus the evening of that Monday [15 July] to save this place from bloodshed and to bring unity—in which I was successful, I believe."[8]

His claims notwithstanding, the inglorious reign of Sampson and his cohorts lasted scarcely more than a week. On 20 July 1974, five days after his installation as president of Cyprus, Turkey invaded the island amidst its own claims of ensuring the sovereignty and constitutional order of

Cyprus and of defending the Turkish Cypriot population.[9] Turkey initially occupied a fifteen-mile corridor around the northern port city of Kyrenia. On 22 July, two days *after* the Turkish invasion had begun, Sampson announced over Cypriot state radio in high-flown *katharevousa* (puristic; official Greek), "the union [*tin enosin*] of Cyprus with her native fatherland [*mitros Patridos*]. The age-old yearning and the aspirations of our people find vindication in this historic moment. Long live the united nation [*inomenon ethnos*]."[10] The next day, Sampson "resigned," to be replaced by Glavkos Klerides, who as president of the Cypriot Parliament at the time of the coup, was the constitutionally designated president in Makarios's absence. Numerous UN resolutions[11] were passed, and the First and Second Geneva Conferences of the guarantor powers were convened on the situation in Cyprus.[12] Within less than a month, between 14 and 16 August, after the rejection of Turkish demands that partitioned areas of Cyprus be put under Turkish control, the Turkish military forcibly expanded its occupation of Cyprus to include some 37 percent of the island. In a small island with approximately 575,000 total population at the time, the month from mid-July to mid-August 1974 resulted in at least 6,000 dead, 200,000 internal refugees, and some 1,600 missing persons. At the time of the Turkish invasion, the citizens of Cyprus were ethnically diverse and lived interspersed with one another for the most part.[13] According to the last official census, at independence in 1960, 77 percent of the population were ethnically Greek, 18 percent ethnically Turkish, and the remaining 5 percent Maronite, Armenian, and "Latin."[14]

In early December 1974, Makarios returned to Cyprus, where he reassumed the office of president and kept that position until his death in August 1977. The Turkish occupation of Cyprus continues to the present day. In February 1975, the Turkish Federated State of Cyprus was declared in occupied northern Cyprus. And in November 1983, a unilateral declaration was made of the independent Turkish Republic of Northern Cyprus. Both the 1975 and the 1983 declarations of statehood and independence in occupied Cyprus were immediately condemned by the UN Security Council, which called upon the member states of that organization to reject the declaration(s) of independence and to continue to recognize the sovereign Republic of Cyprus. Only the Turkish government (and much later Saudi Arabia) recognized the renegade republic in the north. The increasing influx of settlers from Turkey and the emigration of Turkish Cypriots have starkly shifted the social and cultural configuration in northern Cyprus, nationalist claims to pan-Turkish identity notwithstanding. The tension between Turkish Cypriots and Turkish settlers is palpable and apparent in newspapers, politics, and social interaction.[15] Efforts for a negotiated settlement to "the Cyprus problem" have thus far ended in an impasse.

In the years immediately following the Turkish invasion of Cyprus, the reinstalled Cypriot government eloquently and for the most part successfully pled the case of a single and sovereign Cyprus in the international arena. President Makarios's speech to the UN General Assembly on 1 October 1974 sounded many of the themes that would be maintained throughout the next two decades of international and internal debate over "the Cyprus problem." The Cyprus problem, as Makarios maps it in his speech and in subsequent years, is the result of outside interference in the affairs of a sovereign and independent state. Elimination of that interference will result in elimination of the "problem." Makarios acknowledged the right-wing coup of 15 July 1974 as "the prelude to the tragedy" of Turkish invasion and continuing occupation. His references in that context are almost exclusively to the machinations of the Greek junta; there is no mention of the internal political situation in Cyprus that led to the coup. He identifies his own overthrow as a "coup d'etat by the Greek junta" and further characterizes it as "engineered and staged against the legitimate Government of Cyprus by the military junta then ruling Greece. Officers from Greece serving with the Cypriot National Guard, acting on instructions from the military junta in Athens attacked on the 15th of July and destroyed with heavy weapons the Presidential Palace, seeking my death."[16] There is no mention of the precoup period in Cyprus, one fraught with bombings, assassinations, hostage taking, and gun battles, as even the most cursory examination of the newspapers of that period reveals. The ominous warning signals of EOKA-B assaults, gun running, and bomb attacks and of similar actions by EOKA-B's Turkish Cypriot counterpart, the TMT (Turkish Resistance Movement), are ominously apparent in the months and even years prior to July 1974. But Makarios makes no mention of them nor of the Cypriot perpetrators of the coup. As Christopher Hitchens shrewdly observes in "The Axe and the Woods," the second chapter of his *Cyprus,* by way of citing a Turkish proverb ("When the axe came into the woods, the trees said, 'The handle is one of us'"), Greek Cypriots, including Makarios himself, did not expect mainland Greeks to actually turn against them. Still, Makarios's speech—made only some two and a half months after the Cypriot coup and the Turkish invasion of Cyprus and its expansion to almost 40 percent of the island when he himself was still unable to return to Cyprus and the acting president, Glavkos Klerides, was generously (?) suggesting that new elections be held (though Makarios was president as the result of an uncontested election)[17]—is striking for its silences. Makarios's speech is, however, an eloquent testimony to the brutality of invasion and occupation, to their violation of human rights, to the threat such actions pose to the international sphere and to small states in that sphere most of all:

> As a result of the Turkish invasion, Cyprus, a flourishing and happy island, has been turned into a place of ruins, tears, and death. The Turkish invasion forces have occupied almost 40 percent of the territory of Cyprus and have uprooted from their homes over 200,000 people, constituting one third of the population of the country, who, having been forced to abandon their lands, were turned into refugees living in the most appalling conditions . . . the ruthless showering of napalm bombs on undefended towns and villages . . . murdering in cold blood, raping, looting and plunder . . . against every norm of decency in a civilized society.
>
> . . . In no circumstances should the acquisition of territories by force be tolerated nor can it confer upon the invader any post of vantage in negotiating or otherwise. Nor can faits accomplis resulting from military operation be accepted or condoned. If they were to be accepted or tolerated in the case of Cyprus a most dangerous precedent would be set for other small countries whose independence will be at the mercy of their more powerful neighbors.
>
> I have come here to seek the support of the international community in our struggle to save the independence, unity, and territorial integrity of Cyprus. I am here in a cause for justice and freedom to a small-state member of the United Nations.

Makarios's speech also, if rather discreetly and sometimes anonymously, indicts U.S./Turkish/Greek complicity in the de facto partition of the island: "It is obvious that the Turkish invasion was not intended for the restoration of the constitutional order as established by the Constitution of 1960 but for enforcing her partitionist plans in violation of that Constitution." Makarios then quotes President Lyndon Johnson's letter of 5 June 1964 to Inonu, the Turkish prime minister at the time, on the eve of another planned Turkish invasion. In that letter, Johnson explicitly acknowledges "our understanding that the proposed intervention by Turkey would be for the purpose of effecting a form of partition of the Island."[18] Johnson's directive (and threat) forestalled Turkish plans for an invasion of Cyprus. In the opening of his speech, Makarios referred to his "impression that some countries did not raise their voice against the Turkish invasion at first because they were deceived by Turkey as to her real intentions." The delicate reminder, then, is that "international" (i.e., U.S.) pressure prevented a Turkish invasion in 1964; "international" pressure should be able to effect a Turkish military withdrawal and greater compliance in a negotiated settlement in 1974. This view was, and arguably still is, distinctly widely held in Cyprus. Foreign intervention is cited as both the cause of the disaster in Cyprus and the best hope for its resolution. A refugee woman interviewed in Michael Cacoyannis's film *Attila '74* explains this quite directly: "We're waiting for a solution from the United Nations, a fair solution to 'the Cyprus problem' [*to kypriako*], that will rid us of the barbarians who came and invaded our island. If the UN can't solve 'the Cyprus problem,' then why do we go on?"

President Makarios's speech to the UN is astute and powerful in its condemnation of the Turkish invasion and occupation of Cyprus and its plea for the withdrawal of occupying troops and a return of constitutional government to Cyprus. And it is precisely this that makes his circumvention of any explicit reference to the internal situation in Cyprus even more striking. There are only three moments in his speech in which the past and the internal affairs of "Cyprus, a happy and flourishing island," are even obliquely indicated. In reference to "Turkish aims" in its invasion and occupation and to the Cypriot Constitution of 1960, Makarios indicts Turkish claims to upholding the Constitution and its own role as a "guarantor" of that Constitution. Delicately or cunningly sidestepping any reference to his own thirteen-point proposal for the revision of the Cypriot Constitution presented only months before the coup and the Turkish invasion, Makarios speaks of the original Constitution of Cyprus as "giv[ing] many privileges to the Turkish-Cypriot community in a way that some of its provisions impede the smooth functioning of the state, yet it is still acceptable to us as it stands. Any changes must be made with the consent of all concerned." It was precisely because the Constitution was *not* "acceptable to us as it now stands" that Makarios repeatedly proposed specific revisions to that dubious document, most especially in his ill-timed effort of 1963 and again in the months preceding the events of 1974. In addition, exactly who comprises the "all concerned" who must agree to any constitutional changes is unspecified, as is a mechanism to secure their "consent." Do Turkey, Britain, and Greece have to provide their "consent"? Are they constituent members of the "all concerned" category? Clearly, their consent, let alone the consent of Cypriot citizens and of their elected leaders, was not forthcoming in any effort to change the way the Constitution of 1960 constructed Cypriot society and state. Yet the vagaries of his speech are not simply Makarios's foibles; they implicitly gesture toward the skewed and effectively nonindependent state structured in the Cypriot Constitution. The intercommunal violence of 1963–1965 and the events of 1974 are at least in part responses to Makarios's attempts to make changes—though, of course, scarcely disinterested ones—in that Constitution.

And then, in the speech's only direct reference to the Turkish Cypriot citizens of Cyprus, Makarios refers to Turkey's uprooting of "the Greek Cypriot population so that she [Turkey] may transfer and establish there Turkish populations, removing them from their homes in various parts of the island." Only subsequently, three lines later, is the reference to "Turkish populations" specified as "Turkish Cypriots."[19] It is at that point that Makarios intimates his role as the representative of all Cypriots: "I am sure that not only the Greek Cypriots but also the majority of Turkish Cypriots would not be happy to abandon their homes and to be transferred to other areas. What is the purpose to be served by such an inhuman exercise? The autonomy and security of the Turkish Cypriot community as claimed by Turkey?" He then shifts, without attempting to answer his own rhetorical questions, to a comparison of Turkey's claims in Cyprus with those of Hitler in Czechoslovakia. But there is no acknowledgment of the internal strife in Cyprus and, much more crucially, no unequivocal proclamation of his steadfast determination to counter extreme right-wing violence *within* Cyprus on the part of both Greek Cypriots and Turkish Cypriots against each other's communities but also against "their own."[20] Thus, Makarios's rhetorical questions here are vehemently answered by others elsewhere: by that multiethnic right wing in Cyprus, by the machinations of mainland Greek politics (of the junta but also preceding and subsequent to the junta) and of Turkish politics (that of the right wing but also of the center-liberal parties), both in terms of their internal, national concerns but also in their relationships with the "superpowers" of the United States and the then USSR.

Finally, and with no doubt unintentional irony, Makarios's last oblique reference to the fierce problems in Cyprus that predate the Cypriot coup and the Turkish invasion and occupation of the island is in the closing lines of his speech. There he expresses his appreciation to the UN Peacekeeping Forces in Cyprus—stationed there as a result of the conflicts of 1963–1964—and his sorrow at the loss of life that those troops incurred in "discharging its responsibilities in the face of such obstacles placed in its way." The profound internal problems in Cyprus from its inception as an "independent" and "sovereign" state in 1960, though not directly addressed in Makarios's speech, are the virtual foundation on which his speech is constructed. In his nonspecification of that ground, his call for "an international conference within the framework of the United Nations" to resolve "the problem of Cyprus" is poignantly limited at least.

Of course, this could be seen as an example of Makarios's political shrewdness. It is unseemly and perhaps unwise in a public, international speech to acknowledge internal problems and violent conflicts. Yet one of the reasons that Makarios's speech to the UN General Assembly on 1 October 1974 is so crucial is precisely because it articulates what was to become, with some small shifts in focus, internal Cypriot policy toward those same problems for a number of years. And, if Makarios was unwilling to articulate questions or answers concerning the internal situation in Cyprus, there were others only too willing to speak—and vociferously—in social, political, *and* (para)military terms. But finally and tellingly, Makarios's evasion of the internal problems of Cyprus is *not* sustained in Cypriot cultural texts. In fact, in diverse ways, they take up the crucial internal and international issues of sovereignty, invasion, violation, and displacement toward which Makarios's speech gestured and in response to which it was too often silent.

But before I turn to the cultural texts of that period and particularly to the prevalent image of woman-as-marker-for-the-nation and to the question of nationalism and gender roles in general, there is one further point to be made about the functioning of the Cypriot state subsequent to the Turkish invasion and occupation. For the shift in perception and operation of the Cypriot state in the post-1974 period is worthy of note and indeed exemplary as it shrewdly elaborated and enacted a number of productive policies to establish and sustain its role as the (sole) legitimate government of *all* of Cyprus. Following the invasion, for example, electrical power, water, and gas to all of Cyprus were continued from the utility plants and offices in unoccupied Cyprus. This was in spite of the obvious fact that there would be no payment of charges incurred for the consumption of those utilities in that portion of the island under Turkish occupation. The government of unoccupied Cyprus also officially publicized its continuing payment of pensions, social security, and insurance premiums to Turkish Cypriots living in the occupied territory. And Turkish Cypriot houses damaged or destroyed in the firebombing and general devastation of the invasion (and perhaps also in right-wing Greek Cypriot violence against Turkish Cypriot villages and homes prior to the invasion) were repaired and "loaned" to displaced Cypriot refugees, awaiting the return of their Turkish Cypriot owners. This information was officially publicized on both sides of the "green line" dividing the two parts of Cyprus. And, when the first university in unoccupied Cyprus was established in 1992

after some four years of planning and in spite of the constitutional designation of (essentially segregated) education as the separate responsibility of
each ethnoreligious community, the legislation of the Cypriot Parliament
designated the university as explicitly bicommunal. Thus, the university
includes within the School of Humanities and Social Sciences the five
departments of Greek Studies, Turkish Studies, Foreign Languages and
Literatures, Education, and Social and Political Sciences. The laudable
decision by the eight members of the solely Greek Cypriot Interim Governing Board to construct Greek and Turkish studies as separate but equal
departments—that is, rather than what could have been the subsumption,
for example, of Turkish Studies into Foreign Languages and Literatures—
was a noteworthy gesture of intercommunal goodwill and desire for coexistence. Or it was at least a noteworthy gesture of political shrewdness.
Such gestures on the part of the Cypriot government and its official and
semiofficial bodies are matched, if not exceeded, in certain nongovernmental Cypriot organizations—of trade unions or political parties or student groups or journalists, for example—that have attempted relatively
regularly to hold bicommunal meetings within (and outside of) Cyprus.

One of these was in December 1989. The first public discussion between
Turkish Cypriots and Greek Cypriots since the Turkish invasion of 1974
that included Turkish Cypriot opposition politicians and journalists from
northern and southern Cyprus was announced in the capital city of Nicosia. The evening meeting was held on 14 December in the cultural center
in the renovated Famagusta Gate inside the walls of the old city.[21] It began
late; the Turkish Cypriot speakers were delayed by the Turkish military at
the Ledra Palace crossing between the two parts of the divided city. The
room was crowded and hot, even in the chill air of December. The tension
was palpable. When the delegation from the north of Cyprus finally arrived (minus some of its members, who had been denied exit from northern Cyprus at the last minute), the assembled audience was nervously
watching the door and eyeing the amply armed and numerous Cypriot
police in attendance. The delegation from northern Cyprus entered with
the Greek Cypriots who had invited them.[22] After a brief introduction
citing the "historic nature" of the gathering and an outline of the speakers
for the evening, the first member of the Turkish Cypriot delegation rose
to address the crowd on the topic of "The Identity of Turkish-Cypriot Political Parties." He was Alpay Durduran, formerly leader of the Turkish
Cypriot party Toplumcu Kurtulus Partisi (TKP; Communal Liberation
Party). Durduran had recently (10 June 1989) been expelled from the TKP
for his too radical views on intercommunal relations and the future of

Cyprus.[23] His vocal support of a solution to "the Cyprus problem" in the formation of a Cypriot federated republic in which all Cypriots would be equal citizens and move, hold property, and live freely throughout the island was widely publicized and well-known on both sides of the "green line." Nonetheless, his opening words (in Cypriot Greek) visibly startled many of the largely Greek Cypriot audience: "We are the heirs of 7,000 years of Cypriot history and not of only 400 or 500 years, as some would claim."[24]

Durduran's inclusion of *all* Cypriots, regardless of ethnoreligious derivation, in the history of Cyprus elicited a nervous murmur from among the audience. But he continued undaunted to outline his goal of a Cypriot federated state (*omospondia*) that would unite all Cypriots under a common democratic government, noting that the northern Cypriot government and the resident occupying Turkish military that sustains them "forbids us the use of the word 'reunification' [he used the English word] when we speak of federation." There was, according to the official position of the military/government in northern Cyprus, nothing to "reunite." But Durduran insisted that there was and that virtually all Cypriots recognized that fact: "We must win the battle with chauvinism to reunite our country." Later, in response to a question about what Turkish Cypriot society in the north saw as the major impediments to a just solution to "the Cyprus problem," Durduran responded immediately and without hesitation: EOKA-B and the unwillingness of Greek Cypriots to share the responsibility for what had happened in Cyprus: "Just as we can't share [the name for] coffee (it must either be 'Greek' coffee or 'Turkish' coffee) and as we can't share the *tsiftideli* [a dance] which is called 'Arabic' in Greek Cypriot celebrations, so official proclamations throw the blame for what has happened in Cyprus completely on the Turkish Cypriots." Durduran then asked the audience what *they* thought were the main obstacles to a just solution to "the Cyprus problem." To this, people in the audience called out in response: the continually increasing numbers of mainland Turkish settlers in the north of Cyprus (estimated in late 1989 to be approximately fifty thousand) and the presence of the mainland Turkish occupation army. Though Durduran had cited the *internal,* intercommunal causes of "the Cyprus problem," his audience responded with the familiar indictment of foreign—Turkish—interference in Cypriot affairs.

During the question-and-answer period that followed the speeches of all of the participants, a middle-aged Greek Cypriot man jumped up from his seat in the audience and moved quickly to the side of the circular room, apparently to better address the entire group gathered there. The nearest policemen rushed over and grabbed his arms, presumably fearful of his intentions. As he struggled to shake them off, the man identified himself as a Greek Cypriot and a former Cypriot National Guardsman. He had served in the late 1960s under the mainland Greek officers who were, as the Constitution provided, commanding officers in the Cypriot military (though in increasingly greater numbers than the Constitution allowed). The man described his repugnance at the unchecked presence and actions in the Cypriot military of the extreme right wing and their mainland Greek commanders. The audience grew ever more agitated as they began to suspect the direction in which the man's account was moving. He continued in a tone of growing harshness and agitation to tell of the attack ordered by General Grivas in November 1967 on the Turkish Cypriot village of Kofinou. In that action, his (mainland Greek) commanding officer issued an order for the elimination of the Turkish Cypriot villagers. At this point in his story, he again tried to shake off the grip of the policemen, who were now telling him to sit down and be quiet. The Turkish Cypriot speakers at the front of the small hall were silent except for one man, who translated what was happening into Turkish for those who didn't know Greek. Firmly in the grip of the policemen but struggling nonetheless and amidst calls from the audience to let him go, the man recounted his terrified presence at the Kofinou massacre and the atrocities committed by his ethnoreligious fellow soldiers against their Turkish Cypriot cocitizens. This, he concluded as his voice rose angrily, was the major impediment to a just settlement of the situation in Cyprus: the unwillingness of Greek Cypriots to acknowledge their own atrocities against fellow Cypriots. The room exploded. Half of the audience rushed in the direction of the Greek Cypriot man, as many of them to congratulate and protect him as to shake their fists and shout at him. The police eyed the crowd, anxiously fingering their weapons. A circle of civilians formed a wall around the unscheduled speaker, both pushing the policemen away and insulating him from the audience. The man was visibly shaken, not by the audience's reaction to his statement, he assured the people gathered around him as he wiped his sweaty forehead with a handkerchief someone held out, but by recalling the events themselves.[25]

Fifteen years after the coup in Cyprus, after the Turkish invasion and occupation of the island, and after the many substantive changes in the rhetoric *and* practice of the Cypriot government and in Cypriot society, for a Greek Cypriot to recall right-wing atrocities by his own communal group against other Cypriots was still extremely provocative. The meeting was over; it was almost more than the audience and speakers could come to terms with in one short evening. The Greek Cypriot's courage in speaking out at this first public bicommunal meeting was matched by the principled restraint of the Turkish Cypriot delegation. The question on internal Cypriot politics and its role in "the Cyprus problem" was far clearer and more loaded than the official proclamations of the Cypriot government would ever admit. Some register of this is evident in the fact that the Greek Cypriot newspaper reports of the event in the following days made no reference to the statement by the Greek Cypriot ex-National Guardsman. The English-language *Cyprus Weekly,* under the headline "Can We Escape the Past?," quoted Durduran rather extensively and referred in passing to the speech of Niazi Kizilgiourek, a Turkish Cypriot journalist living in the unoccupied south of Cyprus.[26] *Haravghi,* the newspaper of AKEL (Anorthotiko Komma Ergazomenou Laou), the Cypriot Communist Party, ran an article on the event that quoted extensively from Durduran's speech in an outline of his positions on the various issues that circumscribe "the Cyprus problem."[27] The article concludes with a brief paragraph on the speech of Niazi Kizilgiourek.[28] It is only the Turkish Cypriot newspapers that mention the Greek Cypriot ex-National Guardsman's account of Greek Cypriot atrocities against Turkish Cypriots.[29] In the loaded rhetorical battles that have marked the intercommunal Cypriot situation since 1974, this kind of polarization is almost routine. It is also an indication of the extent to which individual and group efforts to improve relations between the two communities are quickly reappropriated by official and semiofficial discourses of intractability or, at least, of extreme circumspection. Still, the frequent citation of Kizilgiourek's speech and especially its conclusion suggests a productive interim direction for efforts to "reunite" Cyprus. It is a direction to which Cypriot culture has often responded more fervently and creatively than the Cypriot state: "There is no doubt that one of the first steps towards a united Cyprus is tacitly the sincere effort to eliminate the symbols of ethnic conflict. . . . The symbolism of ethnic antagonism must be replaced by a cultural dialogue which will emphasize, in the legacy of common social experiences and humanist values, the comparability of common hopes and motivations for coexistence."[30]

So then, what of poetic or fictional gesturing toward Kizilgiourek's stipulation of "common hopes and motivations for coexistence" in the context of literary and cultural production in post-1974 Cyprus? How does "the Cyprus problem"—*to Kypriako,* as it is familiarly referred to in Cyprus—perform itself in particular fictional narratives or poetic expressions in their negotiations of the conflicts and contradictions (historical and liter-ary) of Cypriot nationalism in crisis? One powerful if troubling fictional response to this question leads to others as the ironic narrative of Rina Katselli's *Galazia falaina* (Blue whale), with its fear of female disruption, gives way in other texts to a striking and insistent textual concern with stories of the gendering of nationalism and with female rape and its conse-quences. The central role of fictions and poetic expressions that articulate vexed categories of nationality, ethnicity, sexuality, and gender are a regis-ter of the official political and social discourse of the Cypriot state that cast the island of Cyprus under Turkish invasion and occupation as the woman raped. In that context, the "threat" of resulting "reproduction," both literal and metaphoric, raises provocative expressions of and occasional turns on "the symbols of ethnic conflict."

Rina Katselli's novel *Galazia falaina* is an apt if problematic literary point of entry to "the Cyprus problem." It is as much a disturbing performance of as it is eloquent testimony to the contradictions of the Greek Cypriot posi-tion(s) on and in "the Cyprus problem." First written "from exile" in the Cypriot capital of Nicosia in 1976, the novel was revised in 1978 and published later that year.[31] Katselli, like the unnamed male narrator of *Galazia falaina,* is from the northern port city of Kyrenia from which she and thousands of others were driven when the mainland Turkish army used that city as a point of entry for its July 1974 invasion. Her novel opens in Nicosia a year and a half after that invasion.

Katselli's autobiographical account of her initial enclavement in Kyr-enia's Dome Hotel and subsequent flight to the unoccupied south of Cy-prus is recorded in *Prosfugas ston topo mou* (Refugee in my homeland). *Galazia falaina* is not, then, Katselli's first narrative account of the uproot-ing of a third of the Cypriot population from their homes during and following the invasion. In fact, the differences between these two narra-tives are an interesting commentary not just on ethnic boundaries in Cyprus—though both narrators are distinctly Greek Cypriots—but also, if more implicitly, on gender divisions within the Greek Cypriot community. For the first-person narrator of *Prosfugas ston topo mou* is clearly desig-nated as Katselli herself or, at least, a distinctly female narrator. The narra-tor of *Galazia falaina,* on the other hand, is a forty-two-year-old Greek Cypriot man, a once prosperous landowner and chicken rancher in Kyr-enia, who, with the devastation of the invasion, loses everything except his penchant for "culture" and "art." His often bitterly ironic account of his fall from the past grace of wealth and property to his status in the narrative present as a dispossessed and penniless refugee is in distinct contrast to the anguished urgency of the narrator of *Prosfugas ston topo mou.* That narrator tells a story of violent displacement from home, everyday life, friends and family; of missing relatives; of dead bodies strewn in the streets; of long days of enclavement waiting for the defeat of the invading army and, when it becomes clear that that will not happen, of international assistance to flee to the south; of emotional exhaustion and personal loss. If the narrator of *Galazia falaina* also speaks of personal loss, of missing family and friends, of displacement, his story is rather more distinctly distanced and reframed by the irony of the narrative present rather than the loss and confusion of the story time itself. This difference is not just some predictable transformation in perspective with the passage of time but, at least equally, a performance of implicit gender boundaries in Katselli's narratives. The bitterly ironic tone, the self-absorbed concern, and the almost categorical political, social, and literary pronouncements of the narrator of *Galazia falaina* are not available to the narrator/author of *Prosfugas ston topo mou.* It is, instead, the pressing concern for the narrator's community of family and friends, for their survival and safety, for an effective communal and personal response to the violence and violation of the Turkish invasion that dominates *Prosfugas ston topo mou.*

Galazia falaina opens in an apparently less urgent tone than Katselli's earlier novel, with a short verse-form dedication entitled "Text for/to 19 friends," enigmatically signed "D.G.C." (X.E.K.) If *Prosfugas ston topo mou* openly addresses a wide audience, the dedication of *Galazia falaina* conspicuously foregrounds its own more constrained appeal. The limitations of that appeal are reiterated throughout the narrative. But they are already clearly indicated in the opening when the novel offers an authorial dedication for only one copy—his own. The other copies are to be inscribed by the nineteen friends with their own dedication or invocation in a blank space provided by the author. Such constraint notwithstanding, there is an explicit if ironic attempt from the beginning of this "manuscript" to implicate, to provoke the participation of, that severely delimited audience. And yet, the designated narrative site for the responses of the nineteen readers of D.G.C.'s manuscript is as circumscribed and impinged upon by the narrator as the refugee life of D.G.C. himself.

Divided into thirty-nine short if architectonically constructed sections,[32] *Galazia falaina* does not invoke the urgent immediacy, weariness, and fear of what are presumably the journal entries written during catastrophe of *Prosfugas ston topo mou*. The opening of section 1 is a letter, written in casual, almost leisurely fashion:

Friend,

I'll write first of the blue whale. Not because I want to justify the title of my manuscript, but, well, if you don't like the rest of these pages, or if they strike you as untrue, or—even if you believe them—if you find that they damage the favorable opinion that you have of the world, or if you are like me a displaced Greek Cypriot[33] and you're tired of saying the same thing over and over, or, finally, if you are a member of a powerful country and think you aren't in danger of being served the same dish of injustice that was offered to me, hold onto this page. And you'll have a short handbook about her [the blue whale] whose life is as moving as the lives of all the others who are mentioned below.

Now then, the blue whale before they made her extinct . . . (5)

This is followed by almost two pages of detail about the size, weight, eating and mating habits, and so on of the blue whale. Each time a specific figure is given in reference to the blue whale, the number is written first in letters and then in parenthetical Arabic numerals in what is almost a caricature of scientific numerical precision: "one hundred (100) feet long . . . two hundred (200) tons . . . it would take thirteen (13) elephants to equal her . . . she easily travels eighteen (18) nautical knots an hour" (5–6). In spite of the discreet analogy proposed by the narrator between the blue whales of the title and opening section and the Cypriot refugees—they are, at least, both "moving" stories—the repeatable precision of scientific knowledge proves an impossibility in framing and telling the refugee story. There is no simple and direct narration of the "facts" of his refugee story.

The thwarting of the narrator's desire for precise and objective narration becomes apparent as he accounts for the context in which he learned his facts about the demise of the blue whale: a program aired on Cypriot national television immediately following the Turkish invasion. His response to that program is to "step out onto the balcony and cry, feeling unbearably ashamed of my sudden sentimentality" (7). Repeatable precision cannot be marshaled for the "blunt account of our dismantling." There is, in fact, a double failure of analogy here between the narratives of the blue whale and of the Cypriot refugee. Not only is the language and style of the blue whale's story—putatively precise and scientific—unavailable to D.G.C.'s telling. The narrative perspective of the television documentary—omniscient, third person—is an impossibility as well, at least as he narrates his own story. (Narrating *their* own story is, presumably, an impossibility for the blue whales. The television account and then D.G.C.'s narrative account represent them instead.)

D.G.C.'s proposition of an analogy between the *stories* of the Cypriot refugees and the blue whales elides the disjuncture, the absence of analogy, between the two as *narratives*. It is precisely the language and perspective of the narrative of the blue whales that pose a continuous threat to the narrative of D.G.C. and, by extension, of Cypriot refugees in general. The omniscient or at least impersonal third-person narrative perspective— that of, say, an international Commission on Refugees or even a government refugee report—and the precise language of statistics—"two hundred (200) tons"—are the opponents *against which* D.G.C. marshals his irony and first-person narrative perspective (however limited). At the same time, like his response to the television story of the blue whale, the narrator's ironic first-person account is threatened throughout by a lurch into "sudden sentimentality" or, more often, though hardly as self-consciously, into fierce ethnoreligious chauvinism.[34]

If the narrator can recite the "facts" about the blue whales in section 1, he most decidedly can not do so, or at least not any longer, about himself. And so, not surprisingly, section 2 begins with the question "Who am I?" The narrator confides, "Sometimes I answer in verse, sometimes with curses" (8). This section concludes, however, with neither verses nor curses but with the reproduction of the narrator's refugee identity card. Like his "baptismal name," which has been replaced by the ID number on his refugee registration card and by the initials D.G.C., the narrator's choice of verses or curses has been resolutely impinged upon by definitions of and answers to the question "Who am I?" that are distinctly out of his control. Whatever "facts" he might once have been able to deploy in answer to that question were (scientifically?) disputed by the Turkish invasion and occupation of Cyprus. The remaining thirty-seven sections of *Galazia falaina*, then, are the narrator's attempt to regain or reconstruct some of that control both by telling selected new "facts" about his situation and self and by writing in a suitable audience for those "facts."

Distantly shadowing the outline of the old Cypriot woman's narrative recounted in my introduction, the narrative of the unnamed D.G.C.[35] moves back and forth as well between two topoi and times: the lost (if retrospectively ambiguous) plentitude of a time and space before the Turkish invasion and occupation of Cyprus[36] *and* the narrative present and refugee camp space of a literal uprooting and exile. His is an unavoidably motley narrative—bitterly ironic, pieced together from fragmented stories, marked with inconsistencies, unanswered questions, and sardonic observations. The narrator's language as he tells his stories is similarly pieced together. From demotic Greek: the flyleaf of the novel includes a note on "Orthography," identifying the accents used in the text as the system of the University of Thessaloniki (in mainland Greece). From ancient Greek: with Heraclitus as the narrator's preferred philosophical source. From the Cypriot dialect: with a glossary appended to the novel. From the flowery language of artists such as the narrator's cousin, excerpts from whose work the narrator includes in his own text. The rupture that necessitates a patchwork of history and quasi-autobiography also evidently necessitates one of language as well. In this fashion the narrator of *Galazia falaina* attempts to proceed with the telling of his story as he proceeded with the putatively "orderly" life that was his in Kyrenia before the invasion. Although his initial answer to the question of his identity is to present his refugee identity card, he subsequently cites historical precedents for his status as exile and refugee: the Armenians and Greeks of Asia Minor who fled the Turks, the Jews who fled Hitler, the Palestinians who fled the Israelis (section 3). He describes his wife's ridicule of his preoccupation with writing instead of with heroism (section 4). But, in spite of her ridicule, he describes and then rejects (section 5) the autobiographical realism and descriptive detail of his earlier writing, noting his aborted attempt to represent life in Kyrenia before the invasion, a "Proustian" attempt he bitterly refers to as "*A la Recherche du Pays Perdu*" (Remembrance of a homeland past). But his refutation of realist description notwithstanding, he then engages in considerable descriptive detail about his present condition: his relations with his wife (section 6), the (sexual and psychological) "madness" that allows him to survive his present situation (section 7), the potential destruction of the world and the questionable worthiness of the survival of the human race.[37]

The narrator then recounts his "unorthodox" political beliefs, derived, he claims, from reading history books. And he concludes this account of putative unorthodoxy with a request to be buried in the orthodox "position of an Orthodox Christian corpse, with [my] hands crossed in front of me." Later (sections 10 and 14), fearful that it be forgotten in the turmoil of the invasion and occupation with the multitude of dead who must be buried, he details the "traditional orthodox" burial position and procedures. The implicit suggestion here would seem to be of another unwritten (and unwritable) narrative future for which the narrative present of

Galazia falaina, in all its putative *un*orthodoxy, will have ended. For that future narrative, the narrative present is cast as that-which-will-have-been rather than that-which-is. And the narrator's concern with the moment of narrative closure—of his own death but also, at least for him, of the end of *un*orthodoxy as well—will have been signaled by his own orthodox burial position and funeral rites. And thus he will presumably transcend the narrative present to another narrative space and time (an O/orthodox afterlife).

The rapid succession of scarcely subtle series of oppositions in these sections—sane and mad, normal and deviant, legal and illegal, orthodox (Orthodox) and unorthodox, past and present—unquestionably seems to privilege the initial term in each set. There is an implicit, if uneasy, postulation of relation among those initial terms: past, orthodox/Orthodox, legal, normal, and sane. But the move to link that cluster of signs as simultaneous and almost inherently related is dubiously based on the narrator's ironic pride in his authorial productivity in the narrative present. And that narrative present is grounded in and even generated by the second terms in the string of oppositions—in unorthodoxy, illegality, deviance, and madness. If the narrator desires some future narrative in which the present will be concluded, it is very much in and generated by the narrative present that he articulates that desire. The narrative present, with all its associations of rupture, fragmentation, and deviance, provide access to (desire for) a narrative future. The serial construction of opposing terms that point at the past and present aspires to neither. Rather, it aspires to a future narrative moment and its perspective for which the narrative present will be past. It is that projected future moment, its narrative(s), and most importantly his own "correct" and "orthodox" position in it, to which D.G.C. as narrator struggles to accede. For that future narrative, his (dead) body and his affairs (including his manuscript, *Galazia falaina*) will be in "orthodox Christian" order. It is in this light that he proceeds, then, from burial rites to the contents of his "official" will, legally recorded but inaccessible in now occupied Kyrenia. So, he provides the text of his revised if legally "unofficial" and unrecorded will.

Having thus provided for the orthodox order of his narrative closure (his will, burial position, and funeral rites), the narrator turns to the demands of the narrative present: his manuscript for nineteen friends, the pages of which he seeks to fill "responsibly," urging his readers to do likewise with their own pages. Section 12 introduces the narrator's female cousin, also a refugee and writer, and the argument between the two about the purposes of art. In a gesture that presages one of the pivotal contradictions of Katselli's novel, the narrator's text is interrupted by his cousin's insistence that he include *her* text in his.[38] He acquiesces, if grudgingly, and produces an adamant perimeter to the excerpts from her work with his own ruminations on the purposes of art. In closing, the narrator enjoins his readers to fill the remainder of the page that he has left blank with *their* thoughts on the subject. Here again the narrator's directive is as noteworthy for its circumscription as for its solicitation of his readers' response.

Section 13 warns his nineteen readers, especially those who live outside of Cyprus, of the difficulties of contacting him to register their (*un*solicited and *un*circumscribed) responses to his manuscript: "I have no telephone in my shack." Nor is contact through the mail likely: "My location here in the desolation of state-owned land in Leukosia is too difficult to find for the person who delivers mail." And attempts at contact by newspaper, radio, or television announcement are all futile; the message will never reach its destination, the narrator warns. Still, almost perversely, he urges his readers: "Write me an unrestrained account of your opinion; you have nothing to fear from me." D.G.C.'s narratees are here implicated in a situation very like the situation of D.G.C. himself: write if you want, but it won't reach me or have any effect on what I'm doing. Or: respond only here, in the carefully demarcated spaces I provide for you. (The threat of a reader who does not confine her or his response to the demarcated spaces is made clear in the closing lines of the novel.) D.G.C. thus reiterates for his audience something like the conditions that appear to impinge on his own situation. The spaces for his responses to the refugee narrative in which he finds himself are equally constricted and constricting. In fact, he longs for silence yet fears that, if he falls silent, he will become yet another symbolic martyr: "And so, I'll continue, describing some human types that I know or, at least, I knew" (47). This is the context in which he outlines the correct procedure for burying the dead, especially for himself when he dies (section 14).

Subsequently (sections 15 to 24), the narrative shifts to the narrator's friends and acquaintances, Cypriot and foreign, and the various ways they have come to terms with, responded to, the occupation of Cyprus. This series of vignettes concludes significantly in section 24 with the narrator's decision *not* to tell the story of "some women from *Kyrenia* who've become like blue whales, extinct like Our Lady of Chrysoglykiotissa. . . . [To tell their stories] would take a great deal and I feel it's better that they hold a special place in my heart rather than a page here" (70). The parallels in this passage among women of Kyrenia, virtually extinct blue whales, and the Virgin (though usurped from her throne) suggest a problematic equation that implicitly informs much discussion of "the Cyprus problem." Baldly stated, the implicit equivalencies runs something like this: The properly "enthroned" and "housed" Virgin is (or should be) the marker for (Greek) Cypriot woman, who is (or should be) similarly accommodated in her own house. But this religious and familial order has been violated—invaded—and that space occupied. The Virgin who once "sat on her throne" has been "uprooted from her home, ravaged, and her house made into a mosque" (70). And thus, according to this formulation, both Virgin and woman—here specifically "some women from Kyrenia"—are, like the blue whale, made extinct. This postulation that the woman uprooted from her home is the woman extinct resonates ominously in terms of this narrative, not to mention in terms of post-1974 Cypriot society and culture. Here, in the narrator's rhetorical construct, the reference to the *dis*order or rupture of the configuration Virgin/woman/home results in a refusal (or inability) to narrate.[39] The narrator breaks off his own story of disorder and displacement in a gesture strangely reminiscent of his representation of the breaking off of that other orderly narrative—of "enthroned" Virgin and "housed" (Greek) Cypriot woman—disrupted by the Turkish invasion and occupation. It is the latter rupture or "unhousing" that, perhaps perversely, generated his own narrative in the first place. And so his refusal to narrate is a sort of negative testimony (by self-imposed silence) to the highly charged and threatening power of the formulation that constructs as parallel the unhoused Virgin/unhoused Cypriot women/extinct blue whales.

It is at this moment of narrative disjuncture that our narrator turns from the people around him to "more abstract concepts and how they operate in our times" (sections 25 to 38). With bitter irony he discusses the "Disunited Nations" and the betrayal of its goal and purpose (25); the operations of propaganda (27); the proximity to everyone of disaster in the age of nuclear weapons, regardless of spatial distance—with a diagram of a compass provided for the reader's "precise orientation" to danger (28); the fate of his home and possessions in Kyrenia (29); the desire of some refugees for "compensation" for their losses (30); the nonrefugee wealthy, whom the narrator sees as largely undisturbed by the occupation (31); the nonrefugee poor, who are, for the narrator, unquestionably "rich" if they still live in their own neighborhoods, villages, or towns (32);[40] the narrator's violently angry refusal of an aspersion on his refugee "identity" in the praise of an acquaintance that, in improving his lot as a refugee, he (the narrator) has displayed a steadfastness and tenacity that was his all along (33); his fear of man as more overwhelming than his fear of God (34); a television performance of the ballet *Romeo and Juliet* and the unbearable future (35);[41] the (future of the) narrator's children, the week of the coup that preceded the invasion, the narrator's outline for an unfinished play about extraterrestrial beings (36); the "ancestral" practice of cursing while crossing a bridge, with a blank space for the reader's insertion of her or his favorite curses (37); and finally, the necessity and problem of endings, here accomplished with a dedication from the narrator's dead friend and a quote from Heraclitus (38). The concluding section (39) is set in different type and entitled "Afterword." It recounts the return of the manuscript to the narrator by his dissatisfied nineteenth reader, "an old acquaintance of mine, a quiet, almost boring woman who loved to read." In response to the narrator's query as to whether she returns his manuscript because it is too "caustic" (*apsi*), she answers:

—On the contrary, I found it lukewarm.[42] It's ridiculous for a [grown] man to pretend to be a blue whale. I thought more highly of you than as an animal who submits to his fate and wants to strike an existential pose. Now that you don't have your property and factory you try to impress and overwhelm your acquaintances with literature. We knew that you had that inclination from the time you were a small child; it wasn't necessary for you to remind us again, now that things are so bad here.

—It's not my fault if things are bad.

—For there to be such misfortune, it means that every one of us is to blame [*o kathenas mas ftaei*]. It's not just those who commit the crime but those who didn't stop it [who are responsible]. And we didn't do anything significant to stop it. Now you come to us again, pretending to be a family man, the good Christian, trying to convince yourself that you've made it instead of raising your head and fighting the evil in your country and the world. And on top of that, you write about people as blue whales. (99)

The nineteenth reader of D.G.C.'s manuscript drops it in his lap and "runs off, before I had a chance to say anything else" (100). And there, without "a chance to say anything else," the novel ends. In a gesture that parallels the complaints of the narrator's wife, the intrusive (female) text of the narrator's refugee cousin, and the ominous extinction of "unhoused women" and the Virgin, it is again an unhoused refugee woman who disrupts and here terminally silences the narrative.[43]

In addition to its suggestive gesture to the implied reader in general, there is a peculiar resonance to this exchange between writer/narrator and reader/narratee in the context of the rhetoric of postinvasion Cyprus. The response of the Cypriot right wing to the accusation that it was precisely the right-wing military coup that provoked, or at the very least provided a pretext for, the Turkish invasion and occupation of Cyprus was the protestation "We are all to blame." The extent to which this claim gained circulation is attested to not least of all by the conclusion of Katselli's novel when the nineteenth reader of D.G.C.'s narrative echoes that statement.[44] But even if the obfuscation and leveling of such a statement is bracketed, even if we agree for the moment that the narrator is no doubt liable for at least some of the charges made against him by his nineteenth reader, her use of this phrase in particular in the conclusion of this poignantly ironic account of Cypriot refugee life gestures back to that event that precedes the opening of the novel and its story of invasion, uprooting, and displacement. That is, the short-lived right-wing Cypriot coup itself. And that is an incident figured in *Galazia falaina* in a peculiarly revealing fashion.

In contrast to the statement "We are all to blame," to which the novel grants currency in closing, there are two images that the novel rather assiduously does *not* foreground. But, juxtaposed, they serve as ominously silent markers in *Galazia falaina*. One is an almost incidental reference to the narrator's clean white shirt. He wears that spotless shirt during the week before the Turkish invasion, the same week of the right-wing coup that overthrew the elected president of Cyprus. That the narrator was strikingly exempt from the coup's immediate and organized attempt at the elimination of its many opponents (this, the *coup's* attempt at "cleanliness" and order) is verified precisely in the fact that his shirt remains spotless, "without marks," during that week. And it is verified as well in the narrator's observation that the coup and its imposition of house arrest (another kind of "order") "gave me the time to put my books in order, a job that I'd been putting off for three years" (92).[45] It is to this moment—with a clean white shirt and ordered bookshelves as its predominant markers—as well as to its more commonly understood reference, that the phrase "We are all to blame" could be brought to bear. The narrator's clean white shirt with the outline of a "futuristic play" in its pocket stands as a crucial and contradictory signpost in and of D.G.C.'s narrative. The absence of any marks (*deigmata*) on that shirt is striking in the context of a coup distinguished by violent repression, imposition of house arrest, and threats of execution to any who resisted. But that same week incurs nothing else for the narrator than an opportunity to put his books in order. This is surely as indicative of the narrator's position in "the Cyprus problem" as the later condition of that same shirt.

The day of the Turkish invasion the narrator puts on that same shirt "with trembling hands, while overhead Turkish airplanes whistled as they dropped flames [firebombs]." Subsequently, the "clean, white shirt" is transformed: "That shirt underwent all of the misfortunes of the invasion and the first week of my becoming a refugee, accumulating signs of whatever most tragic could exist in my life: dead members of brave young men, branches of executed savory and myrtle, blood spattered earth, the sweat of struggle, heroic battle, self-sacrifice, forced flight, the tears of women, men and children, my own tears. . . . When I went to take it off it bore a fearful resemblance to my soul.[46] I examined it from all sides and decided to wash it only when we returned to Kyrenia" (92).

The narrator's shirt is inscribed by, and then read by the narrator as a text of, the Turkish invasion and his own subsequent displacement as refugee. It is a poignant trope. Still, his graphic shirt/text here indicts itself in the earlier blank text of the same shirt, "clean" and "white" and "unmarked" during the week of the right-wing coup. Thus the promise of a future return of the clean shirt is more than a little ominous, given that earlier context in which the blank shirt/text and Cypriot society were presumably "put in order" by a repressive coup. But for the narrator, there is no text of, no inscription or marking from, a violent and repressive internal (though clearly externally influenced) coup. That series of events is unremarkable and unmarked/unnarrated. There is nothing to read there for him. Nor is there any intertextual relation between the coup and the Turkish invasion that followed. For the narrator, his shirt, his bookshelves, and by extension Cypriot society, are only being corrected, put in order, by the coup's imposition of house arrest. It is this imposition of (textual and military) order that weighs so heavily on D.G.C.'s narrative in retrospect—perhaps also on Katselli's *Galazia falaina* as well. For D.G.C.'s narrative, the carefully orchestrated implication of the reader/narratee in his equally carefully constructed narrative sequence results in the refusal and return of his manuscript by his nineteenth reader. The ironic undertone of D.G.C.'s narration, of his attempt to order and relate the stories of being a Cypriot refugee, is thoroughly called into question by that nineteenth reader. But the nineteenth reader's challenge to D.G.C.'s irony and her call to "direct action" ambiguously echoes the defensive rhetoric of the same people who engineered the coup in Cyprus and its putative order. The utterly untantalizing opposition here would appear to be between the almost smug irony of the narrator and the aptly critical but ominous call to direct (right-wing) action of the narrator's nineteenth reader.

In a similar fashion, the narratee/implied reader of D.G.C.'s manuscript is presented with a series of circumscribed (and inconsequential) choices in response to the (ironically consequential) questions the narrator asks: In the face of injustice, war, and destruction, is the effort to continue the human venture (*anthropini peripeteia*) worthwhile? "If you want, answer [the question] yourself, friend, with a single syllable in the box below: yes or no?" (28). Or, again in ruminating on the destruction of one small country—Cyprus—and the potential destruction of the entire planet: "In the small space which I leave, write something yourself, friend, something about the human race. A rough draft of a memorial plaque or something better. . . . In order to help you, I am tracing a border" (51–52). There is room here for little more than monosyllabic, circumscribed answers. And yet, of course, in the face of circumscription and radically delimited possibility, the narrator himself manages considerably more than a single syllable or an inscription within a narrowly defined boundary. So, too, his implied readers and narratees can exceed the boundaries traced for them. Within the narrative, some of them do, of course—most notably the nineteenth reader but also the narrator's wife and his cousin. And yet, the alternative readings they perform are little more compelling than the writing of the narrator or the reader responses he solicits. The alternative readings and writing of the narrator's cousin are set off in italics and framed by the narrator's dismissive commentary. The alternative readings of the narrator's wife are relegated by his narration to the margins of his stories; she may be an efficient caretaker of daily affairs but she is an intrusive aggravation to his narrative. And yet, one of the audiences to whom he addresses his narrative is precisely such women. This is most conspicuously the case with the nineteenth reader to whom he gives his manuscript, but his audience is also clearly the other "unhoused" women who "read" (yet potentially threaten) his refugee text. For D.G.C., their readings must necessarily be contained and defused, a narrative task that he ardently pursues but only provisionally manages to accomplish.

D.G.C. tells a narrative of the refugee story—and of the foreign invasion and occupation that created that refugee status for the narrator and thousands like him—not only through its content but also through its reenactment of another sort of "invasion and occupation." That is of the narrator's text by his female narratees. If, for D.G.C. in *Galazia falaina,* the image of the unhoused woman is the trope of choice for representing the invasion and occupation of Cyprus, it is equally and only slightly more subtly the predominant trope for a grave threat to his own narrative. That is the threat of interruption, of potential silence, of narratees who read his story differently and who, in their turn, are potential (or actual) narrators telling other and different stories. For much of his narrative, D.G.C. fends off that threat. The counternarratives (of ethnochauvinism, of "sudden sentimentality," of right-wing "order" and "correction," of women who read and write against the grain of his narrative) that seep into his narration of the refugee story strain against his laboriously drawn narrative boundaries. Ultimately, though, in the concluding section of his manuscript, those boundaries are less violently transgressed than just worn down. "You're crazy; you're absolutely mad," he tells the nineteenth reader breathlessly.[47] And then, minutes later, " 'And I, what do you think I should do anyway?' I asked hoarsely."

The rhetorical question that closes D.G.C.'s narrative is testimony to the awesome power of female narrative disruption, the judgment of that nineteenth reader does, after all and in fact, end his narrative. And it is simultaneously an ominous warning against precisely that female disruption. That women like the nineteenth reader of his manuscript (or his wife or his cousin) can lay claim to such "unhoused" power is implicitly a mark of the massive rupture and disorder that characterizes the Cypriot refugee situation. The specifics of that (female) narrative challenge and disruption ominously echo the far-right-wing exhortation to arms—"raising your head and fighting"—and their generalization of responsibility for events in Cyprus: "We are all to blame." The narrator is left with his "impotent" story thrown back into his lap and the challenge to action more "manly" than telling an ironic story ringing in his ears.

   The ambiguity of this fictional configuration is rather brutally reiterated in a Cypriot short story written about the same time, "Paralogismos" (Paralogic) by Maria Abraamidou. But in addition to the fearful ambiguity of Abraamidou's short fiction, there is simultaneously a potential, however hesitant or implicit, for constructing or assembling other ways of (fictional) knowing, for (fictional) shifts and transformations in modes of production and reproduction. And, in fact, this potential is both threat and promise in more post-1974 Cypriot fiction than just Abraamidou's short story. If boundaries (of nation, gender, ethnoreligious communities, class, patriarchy) are reaffirmed by violence and destruction against them, the crossing over of those boundaries is not necessarily insurance against nonviolence. And yet, boundary crossings can also implicate and undermine violence, putatively rigid identities, and patrilineal production(s). But, as

Katselli's novel and Abraamidou's "Paralogismos" both make clear, the (fictional) challenge to the dominant order has its own destructive logic against which its rhetoric of challenge and disruption strains.

Maria Abraamidou's "Paralogismos" (irrationality, illogicality, or miscalculation) was published in 1979, five years after the short-lived right-wing Cypriot coup and the subsequent Turkish invasion and occupation of Cyprus. The short story opens in the Turkish-occupied northern port city of Kyrenia in the months immediately following the coup and invasion. A young Greek Cypriot woman murmurs to herself, "I'm losing it, I'm losing it" ("Paraloizomai, paraloizomai"), as she waters the flowers in the yard of her mother's house in the evening darkness. She hears hesitant footsteps on the dusty stone path that passes next to the house. The footsteps stop; someone is watching her. She hears laughter and voices ("the others") and a Turkish love song (*amané*) that sounds like a funeral dirge (*moiroloi*). It is then that she makes out the body and face that belong to the footsteps: "eyes like an owl, swollen with sleeplessness looking at her tensely as if he wanted to say something, as if he had finally decided to dissolve the pledge of silence that had existed between them for so long" (20).

"Paralogismos" narrates the story of an encounter between a Greek Cypriot woman, Evtuxia,[48] and an unnamed Turkish (or Turkish Cypriot) soldier. And in telling that "paralogic" story, "Paralogismos" critically and daringly contests the dominant national order that would cast the Turkish occupying force and the Greek Cypriots as implacable enemies: the former as brutal invader, the latter as innocent and uprooted victims. "Paralogismos" also, and perhaps even more daringly, contests the designated spaces for Cypriot women and sexuality. And yet, within the narrative space of Abraamidou's short story, the contradictory and uneasy national(ist) constructions that designate proper place—for men and women; for Greek Cypriots and Turkish Cypriots; for Cypriots, mainland Turks, and mainland Greeks—are taken up, momentarily recast, and arguably rather brutally redrawn in conclusion. In that critical retelling of the dominant national(ist) narrative and of an "unthinkable" relationship of sexuality and love between a Turkish (or Turkish Cypriot) soldier and a young Greek Cypriot woman in occupied Cyprus, "Paralogismos" is, as its title suggests, crazy, paralogic, unthinkable. Its suggestively paralogic attempt to remap gendered national(ist) spaces within the narrative is finally, though, impinged on and recontained by the official national narrative that can scarcely allow such subtleties of narrative maneuver.

Some of this uneasiness, and the ambivalence of ethnonational boundaries, is linguistically played out in "Paralogismos." The narrative moves between the demotic Greek of the third-person narrator and the Cypriot dialect of Evtuxia, her mother, and their covillagers. The sometimes tense opposition between these two distinct versions of a single language, which in more than one account of the national story is also claimed as a single culture and nation, is punctuated by the repetition of two Turkish terms of endearment addressed by the Turkish soldier to Evtuxia. In a suggestive maneuver, they are the only words attributed to him in the story and the only Turkish words in the text. The presence of Turkish solely as terms of endearment is, then, implicitly at least, a substantial textual recasting of the Turkish or Turkish Cypriot presence in Cyprus.

In a parallel of sorts to this linguistic movement, the narration itself moves back and forth between the everyday details of life under Turkish occupation for Evtuxia and her covillagers and dreamy nighttime sequences of Evtuxia's own attempted flight "across the lines": lines between Turk and Cypriot, Muslim and Christian, occupier and occupied, man and woman. In this context, it is of no little significance that Evtuxia's border movement is preceded and prompted by a series of memories of five men from within her own ethnoreligious community. Her memories of them are also the memory and present reality of her social and personal "failure"—as a still unmarried woman—to fill the (only) acceptable village role for young women as wife and mother. Evtuxia is neither wife nor mother; she is not even engaged. And so the overdetermination of her memories of Greek Cypriot men is underscored by a narrative configuration in which she recalls those five men precisely as the Turkish soldier moves away from the wall of her mother's house where he had been standing, half hidden in the darkness: "She saw him break away from the wall of the house, *his large body like a threat* in the twilight. The light of the moon rising over Peristeres was focused on his arms crossed awkwardly over his chest as if he were cold or *like a vague gesture of offering or consolation.* Later she saw him slowly uncross his arms and salute her. It was then, *from his utterly and strangely appealing face, from a gesture foreign and hostile, that the memories leapt out at her,* crowding the narrow pathway with their shadows" (21; emphasis added).

Contrary to conventional expectations, it is not the shadowy threat of the Turkish soldier that leaps out of the darkness at Evtuxia; it is her own memories of five Greek Cypriot men justifying why they did not—could not, they claim—marry her. Where does the most dangerous "threat" lie for Evtuxia? With the soldier who salutes her? Or with her own memories? Of course, the prosaic answer is that the Turkish soldier will "leap out" of the shadows and attack the young Greek Cypriot woman. But, in fact, the rather more urgent threat is Evtuxia's memories of rejection from within her own ethnoreligious community and of the consequences of that rejection. If the Turkish soldier is a threat here, he is a decidedly more ambiguous one. He is, perhaps, the threat of desire, of the very "consolation" and "offering" that Evtuxia attributes to him. Given the operative narrative (and extranarrative) boundaries of "Paralogismos," that is a threat indeed.

What is clear, then, is that Evtuxia's border movement—her attempt to recast herself in a different and less restrictive relationship both to her "own" community and to that of the "enemy"—is inextricably linked to her memories of the contradictions and impossibilities for herself as a young and conspicuously unmarried woman within the space of her own community, her own "home." "Home" and "community" are here not self-evident and sustaining categories but problematic points of contention and possibility. It is in this context that the presence of the Turkish soldier can be a "foreign and hostile threat"—the occasion for Evtuxia's memories of being displaced in her own community—as his presence can simultaneously be a "gesture of offering or consolation."

Still, Evtuxia's border movement is tenuous and problematic even on its own terms. Some of its contradictions are apparent in her fantastic account of Kyrenia's past to the local schoolchildren. They come to school full of anguished accounts of the occupation of their homes, neighborhoods, and village by the Turkish military. Evtuxia is unable to respond to their stories and worried questions about the future. Instead, she gathers the smallest of the children around her to tell them a story. It is, significantly, one infused with sunlight and whiteness:[49]

> She told them the story of how once the village was one gigantic garden that stretched to the plain below and within it strolled [Cypriot Orthodox] monks dressed in white because only white suited so much light, so much beauty. And their village was beautiful and they loved it, didn't they?
>
> And utterly unexpectedly she saw again, over the heads of the children, his face bending over hers. (24)

In addition to the loaded postulation of an ethnically and religiously exclusive narrative past, the dominant tropes of Evtuxia's quasi-history are in striking contrast to her flight into the "dripping dampness" of the "dark nights" and the virtual silence—except for his terms of endearment to her in Turkish—of her meetings with the Turkish soldier. Her movement to the Turkish soldier is away from what she herself narrates as "beauty," "light," and "whiteness," religiously embodied, in her story, in the "purity" of the monks. But it is also, clearly, a flight away from sexual repression, rejection, and loneliness. Away from the ethnonational and religious boundaries of her community. Away from the familial boundaries represented by her sick mother and extended family, for whom, in her dreams and out of them, she is "a whore" or "strangely nervous and excitable"—a hysteric. In a familiarly loaded move, then, the dreariness and dissatisfaction of Evtuxia's daily life are countered in her unthinkable relationship with a forbidden other: the Turkish or Turkish Cypriot soldier.[50]

That "Paralogismos" does not specify the national origins of Evtuxia's "Turkish soldier" is striking. He could be either a member of the Turkish Cypriot community or from mainland Turkey. And, if the former, their relationship could conceivably predate the Turkish invasion. Is this, perhaps, the "pledge of silence that had existed between them for so long"? How long is "so long"? "Paralogismos" offers no clarification. It makes virtually no distinction between Turkish Cypriots and the invading Turkish army. In fact, in the passage that precedes Evtuxia's fantastic account of Kyrenia's history to the young schoolchildren, the Turkish army and the Turkish Cypriots are both identified by the children as the "enemy." This narrative gesture calls up the ethnic chauvinism of a version of Greek Cypriot nationalism that, with no irony, calls for a free, independent, and Greek Cyprus.[51]

Still, the overwhelmingly predominant account of the encounter between Greek (and, less openly, Turkish) Cypriot women and the Turkish army that invaded and occupies Cyprus was not that of a weary soldier standing hesitantly off in the gathering darkness. It was rather that of rape. The apparent recasting or renegotiation by "Paralogismos" of the order and boundaries of a dominant national narrative remains underwritten, however, by the metaphorization of the (violated) body of (Greek) Cypriot woman. The nationalist equation of inviolable woman and inviolable motherland is as unsurprising as it is fearfully problematic. But in "Paralogismos," that vexed configuration is less compelling than the specifics of the cultural and literary responses to the outcome or consequences of that symbolic equation of violated motherland and violated women. Certainly, bracketing literary texts for a moment, the political and social consequences of that metaphoric equation are instructive and even startling. The instances of the rape of Cypriot women by the invading Turkish military and the resulting pregnancies were high enough that the distinctly conservative Cypriot Orthodox Church felt compelled to sanction abortion in the fall and winter of 1974. And, at the same time, the Cypriot Parliament

A Greek-Cypriot card and poster from
the late 1980s: "And on earth, peace.
Cyprus, Free Greek"

passed a bill that ambivalently but open-endedly legalized abortion.[52] But
it is the cultural interventions in and negotiations of the equations of
invasion/rape and occupation/reproduction that suggest that far more
was at stake than unwanted pregnancies. For as Abraamidou's short story
suggests, the abortion of unwanted pregnancies did not (could not) similarly "abort" the violations wrought on the bodies of Cypriot women by
the Turkish invasion and occupation—nor the violations wrought on them
by Cypriot society itself before and after the invasion.

    The right-wing coup that preceded the Turkish invasion by little more
than a week proclaimed itself the defender of Cyprus against "foreign
threats"—those threats being one of the purported pretexts for its takeover.
The coup rather brutally located fellow Cypriots as "foreign threats," ironically illustrating once again the remarkable malleability of what is considered "foreign." It is precisely in this context that the "paralogic" of
Abraamidou's short story is most stark. It is precisely in this context that
"Paralogismos" challenges, however ambivalently, the dominant social,
political, and cultural definitions of Greek Cypriot nationalism. It retells
the gendered national encounter between Greek Cypriot and Turkish Cypriot, Cypriot and Turk, Christian and Muslim, woman and man.

Perhaps the most startling challenge of "Paralogismos," its potentially most radical recasting of the dominant national narrative, is not simply Evtuxia's sexual relationship with "the enemy." It is her exultation in realizing that she is pregnant, a condition of which her lover, the Turkish soldier, is also aware. But as a result, she stops going to meet him at night. And she attempts to avoid his watchful gaze during the day, moving through the village via back streets and out-of-the-way paths. When the Turkish military orders "a weapons search" ("but everyone knew they weren't looking for weapons"), the Greek Cypriot residents of the neighborhood in which Evtuxia lives are herded out of their houses and into the square. And Evtuxia feels the "tense eyes" of the Turkish soldier "watching her from afar, hiding within them something of the helpless humility of an animal" (25). Although the homes of the other residents are vandalized, Evtuxia returns to her mother's home to find it "untouched with the key [still] in the door." Rejected by men from within her own ethnoreligious community, dismissed by her own family, pregnant with the child of her Turkish (or Turkish Cypriot) lover, Evtuxia's account of the Turkish army's search concludes obsessively with a mournful enumeration of young women's dowries thrown into the streets.

The realization that she is pregnant causes Evtuxia to stop seeing the Turkish soldier and to reconsider what she had thought was "the deadness inside her": "How did it happen, since she was no longer alive?; from where did this new life stir? . . . so there was finally hope, even for her; she could wait; it gave her some time on credit" (24). But it is equally the untouched house of her mother during the Turkish army's search of the homes in her neighborhood that makes her "resolve to refuse everything": "She would refuse her heart; that was the price she had to pay for the life that had been given back to her" (26). Ominously but not surprisingly, the "everything" that she will refuse—"her heart"—is precisely the soldier and her relationship with him. In what is a stark strategy of narrative containment,[53] Evtuxia meets the Turkish soldier who is her lover and father of her child one last time. And she bludgeons him to death with a garden hoe. Given the unsettling narrative propositions of the short story—about women and men, Cypriots and Turks, desire and repression, and not least of all about the internal dynamics of Greek Cypriot society—that violent closure is virtually a strategic necessity for "Paralogismos." Thereby the violently disruptive questions raised by the border negotiations of a Greek Cypriot woman and a Turkish (or Turkish Cypriot) soldier are brutally attenuated.

Nonetheless, it is the bloody and violent conclusion of "Paralogismos" that points back to the fiercely ideological struggle at work throughout the narrative. And it is the narration of the soldier's death that makes this most apparent. Rather than cry out as Evtuxia strikes him, he falls to his knees, stretching out his hand to caress her swollen belly. Then he slips silently to the ground and dies. Rather then flee the scene leaving his body behind, Evtuxia performs funeral rites for him: "She stood for a moment, looking at him [lying] at her feet. Then she took water from the yard and washed the blood from his face. She straightened his body and crossed his arms over his chest as she had seen him do himself. She took the hoe and began to dig in the damp soil" (27). The next morning, Evtuxia bends over her mother's sickbed and promises that for which her mother had been pleading and Evtuxia refusing for months: "I'll go and find the Turkish Commanding Officer so that he can arrange our papers and we can leave. All right, mother?" (27).

The border crossings, the *paralogismos*—ambiguous, loaded, and im-pinged upon as it was—is over. The Turkish soldier who emerged from the shadows to contribute to the unspeakable story is effaced, beaten, buried—literally. Evtuxia and her mother will leave their home with the dangerous and paralogic negotiations that remaining there entail and become refugees in the "safe" sameness of the southern, unoccupied part of Cyprus. Evtuxia momentarily retells her role in the Greek Cypriot narrative of Cypriot nationalism with results that are only arguably fortuitous—even for her. Her role as defined by the dominant Cypriot national narrative will almost certainly now be that of an unmarried woman, pregnant but excusably so, with the child of a Greek Cypriot man who died a hero resisting the Turkish invasion. And even if this is not the story that Evtuxia tells, it will undoubt-edly be available to and about her. Evtuxia will no longer be such an embarrassment to herself and others as a nonwife and nonmother. She will now be able to fill at least one of those mandatory roles. But if Evtuxia's role is that of mother-to-be, it will also be that of a helpless and innocent victim. A certain socially acceptable agency and role as mother becomes available to her while another impossible and paralogic role is foreclosed.

Yet, how else could "Paralogismos" possibly end? There is no place in her "own" village, in her own "home," for Evtuxia, neither before the invasion nor after it. It is unthinkable, of course, for her to remain and bear the child whom all her covillagers will know is an impossible re/produc-tion. Her covillagers are as cognizant of her unmarried and unbetrothed status as Evtuxia is. Evtuxia's story of sexual desire for and willing repro-duction with "the enemy" is, in the dominant scheme of things, precisely paralogic. Dubious, attenuated, and ambivalent, "Paralogismos" simulta-neously participates in the dominant narrative of Cypriot nationalism as it locates, explores, and negotiates a contradictory fissure in the official narrative. That negotiation is precisely the attempt to narrate a transgression, a momentary crossing over of the lines. It is here, a fleeting temporal possibility of challenging and perhaps using differently—of transgressing—dominant spatial organization.

That this transgression takes place across the reproductive space of a woman's body is a gesture more than a little loaded.[54] That uterine spatial construct and its correlative of Evtuxia-as-mother are, on the one hand, scarcely a transgression of dominant gender roles. The body of woman is not quite used differently, at least to the extent that it is the site of reproduction. But the narrative agency of Evtuxia, strangely garnered as it is, is itself noteworthy. Does she use or instrumentalize her own body (and that of the Turkish soldier who is her lover) differently in establishing, maintaining, and definitively ending a relationship across ethnic, national, and religious boundaries? She does assume a kind of agency over her own body and desire, although with expressly bloody consequences for the object of her desire, who is himself remarkably acquiescent to her blows. Still, her unborn child will be a tiny production of an impossible "transnationalism," one based not on rape but on desire, seduction, and, arguably, on love. That it is a costly production is indubitably marked by the bloody corpse of the Turkish soldier. Yet, if the violent conclusion of "Paralogismos" seems to lend itself to a dominant nationalist reading, Evtuxia's attraction to and desire and even love for the Turkish soldier simultaneously confound that reading. Like the disruptive women whom D.G.C. attempts to contain in his narrative of refugee displacement, Evtuxia's story too disrupts—if only momentarily and with deadly consequences for her partner—the scheme of the dominant nationalist narrative.

> When I was a small child I wondered
> if she was Greek,
> the cat of our Greek neighbor.
> One day I asked my mother
> if cats are Turkish
> and dogs Greek.
> The dogs had snarled
> at our kittens.
> Days later
> I saw our cat
> eat the very kittens
> that she'd given birth to.[55]

Is there "reproduction" that can accommodate another order of things? That can accommodate the agencies of female desire and sexuality and of reproduction? The reconsideration of boundaries of the "nation" and of what they contain and exclude? One for which the violable/violated woman is *not* the site for and of the nation? Evtuxia's "paralogic" story comes as a provocative response (if not quite an answer) to such questions. Her reclamation of agency—limited, compromised, partial—clearly transgresses national and gender boundaries of "purity" and "integrity." Her story and its narration implicitly disrupt the equation of in/violable woman with in/violable nation. In this transgression and disruption, her story implicates other stories as well, fictional and nonfictional. Evtuxia's story suggests that it is not only the violation of the female body that is at issue but also the violently gendered proscription of social agency and power. The violation of rape is evoked in a scheme of things in which women are pure, moral, and powerless; men are impure, aggressive, and powerful. It is precisely in that context that Evtuxia's story, her border negotiations, and its narration are conducted. She enters the "impure" and "contaminated" nocturnal zone, momentarily leaving behind the dazzling whiteness of pure and exclusionary narratives. But in the "dark" she can be an active agent of her own desires, body, and sexuality. She can also be, of course, an active agent of violence.

The parameters of Evtuxia's story make utterly clear that this is not an isolated issue, a question of an individual woman's autonomy and inviolability. The very definitions and practices of the community of which Evtuxia is a part are at stake. And if, in conclusion, her paralogic story will be recontained by the dominant narrative of nation, motherhood, and (national/ist) sacrifice, nonetheless Evtuxia, the narrator, and the implied readers know that there is another story to tell.

If Evtuxia's paralogic story tells of at least biologically productive border crossings, Panos Ioannidis's "Oi stoles" (The uniforms) tells an eerily suggestive account of another kind of bodily border crossing and transnational production. In Ioannidis's short story, the bodies in question are those of a Greek Cypriot soldier and a young Turkish Cypriot woman. Their transnationalism—or, in a different telling of the Cypriot national story, their nationalism—is figured in their donning the uniforms of the title. *Stoles,* most commonly a reference to uniforms, especially military uniforms, are in this instance the clothes of a Turkish Cypriot mother and her soldier son. In putting on the "uniforms" of a Turkish Cypriot mother and son, the young man and woman are transformed by them. But prior to their transformation, there is another, more conventional appearance of a "uniform." The short story opens in the house of an old Turkish Cypriot man and his daughter as the Turkish army invades Cyprus. Four Greek Cypriot soldiers have been shot outside the door of their house, each one apparently banging on the door, pleading to be granted asylum from the Turkish soldiers chasing them. Their pleas are ignored by the terrified old man and his daughter inside, and the men die at the hands of a Turkish corporal and his men. It is the fourth soldier pounding on their door, peering in their window, begging for help, that opens the story. The father of the young woman responds to her agitation at the killing of this fourth man outside of their house by telling her fiercely, "That soldier outside [the Turkish corporal] is not a soldier—take it from me—he is Allah him-self. It is the Prophet [out there] who runs and beats and punishes [them]. Yes. The Prophet. *He put on a body and a uniform* and came to save the faithful, to clean Kyrenia and Cyprus from these shits" (10; emphasis added). When a fifth soldier pounds on their door, the young Turkish Cypriot woman furtively unlocks the door and, leaving it barely ajar, rushes to the other side of the room. A Greek Cypriot man dashes in grate-fully and then stops suddenly as he realizes—catching sight of a Turkish flag on the wall and the funeral picture of a young man next to it—that the woman and her father are Turkish Cypriots. In the ensuing struggle among the three of them, the recent history of Greek Cypriot and Turkish Cypriot relations is figured in all its conflictual and contradictory familiarity. The civil war that (again) bursts into the open with the right-wing Greek Cypriot coup is no longer "outside"—if in fact it ever was. It is literally in the center of the home (*ston eliako*).[56] This violent confrontation of the political "outside" with the familial "inside" is interrupted by further banging at the door. This time it is the Turkish corporal who charges into the small house with his automatic rifle lowered, demanding to know if the residents have seen a Greek. And with his entry into the house, the foreign invasion and occupation of Cyprus corporeally enters the home as well. It is, of course, already metaphorically present in the memory of the young son of the house, killed in earlier violence; it is present in the marching songs and Turkish military announcements from the transistor radio the old man turns on. But now it is physically there in the presence of the Turkish corporal. The old Turkish Cypriot falls gratefully to his knees at the soldier's feet; his daughter rushes to the old man's side to help him up; the Greek Cypriot man, collapsed behind the couch bleeding from his wounds and the beating he received at the hands of the young woman's father, is for the moment unseen and unheard. When the Turkish corporal attempts to sexually assault the young woman, her father rises to his feet in disbelief and tries to defend his daughter.

The uniform of the Turkish soldier does not clothe the Prophet, as the old Turkish Cypriot had fancifully supposed. It is not the uniform of "the Turkish peacemakers" about whose victorious exploits the radio blares reports. The uniform is here more properly a marker for the Turkish soldier's uncomprehending military incorporation into the expansionist narrative of the mainland Turkish government. As he lunges for the young Cypriot woman, he wonders at his presence in Cyprus at all: "this place to which they'd forced him to come, to kill and be killed, not understanding the reason why, not even wanting to come" (13).

The Turkish corporal's attempted rape of the young Turkish Cypriot woman is interrupted only by the arrival of his commanding officer. The corporal leaves but promises to return later the same night. Thus, the only alternative to the rape of the young Turkish Cypriot woman and the death of the young Greek Cypriot man—to the forcible bodily violation of each of them—is for them both to flee. And they do just that. Together. Dressed in the "uniforms" of Turkish Cypriots, the clothes of the young woman's dead mother and the military uniform of her dead brother. Here another bodily violation occurs, if not forcibly then at least of necessity. For rape and death are fictionally juxtaposed as differently gendered but parallel violations. A blatant formulation of what is a rather more subtle suggestion in the short story would be that rape is to the woman as death is to the man. That is the deadly, violatory possibility from which they flee. Yet, in wearing the clothes that the old Turkish Cypriot man frantically unearths for them from the chests and boxes in his room, the young Cypriot man and woman are bodily incorporated into another narrative, differently. The sexual tension between the Turkish Cypriot woman and Greek Cypriot man are subsumed into a mother-son relationship. The living young man and woman assume the clothes as well as the identities of a *dead* man and woman. In addition to putting on a uniform, the Greek Cypriot also "puts on" the Turkish Cypriot language, as he finds himself responding to the terms of endearment of the young-Cypriot-woman-as-his-mother—though he does so without much more understanding than the Turkish corporal has of why he is in Cyprus.

Thus, from a Greek Cypriot soldier, he becomes a Turkish Cypriot soldier, massacred by Greek Cypriots in the infamous slaughters of 1967.[57] In like manner, the threat of rape for the young Cypriot woman becomes, in a variation on the analogy suggested above, the threat of death. As she puts on the clothes of her mother, the young woman not only puts on her identity-as-mother to the Greek Cypriot soldier-as-son. She also puts on her mother's painfully crippling arthritis and the severe asthma that killed her. In the narrative scheme of things, though, this assumption of the bodies, clothes, identities, and relationships of the dead, with its concomitant loss of what the young Cypriot man and woman were before, is precisely what enables a kind of escape. But the young woman escapes the metaphoric death of rape only by assuming the likelihood of another, more literal death from asthma. In the concluding lines of the short story, which focus significantly enough on the young man and not on the young woman, this transformation "fills him [the Greek/Turkish Cypriot soldier] with courage and love, hope, again without his understanding what she had said" (18). The "she" here is the young Turkish Cypriot woman who has become his mother; she calls out to him, "Karim, my son." Her direct address to him specifies the only proper name identified in the short story; none of the other characters are distinguished by name. And, in fact, when the Greek Cypriot soldier pointedly asks the young woman her name to thank her for helping him, she refuses to tell him. Nor does she want to hear his name; in broken Greek, " 'Don't say,' she cut him off tensely. 'She [I] doesn't want . . . She won't see again . . . If you manage to escape, this uniform of Karim's will save you, this uniform of Karim's differentiates [separates or distinguishes—*horizei*] everything' " (16–17).

Although both the young man and the woman are metamorphosed by their uniforms, the more blatantly transnational or intercommunal body is that of the young Greek Cypriot soldier who becomes a young dead Turkish Cypriot. His body is literally the site for the (re)production or rebirth or resurrection of his intercommunal other. That this is not an utterly violatory metamorphosis is suggested in this narrative of exchange by a closing reference to his sense of well-being, encompassed in the love of his "mother"—a perhaps less threatening alternative than his earlier erotic attraction as a Greek Cypriot man for the young Turkish Cypriot woman.

But the young Cypriot woman too becomes the corporeal space for a narrative of transnationalism, though more implicitly. For she is now "mother" to a "son" who is Greek Cypriot *and* Turkish Cypriot. She is, metaphorically in this instance, the site on and through which the (re)production of a transnational or intercommunal body can occur. And again, the profound ambivalence of the gendering of nationalism—even nationalism challenged—is apparent. For her transformation is incumbent on her ability to reproduce citizens, even intercommunal ones. As ambiguously

as "Paralogismos" though differently gendered, "Oi stoles" affords narrative closure that is literally deadly for the Turkish Cypriot woman by
emphasizing a similar reproductive ability that gives to the Greek Cypriot
Evtuxia "new life." Constructions of biology and gender are here made to
bear an overwhelming fictional burden, as they bear an overwhelming
national/ist burden beyond the fiction.

What amounts to a virtual preoccupation of post-1974 Cypriot fiction
with rape, childbirth, and purity—with the violated body and the product
of its violation—is taken up again by Ioannidis in another short story, "E
Atheate opsi" (The invisible side). But the body in this instance is female
and narrated with somewhat more complexity and ambiguity than in "Oi
stoles." Here the violation, the rape, of the nation/al woman is formulated
as unacceptable defeat and unbearable violation *for the man*—or, at least,
for the man in this short story, that is, for one of its main characters, Lefteris
Foteinos.[58] It is Foteinos's return to a favorite site of his that is the pretext of
the short story. "The Invisible Side" or, in an alternative translation, "The
Unseen Aspect," is literally framed by, begins and ends in, the same narrative moment and topos. The moment is Foteinos's return to his "utopia";
the topos *is* that "utopia" now "violated" by being tilled and productive. It
is a strangely fertile field, a lush strip of green—"geometrically perfect, a
symmetrical carpet"—spread out over what he had known previously as
"an inhospitable, utterly parched plain, littered with skulls and rocks, barren and unproductive for at least a thousand years, from the time of the
great drought that filled Cyprus with reptiles and monasteries" (71).

It is the prior landscape that was Foteinos's favorite place. And his
opening characterization of the landscape evokes that to which the expression "the unseen side" conventionally refers: the unseen side of the
moon.[59] It is some two or three years after the Turkish invasion of Cyprus.
The stark landscape description above is given by Foteinos, one of the
three main characters. The story itself, however, is told not by him, but by
a barely discernible third-person narrator. For the "mediocre artist who
goes by the pseudonym Lefteris Foteinos," the fertile green field is an
unwelcome eruption on what had been "his own moonscape." Returning
to Cyprus and his "moonscape" after two years in Paris, he notices a young
woman, Maria, watching him unearth an animal skull from underneath
the lush field. She takes him to the small refugee settlement on the far side
of the field, to her grandfather, who is responsible for the alteration of the
landscape. As they walk to the settlement, he imagines what amounts to a
rape fantasy in revenge for Maria's putative part in the violation of "his
utopia." He pictures himself "seducing her in the depths of this chimerical

field and, on top of the green plants that had obscured and beautified death, to hold her, to subjugate her under his body, to revenge himself against her and her people for what they had done to his secret place" (73). This bizarre fantasy is tempered somewhat by his meeting with Maria's grandfather, Kyr Barnabas, and by the old man's story. Kyr Barnabas, originally a schoolteacher from Lapitho in the occupied north of Cyprus, lost his wife, sons, and daughter-in-law during the invasion. He made his way to Cavo Greco where, with others from his village, he was installed in a refugee camp. Five months later, his granddaughter Maria appeared, released by the Turkish military. He, his granddaughter, and the others who lived in the refugee settlement with him had worked for two years, carrying in topsoil from nearby fields, to make the barren land productive. This is the origin of "the violation" of Foteinos's "utopia." When Foteinos asks the old man why they hadn't moved elsewhere, Kyr Barnabas's answer gestures to his own notion of "the unseen side": "And cut ourselves off from everything that is here underneath the crops? From our bones and our graves? Underneath the tents and cement are our homes and our roots that reach back to Lapitho, to Ayios Giorgos, and beyond" (80). The old man is only too aware of what lies underneath their "miracle field." But the story Kyr Barnabas tells to Foteinos suggests that the old man, unlike "the mediocre artist," knows the devastating effects of insisting on "the other side," of seeking always to see the invisible.

Foteinos is captivated as much by Maria as by her grandfather and he returns constantly to their encampment. He grows fond of the small child who lives with them, Diamandi (literally "diamond"): "From who knows what branch of their family [the child comes]. He asked often but they never made it clear to him. Only vaguely [they answered], he is ours. . . . And he must have been for them to love and care for him so, for him to resemble them. . . . Certainly the child was the son of one of the many of their family who had been killed. Finally he stopped asking, so as not to open old wounds" (80).

Foteinos decides to propose marriage to the enigmatic Maria. But Kyr Barnabas, in what is arguably a test of Foteinos's own "unseen side," tells the young suitor of Maria's rape during the Turkish invasion of the island and of her subsequent pregnancy which resulted in the young child, Diamandi. Maria has chosen to bear the product of her rape, a "diamond," that she and her grandfather love:

> [Diamandi] is Maria's son! Son of the savage beast who destroyed my family. My wife and my son, Maria's father . . . But we love him . . .

we love him . . . Do you remember what I told you once about coal buried in the earth? This [child] is the irrefutable proof of that, isn't he? Because he too became a "diamond" . . .

As he finished speaking, the old man rose and walked slowly away. Maria's eyes looked at him with hatred, she tore him apart with her eyes . . . (87, ellipses in the original)

Here, the earlier suggestion of "the other/invisible side" as Turkish and/or Turkish Cypriot is rendered even more compellingly. For the "invisible side" of the small child is his biological Turkish father; Maria's "invisible side" is her rape by a Turkish soldier; and that of the "utopically fertile field" is the desolate and sterile moonscape of skulls and reptiles underneath. The parallel suggested between the visible and invisible sides of Maria/the landscape/Cypriot society is relatively clear, if no less problematic in its clarity. But Lefteris Foteinos, in spite of the enlightenment suggested by his name, cannot bear the light cast on "the unseen side." Though he could come to terms with the forcible transformation (or violation) of his "utopic moonscape" and of Cypriot society, the violation of Maria is utterly unacceptable to him. So he abandons her, her grandfather, and the young child: "He remained alone with her, and with her child, who ran as usual to his side as soon as Maria put him down, waiting for Foteinos to play with him, waiting to be picked up, his arms outstretched . . . But Foteinos abruptly withdrew his arms, withdrew his entire body; he avoided touching the child, avoided looking at him; he avoided her eyes which watched him . . . (87, ellipses in the original). Maria, "mortally humiliated," takes her son up in her arms embracing him tightly and, "with a hopelessness, an affection and a love that the painter had never seen," goes inside the house, closing the door firmly behind her. Foteinos gets in his car "like a thief" and drives away. The object of his theft remains unspeakable, an *intra*communal "violation" arguably every bit as "savage" as the rape that resulted in the young *inter*communal boy-child, Diamandi.

And the barren landscape, "his utopia," that opens the story closes it as well. The only difference in conclusion is the third-person narrator's enigmatic observation of a kind of final violation of Lefteris Foteinos himself. He stares out over the fertile "violated" field, remembering Maria and unable to either leave the field and Maria behind or go beyond the field and return to the refugee settlement where she lives: "The first cancer cell was activated . . . at precisely that moment . . . while the sun sank bloodily into the indigo mud which embraced it in successive earthen circles, a moment before the murky darkness fell" (88, ellipses in the original). The titular reference to "the unseen side" of things and of people is reiterated in closing as the unseen cancer cells that mortally violate Foteinos as surely as every other violation that is troped by that image. The implications for intracommunal relations of the refusal of violation in the name of some notion of inviolable "purity," some notion of ultimate and inviolable "truth," is death: the "death" of Maria's humiliation, the death of Foteinos's "utopic" moonscape, the implicitly impending death of Foteinos himself.

The violation—the rape—of (national) woman is here an ironic textual marker of unacceptable defeat for (national) man. And he, in turn, engages in a further and equally egregious violation in spurning and abandoning both her and the "product" of her violation. It is in this context that the *intra*communal "necessity" of Evtuxia's murder of her Turkish lover is most intelligible. It is, for Evtuxia, the story of *intra*communal rejection and violation that precedes the Turkish invasion that spurs her effort at decisive narrative closure—at least of one particular story about intercommunal relations—after that invasion. Such an opening is available only in conclusion for the nineteenth reader of the narrator's manuscript in Katselli's *Galazia falaina,* and then with overtones as implicitly onerous as the murder of the Turkish soldier in "Paralogismos." For the unnamed Turkish Cypriot woman of Ioannides's "Oi stoles" and Maria of "E atheate opsi," any such decisive if brutal closure is foreclosed. Their volition, their efforts at intervention, remain smaller gestures in a larger narrative configuration that foregrounds the contradictory position of the Greek Cypriot man. Yet, without those smaller gestures of the women on which his own position turns, he remains under the mark of both literal and metaphoric impotency.

In this configuration, there is another instructive fictional instance in which the story of the consequences of (female) violation (including, again, the near impotence of male witnesses to that violation) is told to a rather different end. Christos Xatzipapas's novel *To chroma tou galaziou iakinthou* (The color of the blue hyacinth), in addition to attempting a narration of modern Cypriot history, also attempts in conclusion to textually abrogate the fearfully constructed antithesis between "purity" and violation. The binary opposition and utter symbiosis of these two notions is already problematized in the work of Katselli, Abraamidou, and Ioannides. But the variously critical (de)construction in their fiction of a putatively private, protected, and pure female sphere of home in opposition to a public, confrontational, impure male sphere of struggle is complicated even further in *To chroma tou galaziou iakinthou.* Xatzipapas's novel frames its stories with the hospitalization of its main character, Petros, a Greek Cypriot soldier gravely wounded in the fighting of the coup and subsequent invasion. Initially unconscious for weeks and then still unable to see or move and threatened with the amputation of gangrenous limbs, Petros slowly recovers from his wounds in the course of the novel.[60] In that process, he remembers, if often in confused dreams or fragments of his own memories and of stories told to him, the past before the coup and invasion. And he learns from letters and newspapers, from visitors, and from his fellow patient and childhood friend Andreas of what has happened since July 1974, before he regains consciousness in the hospital. Although the novel's main focal point is Petros, it is narrated by a third-person narrator. Yet, to avoid some of the limitations of the focus on Petros's consciousness and experiences, the novel offers footnotes to the dialogue explaining cryptic or controversial references in Petros's exchanges with other characters or providing information to which he and his interlocutors could not have access. Interviews and articles from newspapers of the time are, for example, quoted verbatim (and footnoted).[61] Xatzipapas's novel, then, is a skillful literary and fictional intersection with the nonfictional.

As *To chromatou galaziou iakinthou* follows Petros's recovery from his massive wounds, it accounts as well for his critical reassessment of (and "recovery" from) the recent past. His youthful and uncomplicated simplicity, like his youthful and unmarked body, slowly shift. Chapter 17, "The Ills of Grief," opens with a doctor's early morning visit to Petros's bedside, where he learns that he will not lose his legs (or his potency) to gangrene. After the doctor leaves his room, Petros reflects aloud to his nurse Evterpi on Makarios's miscalculations and myopia in dealing with the designs of the fascist junta in Greece and with their military and paramilitary cohorts in Cyprus. But his analysis is not the simple recitation of conventional views. His criticism of the outcome of events in which he himself was a not entirely witting actor makes Evterpi nervous. She turns anxiously away from him, remembering all of a sudden that a stranger is waiting outside the door to visit Petros. (It is the father of one of Petros's fellow soldiers, seeking information about his missing son.)

But, in a consideration of constructions of female purity and violation as trope for the purity and violation of the nation ("happy and prosperous" and then invaded/violated) and of its sovereign protector state overthrown (in the coup), the most striking section of the novel is its closing chapters. It is at that point in a novel structurally bound by, and allegorized in, his hospitalization and gradual recovery that Petros reemerges, literally and metaphorically, into Cypriot society and history. A letter from his mother calls him home to the bedside of his dying father. His first venture outside of the hospital, then, is to stand witness to his father's last moments as he dies of a "broken heart." Wandering the city after his father's death, unwilling yet to go back to the "enclavement" of his hospital room, Petros decides to visit a close friend with whom he had done his military service. Petros's quantified memories during the taxi ride to his friend's house are reminiscent of D.G.C.'s "scientifically" quantified account of the blue whale in the opening of Katselli's novel: "So then, to Haris's [house]: they'd read there [while together in military training] at least forty-three books at the middle level or higher; they'd eaten souvlaki twenty-four times which was usually courtesy of Haris because he was better off; they'd drunk twelve bottles of Christodoulopais ouzo, because the factory was somewhere near there and they'd gotten half of the twelve bottles free; they'd drunk one hundred forty six coca colas. All together they'd made love two times with cabaret 'artists' from Lebanon, courtesy of the first new year's bonus that Haris had gotten from his unit. They masturbated, each one separate from the other of course, at least around forty times and all this about three years and eight months earlier" (277–78). But if the blue whale is an endangered species, Petros's youthful past with Haris is already extinct. The black-edged notice on the door of Haris's family home announces that Haris "died fighting for democracy against the fascist forces of the coup on July 16, 1974." The past that Petros knew, in which—he thought—he had a plausibly stable and secure position, is irrevocably gone. And so he returns to the hospital from this first venture beyond its confines.

Three chapers later, in the opening section, "The Rape," of the last chapter in the novel, Petros has two more visitors. Their visit, he thinks to himself, is "a most absurd" one. The two men are completely unfamiliar to him. One is "well dressed with a plump and placid appearance." The other man has "a haggard face, a beard of two or three weeks' growth, and dull eyes." The first man is a psychiatrist of whose services Petros hastily insists he has no need. The second is the father of Koula, a female friend of Petros whom he has not seen since the coup and invasion. After a pointless exchange between Petros and the almost obnoxiously suave psychiatrist in which the latter exudes arrogant control and the former growing unease and distress, Koula's father interrupts with a single blunt statement: "Listen, son, Koula's been raped." To Petros's stunned "What?" the old man continues, "Yes, by a Turkish officer . . . and she's pregnant, son" (306). Still, though immediately worried about Koula—"Where is she?

What will happen now?"—Petros doesn't quite understand why the two men have come to him. Koula's father continues, in an exchange that is a terse marker for the fierce social and religious debates in Cyprus about the status of the women violated during the Turkish invasion and occupation. Their exchange—three men discussing, with no little concern and distress, the situation and future of a violated woman who refuses to comply with their "better judgment"—gestures distinctly toward the literal post-1974 Cypriot social response of aversion and detachment to women who had been raped, abandoned, or were without male protectors.[62] Here again, the silenced subtexts and indictments of Abraamdiou's "Paralogismos" and Ioannidis's "E atheati opsi" recurs, if more delicately:

> —Look, Petros, the problem is she doesn't want to accept that she was raped by a Turk.
> —And why, indeed, should she accept it? That's what we're lacking these days, to "accept" such events. She's absolutely correct unless I, because of illness, am not judging things accurately.
> —She doesn't want to abort the . . . child, the doctor [the psychiatrist] said abruptly. She claims that it's not the product of rape. She insists that the child belongs to the two of you. Ask her and you'll see. (307)

At this Koula's father hastens to reassure Petros that he understands that this is not the case, that Petros is not the father of Koula's child:

> — . . . all of us know that you don't have any connection with this . . . this bad luck . . . he said.
> —If you could help . . . said the psychiatrist.
> —How? I must help but how? asked Petros decisively as if the despair of heroism had arisen within him.
> —If you meet, said the psychiatrist, perhaps you could persuade her that . . .
> —When will this happen? Petros asked impatiently. I might be able to do something. . . . I'll wait for her . . . (308)

This exchange—"The Rape"—is immediately followed, not by the encounter between Koula and Petros that closes this chapter and the novel, but by a section entitled "The Supersubstantial" ("Yperousiotis"). Literally then, what ensues from bodily violation in *To chroma tou galaziou iakinthou* is disembodiment. For that is here the literal meaning of *yperousiotis:* to be beyond or above material embodiment. This disembodiment or supramateriality is not only the strategic recasting of the violated body of Koula but also of (a "violated"?) Petros who loves and desires her. The parenthetical question of whether or not Petros is also the object of a less literal "rape"/violation is perhaps slightly outrageous but not altogether inappropriate. For his "manhood," if we take that to be sexual potency, like Koula's "womanhood," if we take that to be female purity, has been violated in the coup and invasion. In the dominant social scheme that defined gendered places before the summer of 1974, Petros *would not* necessarily acquiesce to the request of Koula's father and the psychiatrist. And Koula *would* presumably acquiesce to their request that she have what would have then been an illegal abortion. But neither Petros nor Koula do exactly what they are called on to do. And, implicitly at least, the actions of both of them indict the definitions and, by extension, the social scheme itself that so censoriously and often mortally enforces boundaries of manliness and womanliness. That this is a vexed moment in the novel when unspeakable suggestions must be quieted is evident in the tone of the narration itself. For at this juncture, the usually barely perceptible narrator addresses his narratees directly and almost aggressively: "Let's hypothesize that a human's life is divided in half from one particular point [*oriako simeio*]. This point, from which hangs a lottery, has no connection to a person's age—it could be thirty, forty, fifty. For Hesiod, for example, it was a sun-drenched spring day in which, as he was grazing his flock at Elikona, the Muses came and said to him, 'We know how to tell lies but we also know how to uncover the truth' and they gave him a laurel branch and proclaimed him a poet. . . . For Petros, this boundary stands at his 23rd year, not of course as a number, but as a concentrated crux of life, even though it was mortally endangered" (308–9). The invocation of Hesiod as paradigmatic example of a hypothetical turning point from shepherd to poet—a poet who also records history—is indubitably a charged trope for Hatzipapas's novel itself as it seeks to poetically uncover "truth" while it tells "lies." But it is equally a trope within the narrative for Petros's telling of his own story in which he, too, tells lies, rather literally in this instance. For the narrator cozily offers "a further clarification" to his readers: Petros has, in fact, committed a sin of omission in his earlier account of the moments just prior to his near-fatal injury in battle. After this intimate aside, the narrator turns to an abstract theoretical account of the relationship between materiality and immateriality as not antithetical and the consequent positioning of the "supersubstantial" (*yperousiotis*) on neither one side nor the other of this nonantithesis. The narrator illustrates his discussion with numerous references to the im/materiality of the New Testament Christ. This is not, the narrator assures his audience, meant to throw doubt on the claims or powers of the Christ. It is simply a means for him to "provide a sketch of the hero and his supersubstantial situation and so he [the narrator] will be intelligible" (311).

The subsequent turn from im/materiality and super/substantiality is abrupt. In fact, it is a bullet blast: "We said, or maybe we didn't say, how a bullet through the lock opened the door of the Castle" (310). With this, we return to the story past before Petros's near-fatal injury, to his escape from imprisonment by the EOKA-B paramilitary and their Cypriot and Greek military cohorts in "the Castle." As he emerges dazed from the prison, "he didn't understand to what extent he was embodied or disembodied and which of the two conditions would win out over the other." A man's voice shouts: "What are you waiting for you assholes? The Turks are coming, go and fight." Here, "on the borderline of materiality and substantiality," Petros finds himself "suddenly and unconsciously" in a state of *yperousiotita*—supersubstantial, disembodied. It is at this moment, in this state, that he remembers/encounters Koula. Like Petros, she too is without a body. In one fell swoop, the problem of bodily violation or rape is "poeticized" as impossible. With no body to violate, how can there be violation? But there can, of course, be no physical contact or sexual love either. Petros's memory of Koula is of nothing but a red stain with a green line through it. But that red stain "embraces his hair": "Hair—he thought about that. Now how can two disembodied essences embrace one another's hair? It's a little crazy; it approaches the edge of insanity and *we'd better recognize it*" (311, emphasis added). This last observation—"we'd better recognize it"—could be either that of Petros or of the narrator. Is this again the assertion of the usually reticent narrator in an effort to contain the more threatening implications of the story he tells? Or is it Petros, who recognizes the dangers of the disassociation he seeks to work on his own and Koula's desiring bodies? That disassociation itself is "crazy" enough. But the narrator's effort at disassociation is of a rather different kind. His effort is to disassociate the "insane" propositions about Cypriot society and its gendered citizens implicit in Petros's story from the "sane" world of his narration and its narratees. Of course, insanity or the "paralogic" has threatened virtually all of the literary narratives of post-1974 Cyprus. And disembodiment is a "crazy" solution to an insoluble problem of metaphorizing the nation as woman, which, part and parcel of the original metaphorization, virtually regulates violation of that nation as female body. For what the Turkish officer will violate as embodied woman, Petros cannot embrace as disembodied woman. The fictional resolution of the threat of rape is "poetic" disembodiment. But such resolution presents an insoluble problem in its turn. That insoluble problem is suggested by the trope of "the color of the blue hyacinth" itself, the novel's and Petros's (and finally Koula's) trope of choice: erotic love. Even in a novel, the resolution of the threat of violation in disembodiment cannot last for long. The super-substantiality, the disembodiment, the immateriality of the young man and woman in the midst of a civil war and invasion dissipates: "[They] braked in front of Koula's house in the old car that belonged to her father. The legs first, as they tried to get out [of the car], diffidently but steadily acquired their sleekness and luster on the sacred [lit. devout, *evseves*] inner side of her thighs, revealed from the folds of her wide skirt" (312). It is a most material desire—the sight of Koula's thighs, his thirst for a cigarette—that disengages Petros from "supersubstantiality." As Koula and Petros embrace, kiss, separate, she promises to wait for him there. And again the narrator intervenes: "As he left, he hadn't considered that she wouldn't be able to wait for him there. Perhaps the reason for that was that, up to that moment, he had correctly conceived of the capability[63] of a person, the sovereign capability of people. . . . Because the Turks had made the attempt before and were unsuccessful; they would be unsuccess-ful a thousand times more; they wouldn't manage it; don't laugh; they wouldn't be successful against real human capability. But not in the midst of an illegal opposition, which in this instance was a remote-controlled betrayal. . . . In half an hour, of course, Petros (and Tassos as well) under-stood that their 'human capability' was overwhelmingly predetermined" (313). Petros, unwittingly and based on his "correct conception" of human possibility, implicitly plays a supporting role himself in Koula's violation. His ignorance of the political violation(s) already effected against "purity" and "sovereignty" (of Cyprus) leads him to accept without question or comment Koula's promise that she will wait for him. And she, with her "sovereign human capability" or agency does wait. Only the odds against her sovereign capability or agency, are "overwhelmingly determined." Ig-norance, here, has fearful consequences.[64]

The final section of the novel's last chapter is titled eponymously "The Color of the Blue Hyacinth." It is here, finally, that Koula and Petros meet again. It is November 1974: "Koula was the same dear and beautiful woman that he'd known. She didn't have a swollen belly and why should she in any event? She smiled always in the same way, perhaps even a little more than he remembered. Some kind of imperceptible haziness in her eyes—undoubtedly from the windy and dusty November morning" (314).

But why does Petros immediately claim that her belly should not be swollen or that the haziness in her eyes is from the dust in the wind? The omissions in his story are even more apparent here than they were in his account of the last moments before he was wounded. But the exchange between Koula and Petros is an impossible attempt at simple clarity, not subtlety, at the definitive differentiation of past and present. The past is over; their situations, their perspectives, their "verses" must change, already have changed. Petros's promise to Koula's father and the psychiatrist that he will "help" to "persuade" Koula echoes ambiguously in their dialogue. He states straightforwardly: "First we must begin with the child that we made in the insanity of the summer" (314). But, in this pointed comment, Petros accepts paternity of Koula's child, both literally and metaphorically. He does not attempt to refute the "overwhelmingly predetermined" story of their love, or of her rape, and pregnancy. She answers him: "Yes, this past summer was crazy. We have to take from within us this horrible summer" (315). There is an implicit irony in Koula's response, however, which contributes to the growing ambiguity of exactly what the two are talking about and of exactly what they are proposing to do. For Koula's phrase—"*va vgaloume apo mesa mas afto to frichto kalokari*" (let's get rid of this horrible summer [from inside us])—could of course be a discreet reference to the abortion that her father and the psychiatrist want her to have. (It is never quite clear what Petros wants in this context.) But it could also be a discreet reference not to abortion, but to the birth of the child in spite of its mixed parentage, a different kind of "removing or taking out from within us." Petros's answer to Koula is no more clear, in spite of the narrator's characterization of his response: "We're young, he said in the midst of relieved uncertainty. Let's make a summer . . . without July" (314–15, ellipses in the original).

But what exactly is the "relieved uncertainty" (*anakoufismeni amfivolia*) that characterizes Petros's suggestion of eliminating July from their past? As often in Xatzipapas's novel, the modification of adjective and noun is virtually reversible. Thus, Petros is also in the midst of "ambiguous or doubtful relief." Yet uncertainty and ambiguity are not just his attributes in the closing of the novel. If supersubstantiality is not an adequate response to rape, is the erotic love of "the color of the blue hyacinth"? Is that which "the mediocre artist who goes by the pseudonym Lefteris Foteinos" refuses accepted in the person of Petros and his acknowledgment of paternity for a child wrought by rape? And what will become of that tiny "product" of violation; is it abortion that Koula is proposing? She responds to Petros's suggestion of making a summer without July by drawing even closer to the arm he's put around her shoulders as they walk. And, after extracting a promise from him that he "won't laugh," she tells him of a "dream" she had:

—But it's not a "dream" . . . More likely, it's half and half . . .

—Half real and half unreal, we could say. I'm listening.

—Last night I gave birth to an egg . . .

—An egg?

—Yes. Don't you believe me?

—I believe you. Of course I believe you. You told me that you'd wait for me that day and you *did* wait.

—And you kept your word too. You didn't die.

—So, I believe you, he replied to draw her back to the dream.

—I was burning with fever. When I woke up, I was drenched in sweat. I heard myself shout—take it, take it away from here. On the sheet was a grey, red stain . . .

She spoke with difficulty. As she uttered the words one by one, from amidst the tiny imperceptible hairs around her lips, were droplets of sweat that caught the morning light of Apogonikou [November, in ancient Cypriot designation of the months]. He kissed her gently. For the second time in his life. Like a copy or reflection of the first kiss, before the lottery.

—And in the middle of the stain was an egg . . . she continued. It's color was like . . . wait a minute, let me think a minute. There, just like that over there. And she pointed to a flower in the grass.

—The color of the blue hyacinth, he said and brought his hand to his forehead as if he were trying to remember something. And it was hollow, he said finally.

—Yes, how did you know?

—It was a product of this horrible summer . . . That's why I was saying that now, with the fall, we have to fix things.

A light rain began to fall.

—Let's go, he said to her. (315–16)

Petros's effort to remember remains without specified result: that the egg was hollow, that paternity is always contestable, that "recovery" might also require a reappraisal of notions of health (sovereignty and purity) *and* of illness (the threat to and violation of "health"), that they might be simultaneous rather than antithetical, that Koula might not be pregnant at all (a "hollow egg"). From the narrator there is no final explanatory word; the novel ends with the last line of dialogue between Koula and Petros: "Let's go."

So the ambiguity of origins and endings in Xatzipapas's *To chroma tou galaziou iakinthou* remains unresolved in conclusion. But in the undecidability of that conclusion, what *is* clear is that there are no unambiguous stories and no unambiguous storytellers, as the citation of the Muses themselves suggests. But in that undecidability, the invocation of the (pure and virginal) female body as the sacred space of and symbol for the nation is profoundly if equivocally problematized—not just for Koula or women or the maternal space but also for Petros, men, and paternity. Finally, the identity—the nationality—of the father of Koula's unborn child is less important than the violence with which that child was wrought. But responsibility for that violence, this novel (as other Cypriot fiction) suggests, is not so unidirectional as some would have it. Petros, after all, might be utterly wrong in his desire to make a summer without July. Forgetting does not ensure change; it might lead to repetition. Nor does remembering—his hand to his forehead in conclusion or Koula's remembering of her dream— ensure that the Muses' "truth" is revealed. And the narrator's notion of a lottery dangling from some crucial point in a person's life, after and before which point everything falls in two neat parts, that too is as ambivalent as any other framing device. For lives and their events can only seem so neatly divided in retrospect—and ultimately only when the life is over, in death. For death is of course the apparently unequivocal end of the story of a life. Such neat division with a decisive turning point can only seem so in the fictional construction, as in *To chroma tou galaziou iakinthou,* of an initially unobtrusive omniscient narrator telling a series of stories about his characters with ever increasing visibility and intervention.

For Maria and her grandfather in "E atheate opsi," violation and paternity are no longer the decisive issue. They are not forgotten but transfigured in the transformation of a "lump of coal" into a diamond. It is "the mediocre artist"—who claims to want to see the "invisible side" of things, to make Kyr Barnabas and Maria forcibly speak their secrets—who condemns and rejects the past and its violations after himself compelling the unseen and unspeakable. But even in his impotent claims to purity, to separation from the site of violation, he is violated in turn by the inexplicable reproduction of cancerous cells deep inside his body.

Nor does paternity matter to Evtuxia at the end of Maria Abraamidou's short story; Evtuxia decisively and bluntly eliminates the issue of paternity herself in her murder of the child's father. But she will presumably bear and raise the child within the confines of a national narrative that would allow such a transgression—bearing a child with no father, being a woman without a man—because of the even larger transgression that was the Turkish invasion and occupation of Cyprus.

In conclusion, it is perhaps unnecessary to point out that the narrative representation of rape is not simple repetition of the factual story of the violation of Cypriot women by the invading Turkish army. It is not, in a conflation of literary and historical narrative, some direct, inevitable, and unmediated literary reflection of historical fact. Foreign invasion and occupation do not inevitably or "naturally" produce a proliferation of cultural and literary narratives of female rape, however much invasion and occupation seem to repeatedly (re)produce war as sexualized violence. The primacy of the *story* of rape is as striking in its occurrence in post-1974 Cypriot *fiction* as it is in its lesser significance in the fiction of other social and cultural instances. Whereas gender and sexuality are inextricably and fundamentally a basis of nationalism, the foregrounding of rape as the "national story" is not. It *is,* however, an unavoidable if implicit consequence of the specific gendering of nationalism described above, of the specific metaphorization of the nation and national land in the pure and virtuous body of a woman.

In post-1974 Cypriot fiction, the story of rape, rather than some presumably straightforward literary refraction of its historical occurrence, is a (potentially disruptive) marker in narratives of violently conflicted social and political relationships: the intercommunal relationships of Cypriot society between Greek Cypriots and Turkish Cypriots, between men and women; and the international relationships between Cyprus and its Mediterranean neighbors—Greece and Turkey, of course, as well as the Middle East. Further, these relationships are fiercely gendered in particular ways and not just "naturally" sexed. The narrative image and story of female rape, then, is not simply a "woman's" story. In fact, one of the distinctly foregrounded aspects of fictional and nonfictional accounts of the coup and invasion of Cyprus is the "man's story" of female rape, the male response to the metaphor and the reality of the rape of women as military and political strategy. This is a gendered social and political story.

Something of this political gendering or gendered politics is performed in Abraamidou's "Paralogismos." For, though it does not directly represent female rape, it is very much figured on the story of rape. The charge of the Turkish soldier standing in the shadows of her home, the simultaneous threat and consolation he offers her, the very narrative workings of the short story, are predicated on the context of the story of literal and metaphoric invasion, occupation, and rape and a transgressive response to that story. Yet, in narrating the transgression of (nonetheless firmly inscribed) gender and national boundaries, "Paralogismos" resituates rape to question social and national power and agency, not just bodily violation.

In Ioannidis's "Oi stoles" the threat of bodily violation (rape) for a young (Turkish) Cypriot woman is linked to the threat of bodily violation (death) for a young (Greek) Cypriot man. Here, as in the short stories of Ioannides and in Xatzipapas's novel, representations of rape are inextricably bound up with representations of national and religious, cultural and linguistic boundaries. This is not to diminish the violence and violation of the historical experiences of rape (or invasion). But it is to suggest that post-1974 Cypriot narratives do not simply replicate that historical experience. And it is also to suggest that the image or representation or story of the rape of woman figures something other than just the "rape of woman." Undoubtedly, the violent and coercive penetration—national, sexual—by an invasive other is part of the story. But it is also, and equally, the sexual, political, and national issue of uncoerced female agency, of control over the body, sexuality, and reproduction and, equally, over her political, cultural, and economic place(s) in society.

Narrating the female body as the site of purity and nation violated, as the site of an international maternal (re)production, is certainly a dubious gesture. It conjures figures of eternally fecund and nurturing woman, of the reproductive site of "natural" bodily conciliation. Yet, simultaneously, the narration of the (violation of the) female body in these texts also conjures the contradictions, the violatory representations, of the female body as national site. Those conflicting images mark, as threat *and* promise, many post-1974 Cypriot narratives, as they do a social and cultural discourse around them. But if that narration is a dubious gesture, it is also an indication of a different story beyond *and* within national boundaries that is yet to be told. In the meantime, however, that story is "paralogic" or "insane" or "deadly" and narrated in the dark silence of Evtuxia's midnight border movements.

> They say that one should love the homeland
> that's what my father always told me too.
> My homeland is divided in two
> Which half should I love?

This poem, "Which Half," written in 1975 by the Turkish Cypriot poetess Nessié Yasin, evokes and problematizes the notion of a singular identification and of a past betrayed, as it questions the identification itself and the change that incurred betrayal. The poem's present of loss and dismemberment—"My homeland is divided in two"—is juxtaposed to the authority of the past—"my father always told me." In that past, allegiance was presumably clearly designated. Society and father established the patriarchal boundaries of what "should" be—"love"—and of its specified object—"the homeland." But what in the past appeared to be a source of stability and power—the directive of society and father, the boundaries of the "homeland"—is in the present a source of anguish, conflict, and instability. The present from which the memory of authority and certainty, of familial and national coherence is evoked is also the present of that memory violated. The lyric present is itself predicated on the story past of betrayal. Memory of authoritative surety in the counsel of the collective "they" and of the father and in the homeland toward which they exhort love is, in the present, surety betrayed. And implicitly, the transgression that marks the narrative present marks the only apparently unproblematic narrative past as well. In fact, it is from the present of transgression and betrayal that the past is approached or remembered and critically questioned at all. In this tension between past and present, perhaps in and through their narratives, there is a sense of palpable longing for, faint imagining of, other not yet articulable communities; other ways of producing and reproducing sexual, familial, and social relations; other ways of knowing and living differences. This, too, like Evtuxia's desire, is a kind of midnight border movement, a silent, even unspeakable exchange across borders and within them—an impossibly mortal movement and speech, an impossible community.

3 Between Here and There: National Community from the Inside Out and the Outside In —Palestine 1982

We render special tribute to the
brave Palestinian woman, guardian
of sustenance and life, keeper of
our people's perennial flame.
—Palestinian Declaration of
Independence, 1988

We carry in our worlds that flourish
our worlds that have failed.
—Christopher Okigbo, "Lament of the Silent Sisters"

Here we are, near there . . .
—Mahmud Darwish,
"Hunā naḥnu qarb hunāka"
(Here we are, near there)

Ayyam Beirut, Beirut days, is the arguably affectionate and certainly poignant appellation for the period of Palestinian political and social consolidation and development in Lebanon that came to a bitter and bloody end in early summer of 1982. On 6 June of that year, Israel initiated a massive invasion of Lebanon, the so-called Peace for Galilee offensive. Its aim was to eradicate the Palestine Liberation Organization's political and military presence in Lebanon and to sever the link between the PLO in the diaspora and its increasingly and demonstrably steadfast support in the Occupied Territories. And, as had been the case for decades, the Israeli goal was to shore up or, if that wasn't feasible, to install and maintain a pliable Lebanese government as well as to counter the Syrian presence in Lebanon. The Peace for Galilee offensive, with its multiple objectives, culminated in the fierce and viciously destructive two-month siege of Beirut. That siege ended with the U.S.-brokered departure into the diaspora in August 1982 of Beirut's armed Palestinian soldiers, some eight thousand in number. Most of the staff of the considerable network of PLO social services headquartered in Beirut left the city with the fighters as well. Fast on the heels of their departure—and in spite of the agreements signed by the PLO, the United States, and Israel to protect the Palestinian civilian population in Lebanon—were the massacres in Sabra and Shatila. Nostalgia for those preinvasion years, in spite of their growing intercommunal tensions and marked political and social contradictions, was made sharper by this end to *ayyam Beirut* and by the subsequent bitter years of the "War of the Camps."[1] But nostalgia was not the only or perhaps even the most significant response to that deadly Israeli "peace" offensive and its devastating consequences for Palestinians (and Lebanese) and, at least initially, for Palestinian political and social organization.[2] Some extent of the radical diversity of responses to the crisis of the summer of 1982 and its violent challenges to notions and practices of national community is discernible in Palestinian cultural and literary production in the months and years that followed. They included moving and eloquent testimonials to the horrific experiences of that summer and to its aftermath, often thoughtful (and sometimes less than thoughtful) political and historical analyses, and finely wrought poetic and narrative responses. There was also a critical reconsideration of Palestinian history and political strategy in the decades prior to the Israeli invasion. For no moment of crisis is ever truly isolatable; the "crisis" itself, on closer examination, spills over into the periods that precede and follow it. And critical responses to and assessments of crisis necessitate historical reassessment as well. In this instance too, the crisis of Palestinian national redefinition and organization occasioned by the Israeli invasion in the summer of 1982 ultimately demanded a reconsideration as well of the years leading up to 1982. It was a period fraught with contradictions, mistakes, and losses for Palestinians and their political and social organization but also marked by undeniable achievements. Those losses and mistakes as well as achievements and victories prior to the Israeli invasion of 1982 distinctly affect the shape and tenor of post-1982 visions and practices of national definition and community.

The fifteen years prior to the 1982 Israeli invasion of Lebanon, from the 1967 defeat of the Arab states by Israel in the Six Day War, provided a distinct opening for Palestinian social, political, and military reorganization and for a measure of Palestinian autonomy in Lebanon. To a somewhat lesser degree and for a shorter period,[3] this was also the case in Jordan and Syria. And, though its effects were manifested rather differently and less immediately, it was also the case for the post-1967 Israeli-occupied West Bank and Gaza. No less important, the post-1967 period provided an opening for at least some sectors of the Lebanese population in Lebanon as well.

The openings for Palestinians and the PLO were due in no small part to the severely diminished political and military authority of the Arab states involved in the 1967 war—Egypt, Syria, and Jordan—as a result of their devastatingly swift defeat.[4] The defeat of the Arab state armies graphically demonstrated the limitations of conventional military confrontation with Israel and hence, by implication at least, substantiated the importance of guerrilla action. It substantiated as well subsequent Palestinian demands for civic rights in Lebanon.[5] With the defeat of the Arab armies in the 1967 war a period of consolidation and more effective organization for the PLO and for Palestinians in general was possible.

The PLO itself, established in 1964 by Arab regimes fearful of the radicalizing potential of the Palestinian situation, within a few years after the 1967 war came under the governance of popularly supported Palestinian groups, notably Yasir Arafat's Fateh organization, founded in 1965. Prior to this, the leader of the PLO was appointed by the Arab states. As an umbrella organization for and coalition of Palestinian resistance groups and political parties as well as independent Palestinians, the PLO in-

creasingly began to take on the organization and function of a government
in exile. It served to organize and at its best serve the needs of the diverse
Palestinian population in the diaspora and, rather more slowly, in the
Occupied Territories.[6]

The ability of the PLO to both organize and protect Palestinians in
Lebanon and elsewhere was demonstrated with remarkable effectiveness
in the terms of the Cairo Accords of November 1969. The address and
scope of the Accords were broad: the continuing harsh and discriminatory
conditions under which the majority of Palestinians in Lebanon (and elsewhere) lived; the critically weakened ability of the states and rulers of
Jordan, Syria, and Egypt to direct the Palestinian movement; and the reconfiguration of political and social relations among the various peoples
living in Lebanon, in the Palestinian refugee camps as well as in Lebanese
and Palestinian towns and villages and, of course, in the Lebanese capital
of Beirut. Signed by Yasir Arafat as head of the PLO and by the commander
of the Lebanese army, the Cairo Accords granted autonomy in governance
and administration to the Palestinian refugee camps.[7] Equally, it ensured a
measure of civil rights for all Palestinians in Lebanon.

In addition, for many Lebanese in this period, the continuing crisis of
the postcolonial sectarian system in Lebanon seemed to make clear the
desirability of a secular, democratic state rather than the divisive confes-
sional system left in place after WWII by the departing French colonial
authorities. The growing strength of the coalitions between some sectors
of the Lebanese people and the Palestinians made a shift to a more equitable secular state seem a possibility. It was this period that saw the establishment (in 1969) by Kamal Jumblatt of the Lebanese National Movement,
a nonsectarian (or at least intercommunal) coalition of democratic Lebanese forces with which the Palestinian resistance in Lebanon allied itself
in a search for a more just and equitable revision of social and political
order in Lebanon.

Both in the international political arena and in the social and political
organization in Lebanon and the Occupied Territories, the gains between
1967 and 1982 for the PLO were numerous, particularly in the early 1970s.
Of critical significance in the category of international politics were the
successive Arab League Summits of 1973 (Algiers) and 1974 (Rabat),
which officially recognized the PLO, since 1969 firmly under the leadership of Arafat and his Fateh organization, as the "sole, legitimate representative of the Palestinian people."[8] And, in November 1974, the General
Assembly of the United Nations reiterated this recognition (Resolution
3236) and invited the PLO to participate in its sessions in the official

capacity of "observer." The late 1970s, however, saw Egypt's President Anwar Sadat agree to a separate peace with Israel, effectively undermining PLO efforts for multilateral peace talks and undermining as well the (always precarious) union of the Arab League states. Sadat's trip to Jerusalem in November 1977 was followed by his signing in the following year of the Camp David Accords, the March 1978 Israeli invasion and continuing occupation of southern Lebanon notwithstanding.[9] But the diplomatic setback of Camp David was simultaneously a catalyst for an organizational advance: the ever more steadfast linking of the Palestinians and PLO of the diaspora with the Palestinians and pro-PLO organization of the Occupied Territories. For the Palestinians of the Occupied Territories and their leaders resolutely refused the "self-rule" scheme of the Camp David Accords. Ironically enough for its champions, the Camp David Accords made clear the necessary direction of the organizing and resistance efforts that had gone on for years to link the Palestinians of the Territories with those of the diaspora.

As for gains in Palestinian social and political organization, both political emphasis and greater dynamism seemed to rest, at least initially, with the diaspora populations, particularly in Jordan and Lebanon. But after 1970, with the expulsion of the Palestinian resistance groups from Jordan, the center of Palestinian and PLO activity was most decisively located in Lebanon. This location would shift of devastating necessity in the post-1982 period. And already by the mid-1970s, the situation in the Occupied Territories had undergone considerable change. In the second of only two elections organized by the Israeli Occupation authorities, 1976 saw the election of pro-PLO Palestinian mayors and village councils in numerous West Bank towns and villages.[10] The Palestine National Front, established in the Occupied Territories in August 1973 with high visibility and thus high vulnerability (to the imprisonment and/or deportation of its leaders and the harassment of its supporters), was replaced by the more restrained and organizationally decentered National Guidance Committee. Organized in late 1977 after Sadat launched his separate "peace initiative" with Israel (the Camp David Accords), which included the "self-rule" scheme for the Occupied Territories, the National Guidance Committee saw itself as a support network among West Bank communities and their leaders. Its primary goals were to counter the Camp David Accords and their explicit and implicit plans for the Occupied Territories and to solidify the links between the PLO and the grassroots organizations of the West Bank and Gaza.

Still, between 1967 and 1982, Lebanon was the principal ground for widespread PLO organizing and military actions. During the early part of this period, the Palestinians and Israel largely confronted one another through the guerrilla actions of the former and what Helena Cobban refers to as the "war of spooks" of the latter (55). Thus, apparently, the 1973 war waged by Egypt and Syria with regular armies and conventional military tactics came as something of a surprise to Israel. And though the Egyptian and Syrian armies did not win an outright military victory against Israel, their limited success in the 1973 war allowed them a considerably stronger bargaining position from which to attempt their stated goal for that military effort: the reclamation of their lands occupied by Israel in the 1967 war.

Palestinian/PLO participation in the 1973 war, however, did not generate the hoped for bargaining power vis-à-vis Israel or the Arab states. Subsequently, in fact, the PLO's repeated request for an Arab-sponsored multilateral peace conference that would include the United States and the Soviet Union as well as the European states was deftly undermined by the so-called shuttle diplomacy of Henry Kissinger, U.S. Secretary of State and National Security Advisor to then-President Nixon. Kissinger's accomplishments were swift. In less than six months following the 1973 war, all Arab states but two had lifted their oil embargo against the United States. And, no less an achievement for Kissinger, the diplomatic initiative and primary role in the Arab-Israeli situation was decisively and almost exclusively in the hands of the United States. And the United States officially and publicly stated that it would not negotiate directly with the PLO. Still, the Arab League meeting at Rabat (1974) that officially recognized the authority of the PLO and in November of the same year sponsored Arafat's speech before the General Assembly of the United Nations in New York City were important accomplishments for the PLO. And they officially marked a decisive PLO turn toward diplomatic efforts.[11]

But on the local Palestinian front(s), the situation was more complicated. The public proclamation by the Democratic Front for the Liberation of Palestine (DFLP) and subsequently by Fateh of the acceptability of a Palestinian "national authority" on *any* part of redeemed Palestine as opposed to a secular, democratic state in all of historic Palestine provoked much fierce popular debate, particularly in the refugee camps in Lebanon and Syria. Their fear was that, with a national authority in any part of Palestine, the return of the hundreds of thousands of Palestinians whose lands and homes were in historic Palestine might be permanently deferred and ultimately foreclosed. Nonetheless, through considerable negotiations among the various groups within the PLO, this significantly revisionary position was formally adopted at the meeting of the Palestine National Council (PNC), the legislative body of the PLO, in Cairo in the summer of 1974. But by late September of the same year, the Front of Palestinian Forces Rejecting Surrenderist Solutions, or the Rejection Front, announced its formal opposition to the plan. For the next four years, their opposition was a considerable challenge to the PLO's Executive Committee, the smaller governing body of the PLO "elected" by the PNC via an intense negotiation process. As before, so now too, the differences between the "inside" and the "outside" of the Palestinian situation were marked. For within the Occupied Territories, this shift in PLO position was largely welcomed.

By the spring of 1975, the civil war in Lebanon (1975–1976) had erupted. In spite of the PLO's formal position not to involve itself in the internal affairs of any Arab state, Palestinians in Lebanon were irrevocably enmeshed in that civil strife. Indeed, the outbreak of the civil war is conventionally located in the deadly Phalangist attack on a busload of Palestinian workers passing through a Christian suburb of west Beirut on their way back from a rally.[12] In any event, it was (again) clear that Palestinians were not exempt from Lebanese "internal affairs." In fact, they were more often active players in those affairs. By early 1976, with the siege and subsequent massacre of Palestinians and Lebanese at Tall al-Za'tar, the PLO had little choice but to officially engage in military support of its ally Kamal Jumblatt and his Lebanese National Movement (LNM). This put the PLO in unavoidable conflict with its erstwhile ally Syria, which had militarily intervened in Lebanon in support of the right-wing Maronite Christian forces. Still, by the end of (this phase of) the Lebanese civil war in 1976, the PLO sustained less damage than might have been expected and was able to initiate a period of further consolidation and expansion of social programs in the areas it controlled with the LNM. But the alliance between Lebanese and Palestinians, between the PLO and the LNM, grew dangerously troubled. In *Too Many Enemies: The Palestinian Experience in Lebanon,* Rosemary Sayigh tersely notes of the post-1976 period, "The Lebanese in the areas controlled by the PRM [Palestine Resistance Movement]/LNM joint forces bore the greater part of the costs of destruction and political stagnation, while the PLO/PRM benefitted disproportionately." From the terse to the virtually epigrammatic, Sayigh adds, "In the face of the crisis in its relations with its Lebanese support base, the PLO/PRM proved unable to impose on itself sufficient discipline to nurture rather than exploit its Lebanese environment" (31).[13] The writing was already visible on the wall, then, well before Walid Jumblatt, successor to his assassinated father's leadership of the LNM, disbanded the coalition at the height of Israel's 1982 Lebanese invasion.[14]

By 1981, the situation for the Palestinians and the PLO in Lebanon as well as in the Occupied Territories was tense. On the diplomatic front, Saudi Crown Prince Fahd's announcement in early August of a new eight-point Middle East peace proposal, the Fahd Plan, generated a flurry of debate once again over the PLO position(s) on a negotiated settlement with Israel.[15] In October, Egypt's President Anwar Sadat was assassinated. But no immediate or substantial change occurred in Egypt's relationship to Israel, the PLO, or the Arab states. Throughout the spring and summer of 1981, the expectation of a massive Israeli invasion of Lebanon was widespread. In midsummer of that year, Israel staged a devastating air strike against presumably heavily Palestinian-populated areas of Beirut, which of course included Lebanese as well. This was widely seen among Lebanese and Palestinians and in the Arab world as a move testing international opinion and as preliminary to plans for a wider-scale invasion of Lebanon.

In late January 1982, Moshe Arens, Israel's ambassador to the United States, said out loud what Palestinians and Lebanese already feared, that an Israeli invasion of Lebanon was only a matter of time.[16] Although the United States had brokered a cease-fire between the PLO and Israel in 1981,[17] which the PLO and the Palestinian resistance movements observed with relative rigor, there were successive large-scale Israeli attacks on Lebanon in the eleven-month period preceding June 1982. Only after the massive bombardment of Beirut in early June 1982 did the PLO abrogate the cease-fire.

In the Occupied Territories, deportations of pro-PLO elected officials and terrorist attacks against them increased. In the fall of 1981, Menachem Begin's government announced the installation of a "civil administration" in the West Bank to be headed by Menachem Milson, a professor of Arabic literature at Hebrew University in Jerusalem.[18] Milson summarily dismissed elected Palestinian mayors and officials in the West Bank who refused to cooperate with his administration on his terms. He moved to build up Village Leagues as alternative political powers to pro-PLO elected officials. And he blocked the inflow of funds from a joint PLO/Jordanian committee that had subsidized, among other things, health, education, and child care efforts in the West Bank.

Thus, the 1982 Israeli invasion of Lebanon occurred after a period of considerable transformation and development for the PLO and for Palestinians. That transformation and its organizational advances were fiercely and violently challenged by the events of the summer of 1982 and their aftermath. The devastation caused by the invasion was almost incomprehensibly vast for Palestinians and Lebanese alike. By the end of the first week of the invasion, the International Red Cross estimated that some 600,000 people—20 percent of the population of Lebanon—were homeless and without alternative shelter of any kind and without food, water, or medical supplies; 16,000 were seriously wounded; 10,000 were dead. Of these casualties, the overwhelming majority were civilian. The number of Palestinian and Lebanese armed combatants killed was estimated at approximately 2,000. The casualties only increased—as did the damage to hospitals, schools, and buildings in general, agricultural fields, water and food supplies, electrical power sources, and roads—as the invasion and siege of Beirut continued for more than two months.[19]

The widespread (and illegal) use of U.S.-made and -supplied cluster bombs and white phosphorus bombs, the beating and terrorizing of civilians, the widespread massive destruction of Lebanon's infrastructure, and the high number of civilian casualties sustained by Palestinians and Lebanese turned even public opinion in Israel against the "peace" campaign. By mid-June opposition to the invasion among the West Bank Palestinians, the Palestinians in Israel, and also the sometimes reticent Israeli peace movement had already gathered momentum.[20] Palestinian support for the PLO and against the Israeli war in Lebanon was widespread and adamant.[21]

International responses to the Israeli invasion were varied in both rhetoric and action. Most governments condemned at least the scale of the devastation wrought by the Israeli offensive. Some sent medical workers or supplies or human rights observers. Many more nongovernmental groups sent humanitarian aid of various kinds: financial support, teams of health care workers, medical supplies, international observers. The UN Security Council passed a series of resolutions condemning the Israeli invasion and calling for an immediate cease-fire (508, 5 June 1982). It subsequently called for the unconditional withdrawal of Israeli troops (509, 6 June 1982), the establishment and extension of an Interim Peacekeeping Force in Lebanon (511, 18 June 1982), and the protection of the rights of civilian populations (512, 19 June 1982).[22] As the devastation of the Lebanese infrastructure took its inevitably deadly toll, the Security Council called again for the observation of the rights of civilian populations and for the restoration of the "normal supplies of vital facilities such as water, electricity, food and medical provisions, particularly to Beirut" (513, 4 July 1982). As the siege of Beirut dragged ferociously on, the Se-

curity Council called for the immediate lifting of the Israeli blockade of the
Lebanese capital so that humanitarian aid could be dispatched to the civilian population (515, 29 July 1982), reconfirmed its call for a cease-fire and
the stationing of UN observers to monitor the situation in and around
Beirut (516, 1 August 1982), and, finally reiterating its demand for strict
observance of the cease-fire by all parties, demanded as well the immediate termination of all "restrictions" on Beirut by Israel and the latter's full
cooperation in the deployment of UN observers in Lebanon (518,
12 August 1982).

That the Israeli invasion of Lebanon and prolonged siege of Beirut was
devastating for the PLO and the Palestinians is an understatement. And it
is an understatement that the events of the summer of 1982 challenged the
social and political gains on the ground for Palestinians in Lebanon no less
than their sheer ability to survive. The events of the summer of 1982 severely challenged as well the political and military organization and workings of the PLO. Within less than a year after the PLO evacuation from
Beirut, a Syrian-supported faction within Arafat's Fateh organization
staged a revolt against his leadership and seriously fractured the PLO from
within its main, and mainstream, organization. Arafat and the PLO weathered this challenge, though at the cost of considerable disunity and loss of
initiative in the years that followed. Arafat weathered yet further challenges in subsequent years. But, most significant, the impetus for and focal
point of Palestinian political action shifted decisively from the diaspora to
the Occupied Territories and, initially to a lesser extent, to the Palestinians
in Israel. This shift is forthrightly acknowledged in a memorandum of the
Palestinian Communist Party to the 16th Palestine National Council meeting in Algiers in February 1983: "Since the departure of the resistance from
Beirut, the center of gravity of the Palestinian national struggle has shifted
to the occupied territories; the West Bank and Gaza have become the principal battleground and as such they occupy a special and significant place
in the current struggle and in future decisions."[23] They called, therefore,
for a revival of the Palestine National Front as "the sole central leadership
of the national struggle in the occupied territories." The French journalist
and historian Alain Gresh is even more blunt in his assessment of the effect
of the events of the summer of 1982 and their aftermath: "The departure of
the PLO from Beirut following the Israeli invasion of Lebanon in 1982 cut
the leadership off from the last concentration of Palestinians that had provided most of the fighters and many of the cadres. . . . The 1983 revolt of
the Fatah dissidents and the broad split in the PLO merely reflected this
disarray. The very idea of armed struggle was now in question, because for

the first time since the 1967 war the PLO had no direct access to the borders of the 'Zionist enemy' " (36).

However the story is formulated, within months of the Israeli invasion, there was a general shift in emphasis and impetus toward the Palestinians of the West Bank and Gaza—and this distinctly before the beginning of the intifada in December 1987. In its own way, the Israeli war in Lebanon created the conditions for almost the exact opposite of its stated objectives. Instead of severing the links between the PLO and Palestinians on the outside (i.e., in the diaspora) and Palestinians on the inside (i.e., within historic Palestine), those links were strengthened. And the Palestinians within historic Palestine now took renewed and primary initiative in new forms of articulating those links: "Dissension within the PLO's ranks after the Lebanon war opened new political opportunities on the West Bank. The mutiny in Fatah and the rift between the PLO's mainstream and rejectionist factions, culminating in the boycott by the latter groups of the seventeenth session of the Palestine National Council in Amman in November 1984, shattered the unity of the pro-PLO forces in the occupied territories."[24]

Yet, there is certainly no necessary or inevitable accrual of advantage in the fierce death and bloody destruction or in the political and organizational ruptures consequent for Palestinians and the PLO on the Israeli invasion of Lebanon in the summer of 1982. Eyewitness accounts and testimonials of the invasion and siege detail its devastating extent and often wanton savagery.[25] They are scarcely records of opportunity for revisions of social or political organization or cultural boundaries. The most suggestive, the most compelling, and in some ways the most penetrating of responses to that fearful summer are not the accounts of graphic misery and brutality and stubborn and sometimes heroic survival—though such accounts, and the experiences they represent, are their constant context. Rather, it is in the poetic and the fictional—the unrealistic and "unreal."[26]

"Hunā naḥnu qarb hunāka" (Here we are, near there) is a powerful example of a response to the summer of 1982—the Israeli invasion of Lebanon, the siege of Beirut, and the aftermath of those events—that is also a revisioning of it. A short poem written soon after the siege of Beirut by the Palestinian poet Mahmud Darwish, "Hunā naḥnu qarb hunāka" is, though not only, a poignant marker for a post-1982 Palestinian response to nationalism in crisis (again).[27] It is, though not only, an equally poignant marker for the anguish, death, and utter devastation of the summer of 1982. But, most important, it is, though not only, a poignant and suggestive

marker for a vision, an image, an idea, a configuration of words that iter-
ates the desire of, and perhaps holds open a space for, communities outside in.

> I thought to myself, "It's our duty to know what we long for.
> Is it for the homeland? For our picture outside the homeland?
> Or for the picture of our longing for the homeland
> to be seen inside the homeland?"
> —Mahmud Darwish, *Dākira lil-nisyān*
> (Memory for forgetfulness)

> Ours is a country of words. Speak, speak so I can rest
> my narrow path on the stone of a stone
> Ours is a country of words. Speak, speak so that we can
> know the end of this journey.
> —Mahmud Darwish, "Nasāfiru k'alnnās"
> (We travel like [all] people)

It is a commonplace to define desire as a longing for something that is not
present, something that is missing or absent, something that the one who
desires does not have. This is not far from a (rather more Freudian) notion
of desire as the attempt to represent the satisfaction of a need through the
imagining of gratification. Desire, then, is a representation, a depiction, a
vision, of its own fulfillment. And it is predicated on the absence or at least
distance of that which is envisioned. This might be one way of accounting
for the stories of nationalism: as expressions of a desire for that which is
absent and the effort to imagine the fulfillment of that desire for the absent
in terms of national satisfaction. In the late nineteenth and twentieth centuries, the satisfaction of such national desire was considered something of
a national *right*, as in "the right of nations to self-determination." The
relationship of national desire to national *need*—or at least to material
necessity—is perhaps more tenuous. Certainly, the satisfaction of material
need by the satisfaction of national desire is more tenuous.

The call of nationalism is typically uttered in the context, or at least in
the evocation, of material deprivation, discrimination, exploitation. Over
a century ago, Ernst Renan in his "Qu'est-ce qu'une nation?" astutely characterized the call of nationalism as dependent on a notion of "shared
misery"; he noted, as well, the necessity of nationalism's shared "forgetfulness."[28] To this notion, national fulfillment is most often represented as
the resolution of misery (through selective forgetfulness) in and by a

nation-state and its sovereignty, in and by specific territory and its control, in and by a society of national citizens who identify themselves first and foremost in national terms and who collectively accept the legitimacy of the state as the primary manifestation (and narrator) of the nation.

On one level, this is only obvious. For, at the beginning of the twenty-first century, the claims and desires of nationalism in general are familiar enough. They typically assert the coherence, continuity, and integrity of (a story of) the nation's past and of the nation's relation to a distinct language, culture, and land. This (story of the) past is cited as legitimation for a demand for autonomy or independence or, at least, a change in political status for the nation. And the political configuration of the nation-state (the hyphen here bearing an almost impossible burden of connection) is presented as the dominant form and telos of the national story. And, in perhaps the master stroke of this national tale, its dominant form and telos are "natural" and "inevitable." What other organization of people, pasts, and stories could there possibly be?

But there *are* other ways of telling the story, even of telling a national story; there are stories to tell other than that of a presumably singular and self-contained nation. In fact, as we have seen in the two previous chapters, national desires and national stories might well be characterized by a kind of displacement of desire for (a more just and equitable) social organization that is other than that of the narrowly national. Perhaps, at least in this century, it is only apparently "inevitable" that the defining feature of social organization is a narrowly national community in particular. As the examples of the aftermaths of the Asia Minor Catastrophe of 1922 and the invasion of Cyprus in 1974 have already suggested, even at moments of historical crisis, perhaps *especially* at moments of historical crisis, the stories of the nation suggest other kinds of social organization, other kinds of community, that exceed or at least do not neatly coincide with the boundaries of the nation and its state. They suggest social organization and communities that are not singularly containable or representable by the nation-state. These figurations-in-crisis might be considered for a moment as equally "objects of national desire." In a more literary register, the poetic production of space held open is simultaneously a painfully literal struggle for place that is, but not only, national. Formulated otherwise, what if "national desire" is, but not only, about the nation?

Darwish's "Hunā naḥnu qarb hunāka" is pained testimony to national desire and need as it is poetic witness to its im/possible fulfillment. Thus,

Darwish himself has insisted in his prose and in interviews that his poetry is, but not only, national. "Hunā naḥnu qarb hunāka" struggles to produce poetic place from almost impossible spaces as it struggles to articulate that place as—but not only—national. The opening of the poem proclaims this spatial impossibility in its reiteration of the title: "Here we are near there, thirty doors for the tent." Of course, "here near there" can, quite literally, be read as here in Lebanon near there in historic Palestine. But it is also and simultaneously an impossible place of suspension, of waiting, of being in between. This spatial impossibility is immediately reiterated in the second clause of the opening line. A tent with thirty doors? Thirty doors is certainly an inordinate, if not impossible, number of openings. So many, in fact, that there would be virtually no tent left at all. The literally impossible place in a metaphoric here-near-there of a tent with so many doors is reiterated four lines later in the same "thirty doors," this time for a wind. Even the provisional spatial demarcation of an impossibly doored tent is gone. With thirty doors for the wind, where is the structure that enframes those doors? The wind can rush through the dwelling or tent virtually without restriction. This too, like the tent, is a virtually impossible place. Here near there, then, the "we" of the poem occupy impossible or unlocatable or at least unfixable places (*makān*):[29] "between the pebbles and the shadows," "a place for a voice," "a place for freedom," "a place for any place." An even more graphic spatial qualification follows this last "place for any place": "slid down off [the back of] a mare or dispersed by a bell or a [muezzin's] call to prayer." Does the loss of position, of place, astride the mare, precipitate these latter sounds—the bell or the call to prayer? Or are they simultaneous? For these latter are not simply calls to a specific *place* of worship—to church or to mosque. They are also markers of communal *time;* the ringing of church bells and the call to prayer occur at regular fixed intervals. No matter where the faithful are when they hear the call, they presumably recognize both the time marked by the call and the spatial origin or place from and to which the call is issued. They also implicitly recognize their own membership in the community of believers to whom the call is addressed. And yet, such calls are heard by a heterogeneous audience of listeners. Not necessarily believers, they recognize the temporal and spatial marking of the calls nonetheless. This reversal of the usual function of the (religious/communal) call is subsequent to the loss of position astride the mare. Whether there is a causal relationship in the juxtaposition of these phrases that mark loss of time, space, and community, it is clear that in the here-near-there, in this besieged space with ever more encroached upon place, the sounds of a bell and of a call to prayer mark the dispersal of their audience and its communities. Still, the poem continues in hopeful longing:

> . . . soon we'll penetrate this siege, soon we'll free a cloud
> and depart to ourselves. Here we are near there thirty doors for the
> wind, thirty "was."

The continuing efforts in which the poem's "we" engage to locate and move "us" from the position between here and there is punctuated by a pedagogic project addressed to a second-person-plural audience. It is not only "we" who must move, relocate, find a place, and mark the time, but also "you." That second-person-plural address is equally marked by hopeful longing, if also by irony:

> We are teaching you to see us, and to recognize us, to hear us, and to
> touch/feel our blood in safety
> We are teaching you our peace.

Closed in upon (by "you"), besieged (by "you"), we nonetheless teach "you" so that we both might move to a different place, to a different mapping of space, to a different marking of time. And yet, "we" are forced into dispersal (by "you") to Syria (Damascus), to Saudi Arabia (Mecca), to Tunisia (Kairouan): "We may love or may not love the road to Damascus, to Mecca, or to Kairouan." Yet, in grandly stubborn insistence: "We are here with/in ourselves. A sky for August and a sea for May, and freedom for a stallion."

In this apparently neat order of things, of elemental space (the sky, the sea) that is paired with, that belongs to, prosaic calendar time (August, May), the "place for freedom" of the poem's second line is reiterated. But this time it is paired with, it is "for," a stallion (*lhasān*). The mare of the poem's third line is distinctly not, in some mundane reproductive order, paired with or "for" the stallion. The intervening four lines of the poem, with their invocation of a confounded time and space, interrupt what might have seemed to be such a "natural" equine pairing. In an unspoken analogy, "we" too are caught between here and there, our "pairing" with either place interrupted as well—by impossible spaces, by tents with too many doors, by the necessity of pedagogic lessons about safety and peace, by a siege and coercive dispersal that we "may love or not love."

In the face of such forcible interruption and separation, the apparently orderly assignation of one thing for another grows increasingly pointed—

and futile. The penultimate line of the poem asserts, "we do not seek the sea." For the sea, as we already know, is "for May." "We do not seek the sea," that is, "except to draw from it the blue rings around the smoke." In the poem's litany of surveying and apportioning, what is for us, then, are the blue rings around the smoke in the seat. What is for us is the impossible and ephemeral and intangible, the counterelemental. For, of course, blue rings around smoke cannot possibly be retrieved from or fished out of the sea. Smoke cannot possibly exist in water. Yet, the commonsense organization and location of the elements is here challenged by displacement. And on a literal note, it must be said, in the massive Israeli bombardment rained on Beirut for over two months, the sea certainly could have seemed to be smoke—the blue of the sea, like the blue of the sky, an apparent continuum of haze. In that enveloping cloud, "here we are near there." The poem reiterates in its final line "thirty shapes thirty shadows." And in a final gesture of apportionment, where each thing is almost desperately "for" something else, thirty shapes and shadows are, followed by the vagary of two ellipses, "for a star."

Darwish's poem records, in a manner of speaking, the siege of Beirut and the Palestinian evacuation from the city by sea ("we do not seek the sea"). But this recording is accomplished within the poetic articulation of foreclosure, of the reversal of a time and a place (and a call) of gathering. Most tangibly and literally, "Hunā naḥnu qarb hunāka" is situated in Lebanon of course and it "records" or at least gestures to the call to dispersal (and exile) from Lebanon to the sea ("we do not seek the sea"). Yet it is only in the impossible demarcation of "a place between pebbles and shadows" that there is room for a voice, for freedom, for us to travel to ourselves. In this recording of a historical event, there is much that exceeds that event. There is much that is the event of poetic language and imagining itself. Although such a proposition might sound hopelessly abstract, there is, after a fashion, a way in which the "event of poetic language and imagining" bears an important offering to our understanding of the literal event and its aftermath. Even in reference to the literal workings of poetic language, Darwish concludes another poem written at the same time, "ours is a country/a community of the spoken word."[30] It is this very community or country of the spoken word that demands speech, including, perhaps most especially, poetic speech. For, in the poetic logic of Darwish's poem, there can be no *place* otherwise. The immensity of space is simultaneously overwhelming and fiercely confining, the tasks in that space impossible. "Here we are near there," departing for

an hour of a country [*balād*] and a [poetic] meter of the impossible.
We travel in coaches of the psalms, we lie down in tents of the
    prophets and we
emerge in the speech of gypsies.
We measure [the vastness of empty] space [*al-faḍā'*] with the beak of
    a hoopoe bird
        or sing to while away the distance from us and wash the light of
            the moon.[31]

Both "Hunā naḥnu qarb hunāka" and "Nasāfiru k'alnnās" are something
more than simply Darwish's rendition of a Palestinian national dirge—
though, with painful and evocative beauty, they *are* such a dirge. As horrific as the in-fact experience of the Israeli invasion of Lebanon was, it has
here been recorded and transformed in the recording into a vision of "us"
in a place of longing and liminality for which language, song, poetry, the
journey are utterly necessary and at least metaphorically, perhaps even
literally, unending. The events of the summer of 1982 and their aftermath
have been transformed into a poetic injunction against homelessness and
deprivation. And that poetic injunction is also to remember the piercing
insights and keen assessment that can come in being "unhoused" when
the hold of various legitimations of the status quo is violently torn away.
Darwish's poems are, but not only, a call for an end to the injustice, suffering, and displacement of Palestinians as a people. His poems are, but not
only, a call for a literal space that can be "the end of this journey." They are
also a call for more than literal space at the journey's end with *place* to
accommodate freedom, a voice, a star. And how is that *place* provided for?
This latter question is also, but not only, a poetic one. For freedom or a
voice or a star is neither acquired nor contained by national boundaries, by
ethnic or national belonging, by laws and customs. They exceed the fixation of national boundaries as they exceed the fixation of what is or can be
by the visible or the utterable. The "poetic" insight here of Darwish's poem
is also and simultaneously intensely "political":

Ah, the country [*balad*] where we see nothing except that which is
    unseen: our secret
For us the glory: a throne on legs lopped off by the trails that trans-
    port us to every house but our house!
The soul should renew its soul in its own soul, or die here . . .[32]

The place of "our secret," the country of "our glory," is an ironic indication
of the absence of such a place and a country as, equally, it is a marker of

longing for fulfillment, for satisfaction, for the "journey's end" at "a house of our own."

Yet this desire is not simply satiated in the cancellation of absence—whether of place or of country. Nor is it just any house or country or any uttered revelation of an invisible secret that can "renew the soul." There may, in fact, even be secrets that cannot be revealed or forcibly made visible and present, desires that are insatiable. They may remain just beyond the boundaries of the measurable, the utterable, the visible. In the measuring and apportionment of space and the natural elements that are alternately vast and open (*faḍā'*) and closing in on us (*taḍayiqu binā al-'arḍu; t'asurunā al-'arḍu*), where is the place for the unseen, the unspeakable, the immeasurable? Not meekly present to be contained, bounded, fixed, or governed—either by a poem or by a state. Yet, in the face of fierce desire for the resolute demarcation of boundaries and the tidy containment therein of excesses of sight, sound, and materiality, the poem seems to be rather more successful in holding open a place for the unseen, the secret, the immeasurable, the unallocatable.[33]

There is further counsel in this regard suggested by another of Darwish's post-1982 poems. "Naḵlāf 'alā ḥulm" ("We fear for a dream") opens—and closes—with fear and an admonition: "We fear for a dream: don't put too much faith in our butterflies." The flitting ephemerality of both dream and butterfly that inform the expression of fear and warning is, later in the poem, specified as an address to the dream itself:

We are afraid for you; we are afraid of you. We are revealed together,
    don't put too
      much faith in the steadfastness of our wives.

And finally in closing,

We are afraid for the dream, from it, from us. Yet we dream, oh dream
    of ours.
      Don't put too much faith in our butterflies.

The insistent but elusive distinction here *of* and *between* dreams and butterflies suggests the ineluctability of desire and the intractability of its satisfaction. There is no simple and incontrovertible place, bounded and fortified, which either dreams or butterflies occupy. Nor is there such a simple and incontrovertible place for the "us" of "Hunā naḥnu qarb hunāka." The poetic insistence in "Naḵlāf 'alā ḥulm," as in much of Darwish's poetry, on the aching absence or vast distance of such a place—toward which we strive nonetheless—does not ignore or diminish the injustice and anguished deprivation of hundreds of thousands of Palestinians. Nor does it diminish the urgent need for an end to the conditions that create that suffering and injustice. There is also, though, at least potentially, a radical possibility for a "questioning without end,"[34] for a striving toward that distant place, which is not the ethnic or racial or national property of any single people. Rather, as I hope the examples of this and the previous two chapters suggest, it is a sadly repeatable insight, a recurring radical possibility generated out of dispossession, uprooting, becoming-refugee, continuing occupation, and exile: "Oh dream of ours, give us a kernel of wheat. Give it, give it to us." Do dreams (or poems) yield up sustenance? A grain of wheat, a homeland, a safe border? Literally, they don't, of course. Though that isn't to say that the demand—"Give it, give it to us"—doesn't continue to be made or that dreams can't motivate demands, vision, and sustenance beyond themselves.

Beyond his poetry, Darwish has himself pointedly remarked in his prose and in interviews on the distinction between desire and its satisfaction, or between desire as open-ended and desire as prescriptive, as directing its terminal satisfaction. His formulation of this distinction—part of a still fierce debate within Palestinian communities inside historic Palestine and in the diaspora beyond it—is not specifically that of desire and satisfaction. Rather, it distinguishes the potential retrogression of the "return" from a less circumscribed and more open "journey."[35] For the notion of the return is a contradictory one, with its mythic promise of an immediate (national, religious, ethnic, social, familial) fulfillment consequent on its attainment. In the name of that mythic right to fulfillment, the Zionism that founded and continues to inform its vision of the Israeli state on the "right of return" has uprooted and expelled millions of Palestinians. A parallel right of return for those Palestinians remains a fiercely debated issue with no simple resolution.[36]

Surely no concept is more omnipresent in Darwish's poetry, as it is in the modern Palestinian cultural lexicon in general, than the "journey" (ḍahāb, riḥla, safra, sair). But, in counterdistinction to the "return," the journey is open-ended, speculative, always at least potentially exilic; it is not predicated on the specified (or specifiable) destination of a return. In Darwish's poetry (as, at its best, in broader Palestinian cultural discourse), these notions of the return and the journey, like those of space and place, are not set against one another in some violently tidy opposition. Nor are speech and the unspoken (or the unspeakable) postulated as poles between which ample poetic vacillation can occur. Rather, speech is possible precisely in the face of that which eludes it, which impinges on it, in blunt recognition of the unutterable, on the very terrain of and utterly implicated in silence, even forcibly mandated silence. In a similar fashion, the insistent nudging toward a *place* held open for (but not necessarily occupied by) freedom, a star, a voice, is possible and *takes place* only within and complexly linked to the same vast and confining space that besieges us. What Darwish has called "the revolutionary endeavor" of *al-ḍahāb* exceeds the expectation (or coercive construction) of a simple end, of fulfillment in a return to a place that once was. The "right of return" on which the state of Israel and its definition of citizenship is predicated, like the "right of return" that the millions of Palestinians-made-refugees insist on retaining, is a contradictory and dubious endeavor. As the young Palestinian boy's dream recounted in the final chapter suggests, the dream of return can also be a nightmare, or at least a foreclosure on hope, on striving. From the outside in, from the inside out, that place-held-open can precisely—perhaps only?—be in a poem, in a story, in a song. But the struggle for (social) recognition of the need for such a place-held-open occurs elsewhere as well.[37]

There is a poignant visual illustration of the crowded difficulty of constructing this place-held-open in one of the last works by the widely admired Palestinian cartoonist Nāji al-ʻAli. His cartoon indicates, as well, the fiercely charged reformulation of the gendering of Palestinian nationalism in the post-1982 period. Drawn before the onset of the intifada for the Kuwaiti newspaper *al-Qabas,* the cartoon is as remarkably prescient as it is astute in drawing from many of the predominant concerns and tropes of Palestinian culture.[38] In the foreground of the cartoon frame is the image of a Palestinian woman in traditional dress, a young girl at her side. The woman's feet emerging from the bottom of her *thoub,* like those of the girl, are a sinuous web of tree roots. Both woman and girl are literally rooted to the soil in a familiar enough citation of the Palestinian woman as rooted to the land and to tradition; the woman's dress reiterates that traditional rootedness. But both woman and girl are also linked to an explicit resistance to occupation. The young girl throws a stone at a cringing man with a star of David on his helmet. The woman both beckons with and offers stones that she picks up from the ground to a group of apparently hesitant or ineffectual men massed in front of her. She and the young girl, positioned between the timid men and the Israeli soldier, serve as both mediation and front line. (The gender mobilization of the intifada in subsequent months and years is a further historical elaboration of al-'Ali's

Nāji al-'Ali, cartoon, in *al-Qabas* (Kuwaiti newspaper)

astute cartoon image here. In countless instances, and photographs of some of those instances, women don't hand rocks to others to throw; they throw them themselves.)

In visual alliance with the woman and the girl is al-'Ali's omnipresent witness in virtually all of his cartoons: the ragged, barefoot figure of Hanzala. With his back always to the reader and his hands usually clasped behind his back, Hanzala figures as an ambiguous child/old man, sadly observant. But here, for a change, Hanzala's hands are not behind his back. He is not standing impassively by, silent and saddened spectator to the scene before him as he most often is depicted in al-'Ali's cartoons. This time Hanzala actively intervenes, pushing forward into the confused and hesitant midst of the group of men. The men themselves are also a visually familiar feature of al-'Ali's cartoons, with their heavy, bald faces and their legless and bare-butted torsos seemingly immobilized on the ground. The stones flying ineffectually above their heads, their heavy bodies and hesitant faces embody the typically sharp-edged critique of al-'Ali's cartoons. So too does the Palestinian woman beckoning to the men with a stone in her hand, and so too does Hanzala, who moves forcefully into their midst. He is clearly visually male in al-'Ali's cartoons. But his sexually ambiguous status as a young boy/old man aligns him here with womanhood that is visually cast as resolute, clear-sighted, and dynamic in the face of the vacillation and fear of the heavy-bottomed men.

The astute and suggestive concerns, verbal and visual, of Darwish's poetry and al-'Ali's cartoons are equally present in Michel Khleifi's film *Wedding in Galilee,* a Belgian/French coproduction released in 1987. The title is a simple and direct enough indication of what the film is about: a wedding in a Palestinian village in the Galilee, within the boundaries of the Israeli state. The wedding is planned, takes place, and concludes. The film ends. But *Wedding in Galilee* is no simply nostalgic or quasi-anthropological filmic rendition of Palestinian traditions. Nor is it some sort of unfettered and unfiltered proposition about the extratextual Palestinian situation. Rather, Khleifi's *Wedding in Galilee,* with its imaginary and impossible suggestions, epitomizes the ways in which cultural or literary texts can afford a space for questions and propositions that are precisely impossible to articulate in the contemporary political or social sphere. It is those impossible fictions, in their very ficticity and impossibility, that suggest a story we might not have been able to hear before, a dream we might not have been able to dream, a proposition—in *Wedding in Galilee,* about gendered (meta)nationalism— we might not have been able to consider. It is precisely in this impossible imaginary or, if you like, in this splendidly figural aspect that a literary or cultural text can articulate *otherwise* nationalism and gender, the state and the citizen, sexuality and honor. It is precisely in this impossible imaginary too that the literary or cultural text can articulate other notions of community, other notions of honor, other notions of gendered citizenship than the predominant or putatively commonsense ones. Of these former we are in fierce need. As we are in fierce need of an uncommon or a new common sense.[39]

The wedding is itself an overwhelmingly familiar trope in Palestinian literature, song and popular imagination, a trope that took a striking turn in the period after 1948. In the subsequent figural economy of conjugal relations, 1948 and the establishment of the State of Israel in Palestine was cast as a kind of coercive conjugal separation. As even the titles of popular poems from the post-1948 period suggest—'Abd al-Latif'Aql's "Palestinian-Style Love" or Mahmud Darwish's "Blessed Is That Which Has Not Come," with its invocation of "the Palestinian wedding without end" of his "Lover from Palestine"—the bride or beloved is typically the land of Palestine, the groom or lover is the Palestinian. But what appears to be almost mundanely familiar and even commonsensical in this image— the union of or wedding between a man and a woman, an exiled lover and his beloved, a Palestinian and Palestine—is distinctly more vexed on closer consideration.

Yet this prosaic image of the conjugal union of man and woman as a trope for the union of national citizen with national territory under the authority of a national state is at the heart of virtually all nationalist rhetoric. (And it has situated itself, as well and with considerable regularity, at the heart of nationalist grammar-as-state-order.) Vexed as it is, this trope is arguably the generative basis for the absence and longing on which national desire is erected. And, following mundanely on the terms of that trope, the representation of the fulfillment or consummation of desire is possession and control of the land-as-woman. The profoundly problematic nature of this latter equation is conspicuous; increasingly, there are challenges to its putative naturalness. Yet its currency in the figural economy of nationalist rhetoric and grammar persists. What this trope of conjugal union silences or effaces, however, is an inescapable question in this context. And *Wedding in Galilee* is an instructive response, though scarcely the only one, to just this question. For in the Palestinian instance, there is a premier obstacle to possession-of-the-woman/land-as-national-fulfillment. Rather obviously, the fertile, virginal (if violated), and desirable woman/land that belongs to the virile (if exiled) male lover/citizen is otherwise occupied. Namely, Palestine is also Israel and the largely still Israeli-occupied territories.

So this trope, discrepant from the beginning, has come to be as debated in the Palestinian context as it is familiar. And it is precisely in this context of vexed familiarity and debate that Khleifi's (pre-intifada) *Wedding in Galilee* is situated. It subtly if substantially frustrates the conjoining of the formerly separated man and woman as an unproblematic trope for Palestinian nationalism. The film itself, as a narrative representation of the fulfillment of national and sexual desire, is equally a trenchant suggestion of an absence or lack that cannot be made present. This apparently abstract proposition is distinctly less abstract in the national/sexual contradiction that propels the latter half of the film. The antithesis or resolution of absence in this instance is not, in any event, presence. Rather, it is the continuation of desire itself—a desire for something else beyond the consummation of a "national" wedding. In fact, in the context of the film, such insistently political metaphorization of sexuality, consummation, and marriage ensures the failure of consummation, the impossibility of satisfaction.

So then, the putative fulfillment of national/sexual desire in the conjugal union of bride and groom is drastically and suggestively recast in

Khleifi's *Wedding in Galilee*. For that consummation cannot take place as expected. In the face of the burden of his father's dreams, the expectations of the Palestinian community, the growing and clamorous tensions and barely foiled plans for violence outside the wedding chamber, and his own rage and frustration, the bridegroom, Ádil, is impotent. And so, for "the honor and dignity of everyone" (*karāmat lil-kull*), the bride, Samia, takes her own virginity, asking Ádil, as she prepares to do so: "If a woman's honor is her virginity, where is the honor of a man?" *Ḥaitu*—where, she asks, not what. She knows where her virginity-as-honor is. And, claiming the traditionally male prerogative, she takes it herself. Samia takes possession of her own honor—*if*, as she says, "woman's honor is her virginity." But what of Ádil, her young bridegroom? Or of his friends, angry and abused subjects and opponents of Israeli military rule? Or of the older generation of Palestinian men? The predication of the wedding night—or of the allegorical union of the (male) Palestinian with (a female) Palestine—on the groom's possession of the bride and on that possession or taking and its object (female virginity) as a mark of honor are here radically undermined.

This is then a rather different rendition of "the Palestinian national struggle" than that which might be more familiar from media broadcasts and newspaper accounts. It is also a rather different rendition from that series of gendered national equations noted above. And so, for some segments of a Palestinian audience, Samia's taking of her own virginity toward the end of the film is the film's most scandalous moment. Yet, it is simultaneously one of the film's most adamant accounts of "struggle." It is, however, and not coincidentally, one that occurs behind closed doors, in the house of the patriarch, witnessed within the film only by the frustrated and temporarily impotent bridegroom. But it is precisely this aspect of national-struggle-in-containment that follows on and recasts a more prosaic understanding of gendered national struggle. The trope of national/sexual possession is transmuted. In her literal and metaphoric self-consummation, Samia claims Palestine—herself—for herself. And that "taking," that claim, suggests further a vision of self-possession that is simultaneously sensual, sexual, and personally and communally political. Yet, outside the bridal chamber, the wedding guests and the larger community know nothing of this. They know only that tradition has been maintained. The bloodied bridal sheets are displayed in demonstration of the virginity of the bride, the virility of the bridegroom, and "the honor and dignity of everyone." But, courtesy of the camera peering into the bridal chamber, watching from behind the bride's back—the only "wedding guests" afforded this voyeuristic view—the film's audience knows differently. And to witness Samia's act of self-possession is to be compelled to reconsider the significance of the wedding itself. It is to be compelled to reconsider the significance of the gendered national trope that would postulate the consummation of national desire in the possession by a man of a woman.

There is another wedding in Galilee of some considerable familiarity. Though its import is rather substantially different, the account of that other wedding in Galilee comes after the story of Jesus' selection and gathering of his disciples and is followed by the story of his throwing out the money changers from the temple in Jerusalem at Passover. That other wedding is, of course, the New Testament account of "the wedding at Cana in Galilee" (John 2:1–12). At that wedding, and in spite of Jesus' protestations to his mother, Mary, that his "hour has not yet come," he did as she suggested and alleviated the problem of wedding libations that had run out by turning water for ritual purification into wine. Mary gently forced his hand before he was "ready" so that the wedding might end well. And end well it did. The account of the wedding at Cana concludes with John's summation of the incident and, implicitly, with his reason for including it in his Gospel (for it appears in none of the other three New Testament Gospels): "This, the first of his signs, Jesus did at Cana in Galilee, and manifested his glory; and his disciples believed in him" (2:11). Jesus' compliance with his mother's request to see to it that the wedding ended well also confirmed to his newly gathered disciples that they had chosen well to follow him. And the account of the wedding in Galilee leads directly to Jesus' confrontation with the money changers in the temple in Jerusalem. It is, then, at least for John's Gospel, a pivotal episode in Jesus' emergence into the public eye and into social recognition as a religious leader.

There is no miracle worker in Khleifi's film; the food and drink at this twentieth-century wedding are ample. But in Khleifi's account of a wedding in Galilee there is a clear need too for the wedding to end well. As Samia acknowledges, the "honor and dignity of everyone"—guests and bride and groom and their families—is at stake. And there too, in Khleifi's latter-day wedding in Galilee, though its hour may not (yet) have come, are signs to be read. If this incident is the first occasion in the Gospel of John for the manifestation of Jesus as a "glorious" response to human strife and suffering (as Jesus is characterized throughout the New Testament), something like a decidedly nondivine response to strife and suffering, or at least an honorable conclusion to the wedding, is not quite analogously present in Khleifi's Galilean wedding. Though the incident does not seem to appear in the Koran, nonetheless there is repeated insistence there on the proliferation of signs to those who can read them: "Surely [in this] there are signs" for "all mankind," "for thinking people," "for those who hear," for those "of understanding" (Sura 30, "al-Rūm"/"The Greeks," 30:22–29). The signs in the Koran, of course, are of the glory of God, as they are in the New Testament of Jesus as the son of God. (The Koran, for whom Jesus is another prophet but not the son of God, repeatedly refers to Jesus as, rather, the son of Mary). Khleifi's film does not depict an explicitly Christian wedding by any means (though it does mingle customs and aspects of various and diverse wedding practices). But its title evokes that other Galilean wedding of the New Testament. The literal, if more awkward, translation of the film's Arabic title is just that: "The Galilean Wedding." And, as Ádil's father will insist to the military governor as a condition for the latter's potentially intrusive and disruptive presence at the wedding, "You must be a good guest at the wedding [and stay to its end]." Samia will make sure that the wedding ends as it "should." And we as audience, peering over her shoulder, are witnesses to what it takes to make the wedding end well.

But it is not only Samia's act of self-possession in taking her own virginity that makes the wedding end well, and that forces a reconsideration of the national narrative and notions of community, memory, and honor. Nor is it only her unanswered question of Ádil: "Where is the honor of men?" There are other noteworthy instances of visual and verbal reformulation of the dominant national trope in Khleifi's *Wedding in Galilee.* One of these is the very movement of the camera itself in framing and telling its story. Turning for a moment back to the film's opening, the sounds and images that might be expected to introduce a wedding celebration are not the first ones audible in the film's opening frames. Rather, it is the sound of children playing, interrupted and quickly drowned out by the sound of military jets buzzing the landscape. The first visual images of the film are of the exterior of the Israeli military headquarters. The camera subsequently moves inside to a waiting room in the offices of the military commander. This move from outside to inside and out again—here from the skies dominated by Israeli jets, to the exterior façade of the military headquarters, to the interior workings of military rule (which dominates the land and its peoples), to the outside of the building again—marks the visual organization of the film throughout.[40] And, like the trope of the wedding consummated, this structural device is strategically, though ambiguously, reversed in conclusion. If it is on the *inside* that potentially radical transformations of desire and imaginary figures of its satisfaction occur, if it is on the *inside* that the dominant narratives of nation, family, and gendered community are contested and enacted differently, on the *outside* the dominant narrative arguably continues to hold sway. Yet, the disturbingly familiar and vexed implications of this construct are themselves breached in the film. Is the interior a site of the challenge to the dominant scheme of things (on the sexual and familial level at least, the site of Samia's claiming of her own virginity) and the exterior a site of the apparent maintenance of that dominant scheme (on the same sexual and familial level, the display of the bloodied sheets as sign of male potency and the marriage's consummation)? Or is it otherwise? I bracket this question only for the moment, for there are a number of crucial instances in and aspects of the film that suggest a response.

The opening of the film inside the military governor's office witnesses an exchange between the mukhtar of a Palestinian village in the Galilee, Salim Saleh Daoud, and the military governor. Not surprisingly, given the film's title, the mukhtar comes to request permission for an exemption from the military restrictions that forbid public gatherings so that he can hold a traditional village wedding for his eldest son, Ádil. And, equally unsurprisingly, the mukhtar's request is denied in the name of Israeli (military) law and order and, as the military governor insists, because Palestinians have not demonstrated "respect for Israeli will." The implicit formula here for soliciting the "benevolence" of the ruler/occupier toward the ruled/occupied is one that is reiterated later in the film and within Palestinian society between man/husband and woman/wife. But in opening, the references are clearly to military rule and to national aspirations (and "tradition") in opposition to that rule. The fact that the military governor is a Sephardi, an Israeli of Arab Jewish origins, makes no difference in the scheme of things. The military governor's ability to speak fluent Arabic, to have lived among the Arabs, and hence presumably to better "understand the Arabs" than his Ashkenazi (European Jewish) compatriots does not, in this film (or outside of it?), make any difference in the military administration of Palestinian lives.

Actually, it is a young aide to the governor, an Ashkenazi, who comes up with a brilliantly Machiavellian idea. He suggests that the Israeli military governor agree to a permit for the wedding but only if the governor and his entourage are invited. To their surprise, the mukhtar agrees. But he has a condition of his own: "You've told me your terms; let me tell you mine—that you will stay for the *entire* wedding." That is, the mukhtar asks that the military governor and his entourage behave as proper and respectful guests at the wedding of his son. Though the young aide to the military governor, and the military governor himself, might have expected the mukhtar to refuse the bargain out of national or even just regional village pride, the old man accepts their offer with just one term of his own: You must stay until the wedding ends.

The bargain is struck and the mukhtar leaves military headquarters, boards a bus, and returns to his village. In what is the paradigmatic visual organization of the film, the camera moves from the bus and the exterior landscape as it travels through the countryside to the interior, now the courtyard of the mukhtar's home. There his mother sits with her grandchild, Daoud's youngest daughter, telling her a story about the communal murder of an adulteress's son. This scene and its (ironic) commentary on marital and communal law and order and the consequences of their violation is the first thing that greets Daoud on his return home. It is also the first interior scene juxtaposed to his opening encounter with Israeli military law and order in the interior of the military governor's office. The order of these laws is onerous, deadly, whether it be Israeli military law in the present or the communal law of family honor in the remembered past of the mukhtar's mother.

The scene then reverts to Daoud's bus ride back to the village and his voice-over interior monologue as the camera pans the landscape, its olive trees, its goat herds, and its fields. This is interrupted temporally and spatially again by a scene in the interior of Daoud's house, now in his bedroom. It is there that the mukhtar explains to his wife that he had to invite the military authorities to the wedding in order to get permission for the celebration:

—*Shu ra'y 'indik?* [What's your opinion? he asks her.]
—*Ra'y ra'yuk.* [It's your decision, she responds.]

And she adds meaningfully that he should try not to cause a split in the family because of his bargain with the Israeli military governor.

On this warning, the scene returns to the mukhtar's bus ride, then to his bedroom again, back to the bus, and finally to the main room of Daoud's home and the reedy voice of his old father singing. The room fills quickly with male relatives for the family meeting convened to discuss the wedding of Daoud's son and the invitation extended to the Israeli military authorities. The film cuts back to the mukhtar's bus ride to the village and the landscape of the countryside; it returns to the main room of Daoud's house and his formal invitation to the wedding to all of his kinfolk. Heated disagreement erupts over the invitation to the Israeli military to the wedding and over holding an elaborate wedding at all at a time of occupation and military rule. An angry refrain echoes throughout the room: "At what cost, this wedding?" In response, Daoud recounts to the assembled men his recurring dream in which his grandfather appears to him dressed in white. The old grandfather urges the mukhtar to hold a traditional village wedding for his son with singing, dancing, an elaborate feast, and young women dressed in their most beautiful clothes. And Daoud reminds the men of the traditional extension of village hospitality at a wedding to everyone—even to enemies.

As if in counterbalance to the men's indictment of the circumstances of the wedding, Daoud's old father reminisces to Hassan, Daoud's youngest son, about the multiple occupations of Palestine. There were the Turks ("When the Turks were here they despised the Arabs"), the British, and now the Israelis. And, in a reiteration of proverbial Arab hospitality, echoing his son Daoud's acceptance of an Israeli military presence at the wedding, the old man, in apparently senile confusion, tells Hassan,

—If my home were nearby, I'd go and bring you some raisins.
—But grandfather, the young boy responds with a smile, this *is* your home, so where are my raisins?

Such apparently senile interruptions by both the mukhtar's father and his mother are not so simply senile at all. More properly, they function as punctual reminders of alternative ways of seeing the present in light of the past. Their disruptive outbursts of apparent senility are simultaneously astute commentary on and critique of what no one else wants to admit or remember. Daoud himself, standing in the courtyard of his house, responds to his mother's advice about quickly marrying off Sumaya, the mukhtar's lovely and bold older daughter, with the observation that his mother "only seems to be senile, but is in fact clever as a fox."

Back inside the main room of the mukhtar's house, the men of the family argue; some walk out angrily, others continue to dispute Daoud's decision. The camera moves back to the bus ride once again and an identification check by an armed Israeli soldier of Palestinians on the bus. The bus finally arrives in the village and, as he steps down, Daoud invites everyone to his son Ádil's wedding the following Friday. As he walks to his house, and over the ululations of the women on the bus, a megaphone from a military jeep blares an early curfew in the village that evening.

Although the first third of the film moves back and forth between the present of the mukhtar's bus ride back to his village and the future of his arrival home, from the narrative time of the mukhtar's arrival back in his village from the military governor's office, *Wedding in Galilee* proceeds in

fairly linear temporal fashion. A more historically shaped temporal disruption of the film's narrative present is marked in the persons of the
mukhtar's parents rather than in the movement of the camera itself. From
this point on, the camera's oscillation is spatial—between interior and
exterior—rather than temporal.[41]

And so, as time begins to unfold in a more linear fashion within the film,
the day of the wedding dawns. And the festivities *and* the tensions acceler-
ate. In the context of precisely this tension—particularly that between
the Palestinians and the Israeli military but also within the film's Palestinian community as well—Tlali, an Israeli woman soldier in attendance at
the wedding with the Israeli military governor, faints from the heat and
the celebration's day-long drink and food. The Palestinian women of the
house take the Israeli woman soldier away to an upstairs bedroom. They
gather around the bed where Tlali lies, reciting a passage from the Koran to
protect her. One of the older women massages Tlali's neck and chest and
loosens her military uniform. And then the women leave the room, leaving
Tlali to sleep, with a few younger women to watch over her.

Outside, Sumaya, the mukhtar's oldest daughter, boldly taunts the Israeli soldier waiting anxiously for Tlali to reemerge. "We'll cut her heart
out and eat it," she tells him in Arabic (which he cannot understand). A
few moments later, Sumaya continues to tease him, telling him that if he
wants to dance at her brother's wedding he will have to take off his military uniform. The silly banter of a playfully mocking young woman? There
is an Israeli soldier who removes her military uniform and participates
in—dances, in fact, at—Adil's wedding. But it is not the young soldier
Sumaya teases; it is Tlali, who loses consciousness in one (exterior) setting
and regains it in another (on the inside).

Tlali's initially involuntary crossing over from the more public space of
the courtyard where the wedding proper is taking place to an inner room of
the mukhtar's house allows another and equally "scandalous" possibility
to emerge in the story of *Wedding in Galilee.* The challenge to patriarchal
potency and authority in the courtyard is not only figured in Samia's taking of her own virginity. There is another challenge in an alternative visual
rendition of gendered community and the nation—though a decidedly
more private one. That rendition is, for a moment, a woman's story. The
second time we see Tlali in the upstairs bedroom, she has woken and
appears transfixed by her surroundings. She gets up from the bed where
she was sleeping, looks around her, and stretches out on the cool stone
floor, tracing the texture of its stones with her fingertips.

But, as in the story of Samia's "scandalous" self-possession, the story of

Tlali and the Palestinian women is one framed and at least partially contained by the different and male organization outside the inner room. The
very movement of the camera makes this narrative containment visually
apparent. The camera advances from men dancing in the bright sunlight of
the courtyard to the bridegroom Ádil's face in their midst to the men
dancing again. And then it cuts to the inside of the house and the room
where Tlali has been sleeping. Now the lighting changes from that of the
bright sun to a softer, more sensual, ever so slightly blurred yellow lens, as
light filters delicately through the curtains at the windows. With gentle
laughter in the background, bracelets jangle softly against one another.
One of the young Palestinian women gently sifts through her fingers dried
rose petals from a bowl on the tabletop, letting the fragrant petals drop
slowly back into the bowl. This is one of the film's most sensuous efforts to
visually account for smell and touch. With the help of her young Palestinian counterparts, Tlali removes her military uniform and puts on a *thoub,*
a traditional embroidered Palestinian dress. At the heart of the Palestinian
wedding, there is, for a moment, an improvisational and sensual community of Israeli and Palestinian women for whom exclusionary nationality
is suspended. An Israeli soldier, Tlali, *does* take off her uniform and dance
at Ádil's wedding, in the company of women on the inside of the house,
unnoticed by her male counterparts or by the Palestinian men outside of
the house. That this moment is severely constrained is clear from that
characteristic (almost nervous) movement of the camera from this suggestive scene inside the house of gently laughing women, who do not speak
each other's language but have managed to communicate nonetheless, to
the growing tensions outside the house as the conflicts that underlie the
wedding gather momentum.

This nascently transnational community among women stands out
against the familial community of her new husband into which the bride
Samia enters. It stands out as well against the community of national
oppression of Palestinians by Israelis and the potential for violent opposition to that oppression, signaled by the young Palestinian men who are
Ádil's cohorts in the film. And it stands out against Israeli national community with its own internal ethnic and religious tensions, which are, but
not only, between Palestinian Israelis (the proper subject and site of the
film) and European Jewish Israelis (Ashkenazis). If for a moment inside
the house there is a different order—one not necessarily predicated on
national desire but on desire and longing for community of a different
sort—that community is abruptly interrupted and reframed by events outside. And it is not only the threat of the young Palestinian men's retaliation

against the Israeli military that overshadows both this sensual community and the wedding and union of Ádil and Samia. There are other grim reminders of the fierce foreclosure of alternative community. The social and sexual order of a society under siege, the burden of claustrophobic and loveless marriages—these signs too mark the landscape of *Wedding in Galilee:* in the desperate plotting of the young Palestinian men for reprisal, in Sumaya's attempts to refuse the sometimes stifling burden of traditional women's roles, in the frightened and lonely weeping of a wife assaulted by her husband.

The onerous cost of this foreclosure is poignantly and tellingly suggested in the effort of Palestinians and Israelis to recapture the mukhtar's beautiful prized stallion from the Israeli-mined field where the horse has run after the mukhtar's young son, Hassan, and his friend have accidentally let the animal escape from its stall. The Israeli soldiers have the map of the mined field; they know which areas the horse must avoid to escape the mines. But they try and frighten him out of the field by firing shots into the air. The horse, ever more confused and terrified by the gunshots, only runs nervously back and forth. It's the mukhtar himself who, with directions from the Israeli soldier reading the map, gently and lovingly coaxes the horse from the field. The suggestion is scarcely obscure: gentleness and kindness, not gunfire and harsh orders, save the animal (and, potentially, the relations between Palestinians and Israelis?). This, too, like the figure of the military governor who presumably knows and hence "understands the Arabs," is a marker in the film for an alternative cooperation between Israeli and Palestinian.

Yet, what is for the most part the grim foreclosure of such gentle, shared effort is qualified by the repetition of two other crucial images and moments in the film. The least obvious of these repetitions is perhaps the most suggestive. That is the duplication of Samia's bridal dance by Tlali. As the camera frames Samia early in the film, so it frames Tlali later—seen through a doorway, in traditional Palestinian dress, dancing with a candle in each hand. Subtly but nonetheless clearly, there are, then, two brides at this Palestinian wedding. One, Samia, is Palestinian. The other is Tlali, the Israeli soldier. And, other than the implied audience for the film afforded by the camera eye, there is only one person in the film who recognizes, or at least witnesses, the parallel between Samia and Tlali. He interrupts the dance of both women swaying with candles in their hands. It is the same Israeli soldier whom Sumaya teases outside the room where Tlali sleeps. It is this Israeli soldier who interrupts the dance of Samia as he searches for Tlali inside the house. Samia is framed in the doorway, surrounded by a group of Palestinian women, two candles in her hands. Following this intrusion by the Israeli soldier, Samia's mother-in-law decides that the time for the consummation of the wedding has come. Samia extinguishes the two lit candles she has been holding by stepping on the flames, presumably marking the transition from one life to another. When we next see someone (an *other* bride) swaying with two lit candles in her hands, it is Tlali frozen in the doorway as the same Israeli soldier who burst in on Samia and her company of women bursts in on Tlali and her female Palestinian companions. But Tlali's candles are not ritually extinguished to mark a transition from one life to the next. She drops the candles as the Israeli soldier, presumably her boyfriend, roughly grabs her arm and pulls her from the room. One of the young Palestinian women runs after Tlali to give her her military uniform (Tlali is still dressed as a bride in a Palestinian *thoub*).

The figure of this male Israeli soldier is evocative and ambiguous in *Wedding in Galilee*. As he searches for Tlali in the night-dark passageways of the house, he listens outside the bridal chamber in which Samia takes her own virginity. He listens, as well, moments earlier, at the window of the room in which, for the third and final time in the film, the mukhtar repeats to his sleeping youngest son his desire for his story to be understood and remembered by the young boy. As Hassan wakes from his sleep, startled to see his father's face bent over him, the mukhtar asks his son: "Are you afraid of me?" Hassan runs out of the room.

Hassan, arguably younger, prepubescent, and Palestinian, nonetheless has a kind of mobility similar to the Israeli soldier's. Presumably too young to understand what is happening, Hassan is witness to many of the crucial scenes in the film. But it is only the Israeli soldier who witnesses what I would suggest is the most daring proposition the film makes about conjugal unions and partners, about im/possible Palestinian and Israeli futures. More than any other guest at the wedding (other than the film's audience, of course), this soldier has seen the crossing over of boundaries between past and present, between male potency and female possession, between transgression on the inside and the maintenance of honor on the outside, and of course between Israeli and Palestinian. But the consequences of the Israeli soldier's inadvertent (and almost violently intrusive) witnessing of these scenes is never clearly registered in the film. Yet, whether he realizes it or not, he is indubitably a privileged witness and wedding "guest." Whether or not he serves as a marker for the film's implied audience—for other guests present at the wedding in Galilee, as occupiers, as coercive cohabitants, as compelled to stay until the end—is a suggestive question.

For the Israeli soldier is both privileged witness and unwelcome occupier, both guest at and violent threat to the wedding and all that it represents. Why he, in particular, should be sole spectator of the two brides of Palestine is an intriguing question.

The doubled image of the two brides—framed in the doorway, dancing with a candle in each hand—occurs across considerable distance in the film, visually linked by bridal repetition and by the spectatorship of the Israeli soldier. It is a distinct doubling nonetheless. And, as if to subtly underscore the connection, the scene in which Tlali is framed in the bedroom doorway as a second bride follows immediately on that in which, in another bedroom of the mukhtar's house, Samia takes her own virginity. The camera moves from behind Samia's back to the window of the bridal chamber directly to the door of the room where Tlali is dancing with the other young Palestinian women in attendance. Dressed in Palestinian clothes, dancing gently with the lit candles in her hand, Tlali's stance marks the vexation of the land-as-woman trope. It marks the vexation of the wedding and conjugal consummation as trope. It marks the vexation of male possession of female honor—even as it reenacts that possession. Palestine/Israel has two brides. What happens, then, to the nationalist trope of the reunion of Palestinian man with Palestine-as-woman? With which woman is national desire to be satisfied? (And why should national desire be satisfied with a woman at all?) Of course, the conventional answer to that question is clear. But in spite of the abrupt interruption of the sensual and nonexclusive community of women, the suggestion of alternatives to the present order of things remains a flickering image for those who can see it.

The rather more grim conclusion of the film and of the wedding, in which the guests are forced to scatter as Israeli troops reenter the village, firing their weapons as they reoccupy the village streets, cannot quite manage to efface that glimmering image of another kind of community. That that other community is not simply a narrowly nationalist one is figured precisely in the repetition of the same stance by the Palestinian and the Israeli women and by the gentle seduction that allows both Israeli and Palestinian women to briefly enact a community, not of honor, but of gently shared sensuality and pleasure. But pleasure, of course, is fleeting; it cannot sustain itself indefinitely. It suggests, though, the consideration of other bases for the sustenance of community.

Finally, in the triple repetition of the night reveries of the village mukhtar as he watches his sleeping youngest son, Hassan, there is a further and equally striking instance in *Wedding in Galilee* of the play of other desires, of inside and out, of visual and verbal reiteration, of dreams and memory and the burden of both, and of desire that will not be simply and finally satisfied. Each instance of the scene functions as punctuation of sorts for the film, introducing another crucial turn in events. The setting is always the same. In a dimly lit room, the mukhtar murmurs tenderly over his sleeping son: "How strange that every time I want to tell you a beautiful story, one you've never heard before, you're asleep in my arms. What are you dreaming? Are your dreams like mine? Why is it that I want you to learn my story by heart?" The third and final time in which this scene occurs is near the end of the film. It is immediately preceded by long, dark shots of the increasing turmoil and agitation outside as the wedding guests wait clamorously for the climax of the wedding in a demonstration of its sexual consummation. The Israeli soldier who has waited anxiously for the reappearance of Tlali searches for her in the dark corridors of the mukhtar's house. He pauses outside the window of the room where the mukhtar murmurs over his sleeping son. This time, though, Hassan wakes up and faces his father without speaking. In response to his father's question, "Are you afraid of me?," Hassan darts out of the room. The scene immediately following this one is situated in the bridal chamber as Samia takes her own virginity. The mukhtar's dreams are, in that room too, both a fearful burden and a charge. But the mukhtar will never know how honor is maintained or who exactly sustains his dreams. Only Ádil and the implied audience for the film are witness to what actually happens inside the wedding chamber. So, in addition to its grammatical function within the film, the repetition of this scene also gestures strategically toward the film's implied audience: those voyeuristic wedding guests who have followed the rapid, fluctuating movement of the camera inside and out, close up and far away, from men to women, from Israelis to Palestinians, until finally the darkness and confusion close in at the end of the film.

The wedding is over; the bloody sheets are displayed; the union of bride and groom is consummated; "honor and dignity for everyone" is upheld. And the Israeli military reoccupy the village; jeeps rush through the streets as shots are fired into the air.[42] The film closes with a prolonged shot of the drawn-out gauntlet that the military governor and his entourage, now only nominally wedding guests, walk as they leave—or are symbolically expelled from—the village. The shot is punctuated by Tlali, still in Palestinian dress, walking next to her compatriots. But as the Israeli military take control once again of the streets and the outside and as the Palestinian wedding guests rush to their houses, there is one Palestinian figure who runs *out*side. That is Hassan, the mukhtar's young son, witness to his father's frustration, his sister's desire, his brother's impotence, his mother's interventions, his grandfather's memories, the wedding guests' tensions. It is Hassan who weaves in and out of the wedding, darting from one place to another, carrying messages, overhearing whispered conversations. Hassan, like the Israeli soldier and the camera eye itself, is witness to more of the disparate events of the wedding and thus potentially at least to their significance than almost anyone else there. And in the closing frames of the film, in the confusion and disorder of the dark night, he runs to the olive grove, away from the house, away from his family, reclaiming in a small way his residence on the outside. Reclaiming in a small way his right to relationship with the land. And perhaps because he is too young or perhaps because he will (re)tell the story differently, he does so without metaphorizing his action as an act of possession or the land as woman and bride. His is a young and prepubescent challenge to the dominant scheme(s) of things, Palestinian and Israeli. And it is one that defiantly takes place on the outside.

Like the mukhtar's charge to the military governor and his entourage, the charge for bearing witness to the wedding in Galilee, like the terms for being a wedding guest, is perhaps to stay until the end; to witness, to recognize, to remember, to "know by heart" the stories that unfold there. And, at least implicitly, the charge is to (re)tell the story. But how will the story be retold? In simple repetition of a single point of view? And whose point of view? That of the mukhtar? Of his old father? Of the Israeli military governor? Of Samia or Sumaya? Of Tlali? Of the insistently mobile camera eye (not unlike the insistent mobility of Hassan himself)? Or will it be told otherwise? *Wedding in Galilee* offers its audience visual complicity but not singular identification with any one of the guests at the wedding. There is no special insight into what occurs in the minds of the wedding party. The audience is conspicuously cast as an observer, an eavesdropper, an interloper, a distanced eye and ear to the wedding in Galilee. The only interior monologue available is that of the mukhtar to his young son. For, while Hassan sleeps, the audience does not.

How, then, might the story of *Wedding in Galilee* be (re)told? As a story of national oppression and resistance, of the re-creation of a traditional wedding, of patriarchal repression and abuse, of women's different occupation of patriarchal space? What is the proper role and adequate response of the wedding guest? The film presents a range of positions to choose from. But finally, it privileges the visual image of Samia and Tlali, the two brides, as it privileges the dreams of the mukhtar, the mobility of Hassan and of the camera itself. The desire that punctuates *Wedding in*

Galilee is, but not only, for the consummation of a marriage, for the liberation of an occupied land and its people, for the celebration of honor maintained and justice achieved. It is, but not only, for the fulfillment of national aspirations. Or, perhaps, to imagine the fulfillment of that desire is simultaneously to imagine its limits, as in the suggestion of the two brides or in the reminders of other kinds of conjugal unions whose consequences are rather more grim: to imagine the articulation of desire and its fulfillment otherwise, as in the otherwise of the old grandfather's or grandmother's memories, as in the otherwise of the brief moment of community among an Israeli and Palestinian women.

Though it might seem perverse to suggest *Wedding in Galilee* as a marker for national narratives that are, but not only, marked by desires for a state, for freedom from an occupier's oppression, for national citizenship, I would nonetheless make that suggestion. And another as well: that it is equally there, circulating among those *other* desires that are not simply a desire to occupy the gendered subject position of the nation-state, that nationalism and its narratives can point to communities and social organization configured otherwise. Perhaps this is the charge, the terms, of being a guest at the wedding, of being a witness to the story of *Wedding in Galilee.* But those terms are as dependent on the retelling of those stories as on the reading of and listening to them in the first place. If "we carry our worlds that have failed in our worlds that flourish," as the Nigerian poet Christopher Okigbo suggests, it might then be possible, even in a failed dream or world, to see otherwise. "Here we are, near there."

4   Thinking Citizens Again: Culture, Gender, and the Silences of the (Never Quite) Nation-State

> . . . in the shimmer of
> our days while the world we
> cling to in common is
>
> burning . . . I have not
> the ancients' confidence
> in the survival of
> one track of syllables
> nor in some ultimate
> moment of insight that
> supposedly will dawn
> once and for all upon
> a bright prosperity
> making clear only to
> them what passes between
>
> us now in a silence
> on this side of the flames
> —W. S. Merwin, "Cover Note"

Thomas More designated utopia as a place, an island in the distant South Seas. This designation underwent changes later so that it left space and entered time. Indeed, the utopians, especially those of the 18th and 19th centuries, transposed the wishland more into the future. In other words, there is a transformation of the topos from space into time. With Thomas More the wishland was still ready, on a distant island, but I am not there. On the other hand, when it is transposed into the future, not only am I not there, but utopia itself is also not with itself. This island does not even exist. But it is not something like nonsense or absolute fancy; rather it is not *yet* in the sense of a possibility; *that* it could be there if we could only do something for it. Not only if we travel there, but *in that* we travel there the island utopia arises out of the sea of the possible—utopia, but with new contents.—Ernst Bloch, "Something's Missing"

The question of boundary fixation turns between the often conflictual notions (and no less conflictual practices) of culture and of citizenship, between the poignant poetic reservation of W. S. Merwin and the equally poignant philosophical confidence of Ernst Bloch. In that between (though not only there), they are palpable—the questions of the fixing of and fixation on demarcation lines, of fixing and fixation at all, and of boundaries considered natural or necessary or inevitable or permeable or intransigent. It is an encroached upon space, one recognizable as much in the breach as in the designation. It is that rupture to which the poetry of Mahmud Darwish bears witness as the simultaneously expectant and devastating in-between of a "here . . . near there."

But most simply and obviously, the question of boundary fixation is one of drawing boundaries (who does the drawing? who gets drawn? what are the responses of drawers and drawn?) and of insisting on their irrevocable efficacy. Duly noting such insistence and its simple and obvious object, the question of boundary fixation here is most especially of the tenacity of boundaries in times of crisis. It is a question of the authority of those boundaries that are the object of fixation—as they are the object of nationalism. For nationalism, boundaries define and enclose the nation and protect its women and men from variously understood threats of violation. But perhaps most obviously, boundaries and their enforcement render authority to the figure, usually the state, that maintains and polices them. Boundaries are, of course, also, though not identically, maintained and transgressed by the residents of the state. But it is to the (diverse locations of the) state that authority accrues most assiduously in the exercise and policing of boundaries.

Do boundaries, then, persist in times of nationalism-in-crisis? For the "crisis" of nationalism-in-crisis is most often precipitated precisely by the violation of either literal or metaphoric national boundaries. Whether the boundaries hold or not, does the fixation itself on boundaries persist? Can fixation still compel attention in the absence (or transformation) of the boundaries that are its object? Bracketing for the moment the arguable accord that boundaries are natural and fixated adherence to them only exacerbated in times of crisis, what if boundary fixation is generated not prior or subsequent to but precisely *in* times of crisis? And, further, what if that fixation and its concomitant borders are only one of multiple positions or spaces generated in times of crisis, even if they seem to constitute the dominant position? The cultural and historical examples of the previous chapters are an effort to answer this question in the affirmative and to illustrate some of the most interesting and suggestive positions or spaces otherwise (and sometimes elsewhere) generated by nationalism in crisis. To understand that there were historical alternatives, other ways of conceptualizing and living differences—even at times of the most fierce crisis and even though those alternatives were often subsequently or simultaneously forcibly effaced, drowned out, or simply ignored—is perhaps also to begin to understand that an otherwise might be implicit in the present as well.

But, in an increasingly and overwhelmingly vociferous proliferation of global information—of global "noise"—the difficulty of discerning the reading or seeing or hearing of an otherwise in the present might seem impossible. The sway of expertise that offers its own reading, listening, and seeing as definitively informed might seem all the more compelling. But the expert "mastery" of one region's plethora of social and cultural "facts" and "information," of insisting on the "discovery" of what we already know theoretically, of looking in all the same places for raw content, can preclude an understanding of an otherwise.[1] Of course, a penchant for expert testimony, with its translation of the diverse and multivocal into the familiar same, and the penchant to produce it is not the only instance in which the otherwise is precluded; there are other preclusions.

Certainly W. S. Merwin's warning about the im/possibility of intelligibility or communicability—or even of ironic retrospective comprehension—of what passes or passed "between / us now in a silence / on this side of the flames" is an instance of those other preclusions. His warning is familiar counsel to those who have lived the immediate instances of nationalism-in-crisis considered in the previous chapters. Merwin's poem contemplates the likelihood that others will not—cannot—perceive or understand later what happened earlier from its written or spoken traces. Even others in a simultaneous elsewhere, consumed by very different and apparently unaffected lives, cannot be bothered with the language of silent and rocky confines on the far side of the flames. So how can future readers or audiences or descendants be capable of any better comprehension?

Something like Merwin's admonition, or the uneasy suspicion of it, permeates the films, cartoons, short stories, novels, newspaper articles, and poetry of post-1922 Greek, post-1974 Cypriot, and post-1982 Palestinian society and culture. Yet, for Merwin's poem and certainly for each of the three instances of nationalism-in-crisis taken up in the preceding pages, the flames are not only a boundary of enclosure to those on *one* side of the flames. The fires fan out and spread; they are mutable and permeable. No neat and putatively safe boundary lines there. They reach to and encompass the simultaneous elsewhere of indifference or incomprehension or imperception. In the space of "here . . . near there," the "we" in between is not distanced or distanceable from a safe, nonflammable place—even if, for the moment, that safety appears to be the case.

It is, most of all, an inevitable communicability that Merwin's poem challenges, the arrival of that "fullness of time"[2] in which all things will (inevitably) be made whole and clear and meaningful. Something very like this challenge lies at the heart of Fredric Jameson's cautionary reminder: "But the [Freudian] cure is in that sense a myth, as is the equivalent mirage within a Marxian ideological analysis: namely, the vision of a moment in which the individual subject would be somehow fully conscious of his or her determination by class and would be able to square the circle of ideological conditioning by sheer lucidity and the taking of thought."[3] Jameson's emphasis on the limitations of thought of the "individual subject . . . fully conscious" is utterly apt, in and of itself. But even further, the limitations of such individual analytical transcendence—the "mirage" of a moment of conceptual "cure," allowing a "sheer lucidity" that overcomes "ideological [or any other] conditioning"—point implicitly to the necessity of constant reminders of those very limitations. This is certainly one of the implicit tasks the poetry cited in the preceding pages claims for itself. This "mirage" may even point implicitly, and poetically, to the necessity of collaborative endeavors of concept and practice. If not to "square the circle" individually, then perhaps to struggle to do so otherwise, beyond the individual subject and her or his "taking of thought." Metaphorically at least, such "squaring of the circle" is an effort to redraw boundaries that are always already there and tremendously overdetermined in their circumscriptive power. Yet maps and boundaries *are* redrawn, though usually not by individuals and not with sheer lucidity (often, in fact, in the striking absence of even opaque lucidity). They are redrawn figuratively and symbolically as well as literally and concretely. They are drawn over bodies as well as over land, in language and images but also in reconfigured social practice.

Whether such alternative redrawing is registered in official discourse or in dominant social practice is another question. The potential for (and historical precedent of) an official party or a state or a dominant social group to absorb and contain or recuperate any such efforts at redrawing is never absent. The at least ambiguous denouement of the powerful challenge of the mass mobilization of the Palestinian intifada is surely a case in point. Radical mobilization, cooperation, and reorganization are not automatically—or even with sometimes great effort—translated into long-term political gains for those who mobilized, cooperated, and reorganized themselves. Still, those moments of crisis and their fictional and nonfictional retelling in diverse forms can suggest a glimmer of something and somewhere else. As Bloch insists, it is "not only if we travel there, but *in that* we travel there [that] the island utopia arises out of the sea of the possible." One of the ways that "we travel there," as Bloch himself so masterfully displays, is through a literary and cultural imaginary—always ambiguous and contradictory, often implicit, never sufficient in itself. Alternatively, we can cast that literary and cultural imaginary, that articulation of hope, as *desire*. Desire for something more. For something that is missing. Even if hope for an otherwise seems impossible.

It is in this context of desire, longing, and hope that the introduction on national culture and this concluding chapter on citizenship seek to suggest not only the links *between* but the necessity *to* one another of culture and citizenship, of, in a cruder formulation, the cultural to the political. Culture and citizenship: the former is often linked to identity, subjectivity, and communal belonging, the latter to a rough-and-tumble public sphere of collective civic rights and responsibilities. Both, sometimes implicitly, sometimes openly, are often juxtaposed as inexorably conflictual. But in the fierce debates about national "homogeneity" and who belongs where (chapter 1), about national "purity" and its putative protection that is simultaneously violation (chapter 2), or about the inside and outside of the nation and its communities (chapter 3), there is or was little popular distinction between cultural and political demands. There was and is an overwhelming effort, both literary and social, to account for the radical change in which the Greeks of Asia Minor (and mainland Greece, for that matter), the Turkish and Greek Cypriots of 1974 Cyprus, and the Palestinians inside and outside of historic Palestine after 1982 find themselves. And there is an overwhelming effort, sometimes sporadic and uneven but nonetheless amazingly durable, to redefine community and community membership, to redefine the parameters of the state and society, to redefine the gendering of both, to redefine a just and democratic society and the roles of its members. In this, as in the insistence on the mutual necessity of the cultural to the political, the very concept of active citizenship is redefined as well. For if capitalism was the definitive economic mode of modernity, the nation-state was its definitive political mode. In fact, nationalism can be seen (if a little scandalously) as one of the political motors of modernity in concert with the increasing spread of capitalism, rather than as an aftereffect of both modernity and capitalism.

If modern capitalism effectively rent the organization of religious and aristocratic or monarchic communities, it did not—could not—make good on the sweeping promises of broad economic and social opportunity formulated in its name. It did not, does not, and cannot make good on the promises formulated in its name of more just and democratic societies, though its diverse turns from concepts of justice and even of democracy for earlier societies are clear. But this is not a claim to some inexorable march of progress toward a glowing horizon. It seems far more productive, in fact, in contemporary reappraisals of pasts that consume much attention, to at least consider that modern capitalist social development with its political form of the nation-state did not simply emerge from some Darwinesque struggle of the fittest form into which malleable (or even nonmalleable) human content could be pressed. It is at least provocative to consider that, in the particular conjunction of diverse forces in a given place and at a given time, contingency rather than inevitability played at least some part in the emergence of the victorious groups and model(s).[4]

Certainly, the modern concept of citizenship has been almost as vexed a term in the past two centuries as its sometimes presumably concomitant concept of democracy. Both are, but not only, conspicuously modern designations in the age of the nation-state that is with us yet. The eighteenth- and nineteenth-century political theorists and philosophers of citizenship and democracy often presumed a variation on a lofty trajectory that, typically, was located in the generative nexus of the classical Greek city-state and its various leagues and then in the Roman Empire and its radical departure in making Roman citizenship available for bestowal by the empire on selected subjects and subjugated peoples. Seductive as that trajectory back in time might be (and ironic as its predication on a past irrevocably distant and missing is), the focus here is on the resolutely *modern*[5] (and capitalist) context of citizenship as it is decisively shaped by the equally modern (and capitalist) experience of unequal development, dislocation, and migration. Even then, having narrowed the focus from 250 centuries to two, the attempt to address in a concluding chapter such a complex and endlessly debated concept might seem audacious. Or urgent. "On this side of the flames,"

> in the shimmer of
> our days while the world we
> cling to in common is
> burning

as Merwin poignantly puts it. Both characterizations are probably appropriate.

From the emergent formulations of the notion of the modern citizen in the last years of the eighteenth century, most conventionally with the American and French revolutions—the former, anticolonial of a sort; the latter, antiaristocratic and, though unevenly, antimonarchic—citizenship has been contested in concept and practice. The multiple versions of the "Rights of Man and the Citizen" in France or the fierce debates and movement away from the Declaration of Independence to the Preamble to the Constitution in the United States clearly testify to that contestation. Already apparent to some late-eighteenth-century observers and participants was what Julia Kristeva points out in her essay "Women's Time" nearly two hundred years later: "The social contract, far from being that of equal men, is based on an essentially sacrificial relationship."[6] Olympe de Gouges, for one, the fervent if sometimes ambiguous radical of the French Revolution, arrested in 1793 and beheaded, would have had no difficulty accepting at least this initial part of Kristeva's formulation.[7] In fact in retrospect, de Gouges is a kind of literal example of the sacrificial relationship on which the social contract is based. Her challenge to the various manifestations of "The Rights of Man and the Citizen," "Les Droits de la Femme" (The rights of woman [and the citizen]), was an urgent call to her fellow women and to male citizens, framed in an address to the queen-as-woman, to recognize and combat the unacceptable exclusion of women from the social contract and from the category of citizen. Following on the "Rights of Man and the Citizen," de Gouges formulated a parallel list of the seventeen rights of woman and the citizen. As did others at the time,[8] de Gouges forcefully states the case for the centrality of gendered subjects in the construction of the modern nation-state. As de Gouges's document makes clear early on, gender, like race, is not an ancillary subset of modern nationalism; it is the very fundamental ground on which concepts of the nation, the state, and citizenship are constructed. De Gouges's proposal of a sample marriage contract between equal citizens, appended to "Les Droits de La Femme," is an amazing late-eighteenth-century effort to articulate a more egalitarian alternative to the regulation of (hetero)sexuality, which she astutely saw as the egregiously mistaken basis of the category of the male citizen and the state to which he offered his allegiance.

The ambivalent linking of de Gouges's understanding of the category of citizen as founded on race as well as on gender is distinct in the long postscript to "Les Droits de la Femme" in her hesitant and even regretful citation of the end of the French colonial empire (which, of course, was not yet really at an end). De Gouges specifically cites the issues of race and empire and upholds the French Revolution's emancipation of slaves (which the U.S. Declaration of Independence [in]famously failed to do and the French state later attempted to undo): "It would be very necessary to say a few words on the troubles which are said to be caused by the decree in favor of colored men in our islands. . . . A divine hand seems to spread liberty abroad throughout the realms of man; only the law has the right to curb this liberty if it degenerates into license but it must be equal for all; liberty must hold the National Assembly to its decree dictated by prudence and justice" (96). There is no specific mention here of the "colored *women* in our islands." And de Gouges reiterates the qualities of reason and restraint by now so familiarly (and ambiguously) cited as attributes of the citizen. She postulates threat to those qualities in a "license" that can be curbed only by law. Still, de Gouges's vision of citizenship was already a remarkably inclusive one and one that called attention to the fundamental dependency of the category of modern citizenship and the modern nation-state on gender, race, and empire.

Some two hundred years later, Etienne Balibar reminds us again that "in a sense, every modern nation is a product of colonization; it has always been to some degree colonized or colonizing."[9] The citation of "the decree in favor of colored men in our islands" in de Gouges's postscript is one of the rhetorical spaces in which the modern French nation-state and its citizenry were produced by colonization as colonizers.[10] In this context of the nation-state and its citizenry, and in the context of twentieth-century Greek, Cypriot, and Palestinian nationalisms-in-crisis, the question of what has been called "transculturation" is a pertinent one. For transculturation was historically formulated to account for the ways subordinated or marginalized or colonized peoples selectively incorporate and invent from—rather than simply adopt or refuse—materials propagated by the dominant or metropolitan culture.[11] It has also historically been the case that in that process of transculturation (but not only there), dominant or metropolitan cultures have been decisively shaped by the marginal, subaltern, or colonial spaces and their peoples. Of course, this occurs not with anything like commensurate force. Modern colonialism and imperialism have had no equal match in terms of sheer force. Yet, it *has* been undermined, contested, challenged, and (formally at least) overthrown. What has *not* been overthrown has been the logic and power of capital, which informs and propels that unequal force. Even the power of nationalism and the nation-state as produced by and in response to colonization yet remains within the framework of colonization and of capital. The understanding of transculturation, then, as the selective reformulation of materials not even primarily of our own choosing, seductively or coercively arrayed by a metropolitan center or a dominant culture, is crucial. For it suggests the ways in which, with limited, always already charged and laden materials, we seek to make and reformulate our present and our history.[12] The nation is always already produced by colonization as it is always already informed by transculturation.

Modern colonization and its aftermath and the nation-state form, both concomitant with the logic of capital, also redefined the "diaspora" with an immeasurable difference, both quantitative and qualitative, from earlier meanings of the term. It is ironic and suggestive to remember that "diaspora" was used in classical Greek in reference to money (Herodotus and Xenophon) and to soldiers (Thucydides). It comes to mean dispersion of peoples rooted in or belonging to another place, as we understand it today, only later in the New Testament. The antecedence of the national community in the religious community, of the member of the nation in the believer of the faith fixed by and in the eye of god is noteworthy again here—the past two centuries of presumably secular state proclamations notwithstanding.[13]

The original context of the concept of the diaspora as a scattering or dispersion of peoples was a religious one. Of course, the diaspora marks as well the modern national phenomenon of the diaspora of peoples, with the various situations of gendered refugees, exiles, migrants, and immigrants that have come to be included under that rubric. The concept and workings of the diaspora are also distinctly within the context of the modern nation and nation-state that gathers, orders, and regulates its national people.[14] But within that same context is always already the recognition that the borders of the nation, its language, its culture, and its laws are transversable; they never completely succeed at gathering, ordering, and regulating. The notion (and realities) of the diaspora, like transculturation, suggest rather directly the extent to which the borders and boundaries of nation-states, however fiercely militarized and policed, are not (have scarcely ever been) adequate to their self-defined task of containing and regulating the economic, political, social, and cultural life of the peoples who live within them. These boundaries are marked by dispersal, by transversal, by impossibility.

Like the space of the nation, national time is as remarkable in its excession as in its boundaries. The construction of the time of the nation is familiar enough, though no less powerful for its familiarity. National demands in the present moment are predicated on and justified by a citation of the story of a national past of shared history, often of shared language and/or culture, and certainly, as Ernst Renan had already pointed out in the late nineteenth century, of shared misery and suffering.[15] Equally and no less important, Renan also pointed out the fundamental predication of the nation on forgetting and historical error or "mis-remembering." Nonetheless, the past—misremembered or not—is "retold" so as to justify the demands of the present and the changes projected for the future. National time, then, most often presents itself as linear and causal; it is most often shaped by and in narrative.

Even if, as for some peoples beyond Europe, her states, and her present-day union, there is no necessary past of such national history—the past is, in fact, precisely that of European colonialism, which drew its own spatial and temporal lines across the rest of the globe and the bodies of the peoples living there—still, a linear historical claim of coercive community is made if for no other reason than to gain access to economic and political rights. Nationalism, then, provides an internationally acceptable form in which to express demands, desires, needs, rights. It is neither organic nor inevitable, though it has tremendous appeal and power at a given time in a given place. But if this process of nationalism, of its geographic space, and of its historical time is a construction, an "invented tradition" (after Hobsbawm), then it can be subject to construction otherwise. Perhaps its construction site can be one of nonlinear and noncausal time and of shared space. In fact, perhaps it can be constructed without the call to nationalism at all. That is, not only in some distantly utopic future but in a tremendously vexed and unequally accessible present, there can be questions asked and decisions made about desires and needs, about moving through careful processes toward goals that might include economic and political justice, social and cultural freedom, the right to education, health care, decent housing and wages, cultural expression for everyone who happens to be living in this space at this time—regardless of how, from where, and why anyone came: cohabitants of and in a relatively shared space and time, with various cultural and linguistic diversities, needs, differential relations to the state in control (however ambiguous or dubious). What might happen next in this hypothetical (but not really hypothetical) effort to refuse singular place of origin and belonging and to work through processes for change?

What has not worked is clear enough, for instance, the construction of some mythic past of oneness and purity, to which past return is passionately desirable (at least rhetorically). For Japan in the 1920s and 1930s, in the long buildup to fascism in that country, it was the mythic and quasi-divine past of the goddess Amaterasu and her latter-day, presumably divine manifestation in the emperor—Hirohito for the duration of the Showa period. For Germany, it was an equally mythic past of the great Teutonic peoples who were to be united once again in the Thousand-Year Reich. For Italy, it was the Roman Empire, whose glory would be recreated in the new/old present. The interjection here of fascist national histories and their mythic pasts of community is not flagrantly obstreperous, for they are absolutely a part of the nationalist project. They could even, if perhaps perversely, be seen as a brutally violent form of transculturation, the selective reformulation by a "subjugated" people of materials drawn from a dominant culture of a triumphant post-WWI Europe. Fascism's gendered constructions of proper and singular places for the people who lived within their (expanding) boundaries and for the peoples who were to be eliminated from within those same boundaries are not dismissable as an aberration. They were a mortally extreme but plausible enough development from the premises of national time and space and from the inevitable threat to the excession of that time and space.

The dangers and outright failures of the liberal reign of a universal and abstracted notion of the public and political sphere of rational men is another clear enough failure. Its refusal or denial or marginalization of the private, the domestic, the "irrational," and the bodily, desire—its marginalization of that which is troped by the figure of the woman and the non-white man—is not so very far in foundational logic, if farther in extremes of practice, from the fascist state. Knowing what could seem to be a great deal from—or at least about—these instances, what do we actually know?

There are both literal social instances and metaphoric literary instances that address the question of what we know or can deduce from challenges to the dominant concepts and practices of citizenship and the social contract. I have here claimed the privilege and limitations of my academic training in the field of comparative literature and culture to foreground fictional and metaphoric responses to these questions. For listening to and watching with care the form and content of social movements, as the form and content of cultural and literary texts—though the latter are textually rather more fixed, the former not necessarily so—are not only the cultural or aesthetic acts of an audience but, as Cynthia Enloe formulates it in a related context, "a political act."[16] Still, at their best, the latter and the former can provide glimpses of something that exceeds not just their immediate content, not just a nationalized time and space, not just our current, too miserly definitions and practices of the citizen. They can provide glimpses as well of the excession of our restricted notions of time and space and community at all.

To her own rhetorical question in the essay "Women's Time," cited briefly above, of why literature most strikingly displays women's desire for creative affirmation, Kristeva answers with a series of three further questions: "Is it because, faced with social norms, literature reveals a certain knowledge and sometimes the truth itself about an otherwise repressed, nocturnal, secret, and unconscious universe? Because it thus redoubles the social contract by exposing the unsaid, the uncanny? And because it makes a game, a space of fantasy and pleasure, out of the abstract and frustrating order of social signs, the words of everyday communication?" (207). This shrewd answer-by-way-of question is a comment not only on women's literature but on literature in general. And if we understand the uncanny (with its obvious reference to the *unheimlich* in Freud, which is translated more clumsily but perhaps more suggestively in the present context), as the unhoused or unhomed (the *un-heim*), literature can intensify our understanding of the power and limitations of the social contract by pointing to the unhoused—migrants, refugees, exiles, contract laborers, immigrants—who both occupy and enable the social contract. In fact, the social contract is not possible without them. It is their bodies on which and by which that contract is inscribed and constructed. This is not only a reference to notions (and experiences) of transculturation or the diaspora but also to the incredible mobility of capital, which holds in place (or sometimes moves at will) workers in Indonesia and the Philippines and Mexico and China and Malaysia while it constructs the particularity of "our" social contracts. It equally immobilizes, though in a less literal way, the hundreds of thousands of contract workers—now more than ever women—who move (or are moved) from one place to another but are immobilized nonetheless by their utter lack of social rights and protections, by their often brutal abuse or exploitation in their mobile state. Mobility, then, is exceedingly differential. Though it can be, it is not simply or necessarily a freedom.

So then, to return to an earlier question: Is there a social contract not predicated on the sacrifice of women and other unhoused and silenced peoples? In the time and space of the nation-state, what happens to the uncanny-unhoused? To the silent and silenced? To the migrants and exiles and refugees? Well, actually, these *are* rhetorical questions. For in Greece, in Cyprus, in Israel/Palestine (not to mention in the United States, in France, in Italy, in England) of the twenty-first century, we already know the answer. And too often, it is an answer neither as optimistic nor as generous as that of de Gouges some two hundred years ago in her response to the question of for whom "rights" and citizenship and freedom are proffered. Though it is the only political game in town, the winnings afforded by citizenship in the nation-state are not quite so unquestionably victorious.

From the "early" to the "late" Marx, there is a strikingly consistent insistence on the nonprogrammatic future of what is stated forthrightly and adamantly in *The German Ideology*. What will come after that "movement which abolishes the present state of things" is not "a state of affairs to be established or an ideal to which reality will have to adjust itself" (56–57). *The German Ideology* and "On *Die Judenfrage*" (On *The Jewish Question*) are still remarkable reminders of the considerable differences between seeking alternatives to dominant definitions of the citizen and the social contract and the fearfully radical charge of Marx's texts for that "movement which abolishes the present state of things"—an abolition without any possible blueprint of what comes next. On that impossibility, Marx is insistent from his "early" writings through to his late letters to Vera Zasulich on the Russian peasant communes. In the far earlier "On *Die Judenfrage*," Marx states with greater force if less subtlety than he will demonstrate in later work the differences between the political emancipation of "egoistic" or "atomistic" man and the "abstract moral position" of the citizen on the one hand and, on the other, the radical transformation of both in the assumption of one into the other. Only then will "human emancipation be complete." Not the emancipation of the citizen, for that is within the domain of political emancipation: "Political emancipation is a reduction of man, on the one hand to a member of civil society, an *independent* and *egoistic* individual, and on the other hand, to a *citizen*, to a moral person" ("On *Die Judenfrage*," 31). "On *Die Judenfrage*" offers a sharp critique of the nature of bourgeois society, of the relation of religion to the state, and a rigorous comparative reading of various versions of the "Rights of Man and the Citizen" and selected state constitutions of the member states of the United States. In an often smugly "post-Marxist" moment, this nineteenth-century historical example is a still cogent reminder of the necessity and limitations of political emancipation, of a human emancipation beyond the political, of the religious framework that the modern state claimed to have transcended but that, as Marx quite stunningly and sometimes caustically points out, still imbues the concept and workings of the state as it does of its citizens. As the texts cited in this and in each of the preceding chapters suggest, there is a difference still between political and human emancipation. There is an elsewhere and an otherwise, poetic and literal, that is perilously repressed or effaced or ignored. The former—political emancipation—may be necessary to but does not, cannot, ensure the latter: human emancipation.

What are the implications for the concept of citizenship in our own century of the past and the present of ever more complex realities—cultural and social—of "transculturation" and the "diaspora," of the migrant and the refugee, of the exile and the "alien," of the forcibly unhoused and the persistently displaced? What are the implications of understanding the fundamental inequalities and abusive exclusions of citizenship and the social contract, of understanding the extent to which the social contract is grounded in a series of other contracts: the sexual contract, the family contract, the demarcation of a private sphere on which the social contract presumably does not impinge? Is there an understanding of the privilege of the social contract and its constituent citizens as limitation that enables a transformation of the contract? Or its replacement with something otherwise? There are certainly fictional responses to such questions. Many, in fact, and suggestive responses.

Written neither in the language in which she was educated (French) nor in the languages into which she was born (Arabic, Greek, Turkish), Etel Adnan's collection of essays *Of Cities and Women* enacts the gendered spaces of the diaspora for a woman who cannot return "home," as it demonstrates with tremendous accomplishment the processes of transculturation. *Of Cities and Women* is written as a series of letters to a friend, Fawwaz, as Adnan travels through the villages and cities of Europe and the Mediterranean at the onset of the Gulf War in the early 1990s. Adnan's letters to Fawwaz are by way of compensation for the essay on feminism he asked her to contribute to a collection he is editing. She cannot write that essay: "Theories get lost when confronted with privileged experience. I thus renounced the idea of writing you a formal letter on 'feminism,' and began living that which was given to me" (3). If privileged experience is here given priority over a kind of theory, it includes simultaneously an acknowledgment of a differential concept of mobility. Narrative mobility in *Of Cities and Women* is privileged by virtue of education and cultural fluency in five languages, of dual citizenship and a reasonably secure

financial status, and by the narrator's reasonably comfortable literary acclaim as she reads her poetry and fiction and meets with women's groups
throughout her travels. But privileged mobility makes the diaspora no less
poignant, nor the return home any less impossible. The narrator writes to
Fawwaz of their mutual homeland and its capital city, "Our old Beirut is as
remote from us as the Stone Age" (82). The time and place of "our old
Beirut" is impossible to return to. And if the space of Beirut-as-home is at
the far side of a tremendous temporal gap, so too is the experience of a
mother's tongue out of reach:

> I went to Greece, after so many years, partly, or perhaps even mainly,
> because I was looking for (and am still looking for) the voice of my
> mother.
>   I have lost the memory of the voice of my parents. I went to Greece
> hoping to hear the Greek spoken by my mother. I listened closely, and
> it seemed that no one spoke the way she did. I was telling myself that
> perhaps the Greek spoken in Smyrna was different: more musical,
> more passionate. . . . (45)

The delicate unspoken irony here is that Adnan's mother was herself a
mobile woman of the diaspora. But her mobility was of a different sort
than her daughter's. For the mother was a refugee from the Asia Minor
Catastrophe (discussed in chapter 1). Her mobility was the effect of one of
the first international experiments in ethnic purification in the twentieth
century, following on the disastrous and disastrously ill-advised Greek
invasion of Asia Minor in 1919.

Adnan's mother never returned home; her home was no longer there
to return to. Nor can Adnan herself return to or find the "home" of her
mother's tongue. But if even privileged mobility doesn't allow that return,
alternatively it allows home(s) to be produced elsewhere, in the "living of
that which is given": "In the meantime I feel that I haven't settled any-
where, really, that I'm rather living in the world, all over, in newspapers, in
railway stations, cafés, airports. . . . The books that I'm writing are houses
that I build for myself" (111). In Adnan's *Of Cities and Women,* the aching
desire for return, for home, is not satisfied. It is not satisfiable. But neither
is it denied and repressed. It persists. Mobility (privileged or not) and
experience that seeks to find its home as it seeks to articulate a different
kind of theory have no tangible satisfaction. Yet they remain a nonetheless
compelling desire. In fact, it might be just this nonsatisfaction or impossible satisfaction of desire that leads to what might seem to be Adnan's
"postfeminist" observation: "It was no longer a question of clarifying

the distinction between the feminine and the masculine, but of redefining the human species" (37). This is reminiscent of nothing quite so much as the insistence of "On *Die Judenfrage*" on the limitations of political emancipation—here, gender distinctions—in the face of the possibility of human emancipation.

But for the poet and writer who narrates *Of Cities and Women,* there is a kind of home—or at least a house—produced by desire. It is in the books that she writes. And there is a kind of transient community in the women activists with whom she meets as she travels back and forth across Europe and the Mediterranean. And, of course, there is a kind of transient and intermittent community with Fawwaz, the addressee of the letters that make up this epistolary text. *Of Cities and Women* both underscores the urgent need and wrenching desire for home, for community, for belonging as it simultaneously writes letters of the slippage that makes home, community, and distinct belonging a continual struggle with an ultimately unrealizable end. *Of Cities and Women* accounts for that desire and struggle on the part of a woman of relatively privileged mobility if yet also of the diaspora and of exile. And it accounts for the partial poetic or literary resolution of that condition ("the books that I'm writing are houses that I build for myself").

There are two further instances of women's diasporic mobility and communal membership that are suggestive for comparative purposes of considering the gendered silences of the nation-state. A second and less delicately resolved fiction is Andrée Chedid's *La Maison sans racines* (The house without roots). It is the story of a French citizen, Kalya, a professional photographer, who returns with her young American granddaughter to her familial point of origin: a Lebanon that, unbeknownst to Kalya, is on the brink of civil war. The story of these two generations of women is recounted by a wiser, third-person narrator, who tells a story that moves back and forth across time as it follows its main character across geographical space: back and forth from Kalya's childhood in Egypt and Lebanon and France of 1932 to Kalya and her granddaughter's present in the Lebanon of 1975. Kalya is a mobile woman triumphant, one who is sure she has slipped her boundaries and her bonds:[17] "What are roots? Distant ties or ties that are woven through life? The ties of a rarely visited ancestral land or those of a neighboring land where one spent one's childhood, or are they those of a city where one has lived longest? And, indeed, had not Kalya chosen to uproot herself? Had she not wished to graft those different roots and sensibilities one onto another? A hybrid, why not? She reveled in that crossbreeding" (46). If this celebration of mobility is not yet ominous in the novel, it shortly grows increasingly so as Kalya's inability to read the signs of impending war around her, in spite of warnings from her family and friends, grows increasingly as well. The narrator observes:

> Kalya looked as if she were "passing through." . . .
> Passing through and at ease in that transitory state, as if she thought that existence itself were just that: a brief passage between two kinds of darkness. As if in the house of the flesh which was so perishable, or that of the spirit so changeable, or that of language in constant transformation, she recognized her only true habitats. Despite their precariousness, she felt more alive in them, less alienated, than in those stone dwellings, than in those places that were inherited, handed down, and which were often so deeply attached to the past and to their clods of earth that they forgot the space around them. (68)

Yet Kalya too will "forget the space around her." For Lebanon is on the eve of a brutal civil war. Bombs explode throughout the city and outside the windows of the rooms where Kalya and her granddaughter are staying; gun battles can be heard in nearby quarters of the city. But Kalya, unlinked and untied, sure of her ability to move back to Paris with her granddaughter, is virtually oblivious. Her mobility, her liberated rootlessness, is sharply rebounded and rebonded by the recurrent repetition of a single scene that begins and ends the novel. That recurrent scene is one in which Kalya and her granddaughter, who runs out after her grandmother into the early morning light of the square underneath their apartment, are both gunned down and killed by a sniper. What was to have been a celebration, a brave demonstration of the intercommunal solidarity of women in that same square, by Muslim and Christian women alike, turns into a heap of dead (female and black) bodies.

One of the other women shot down in that morning that frames and recurs throughout the novel had earlier wondered to herself, "Could she [Myriam] explain such things [about what was happening in Lebanon] to Kalya so that she wouldn't leave as lightly as she had come?" (75–76). Neither Kalya nor her young granddaughter leave Lebanon "as lightly as she had come." Literally, they're weighted down by the sniper's bullets and by a history and a contemporary political situation, times and a place, that they thought to enter and exit at will. They are mobile women, (dead) citizens of the world.

To Chedid's ultimately grim account of mortal mobility, fixity, and communal membership, Barbara Kingsolver's short story "Homeland" comes as a gentle coda. It is narrated by another grandmother, Gloria Murray St.

Clair, who recalls her childhood and her relationship with her own great-grandmother, a Cherokee woman of the Bird Clan. Great Mam has come to live her final years with her grandson, Gloria's father, in a dusty coal mining town called Morning Glory. The gentle floral irony of the town's name is a comment as well on mobility and fixity and belonging, on a people made refugees and wanderers by the U.S. myth of the melting pot (or, the more appropriate slip of the tongue, melting *plot*), which forgets the violent founding of that myth in the decimation of native peoples and in the slave trade: "The creeping vines for which the town was named drew themselves along wire fences and up the sides of houses with the persistence of the displaced. I have heard it said that if a man stood still in Morning Glory, he would be tied down by vines and not found until first frost. Even the earth underneath us sometimes moved to repossess its losses; the long, deep shafts that men had opened to rob the coal veins would close themselves up again, as quietly as flesh wounds" (2).

That "persistence of the displaced" characterizes not only morning glories but Gloria's Great Mam. Yet, it is a different sense of displacement than that of *La Maison sans racines* or *Of Cities and Women*. For Great Mam teaches her great-granddaughter, in carefully sparse language, the importance of memory, of retelling stories, and of the ways displacement can make itself at home, the ways "the refugee years" are not geographical uprooting as much as they are forgetting. Losses can be repossessed in their retelling: "If she felt like it, on these evenings, she would tell me stories about the animals, their personalities and kindnesses and trickery, and the permanent physical markings they invariably earned by doing something they ought not to have done. 'Remember that story,' she often commanded at the end, and I would be stunned with guilt because my mind had wandered" (5–6). But Gloria does remember and so she begins "Homeland" with the retelling of the story of the forced exodus of Great Mam's clan: "They called their refugee years The Time When We Were Not, and they were forgiven [for being forced to leave behind to die their people who were too old or too sick or too young as they fled the capture of the American military] because they carried the truth of themselves in a sheltered place inside the flesh, exactly the way a fruit that has gone soft still carries inside itself the clean, hard stone of its future" (2).

Great Mam's clan was driven from their forest lands in the Carolina mountains to Tennessee, where Great Mam was born and raised. "Homeland" is ultimately the account by her great-granddaughter, Gloria, of the visit that she and her family made with Great Mam to the old woman's "homeland" in Tennessee. After driving all night to reach the place, they find "real tepees" "made of aluminum and taller than a house. Inside, it was a souvenir store" (17). And they find "real Indians": "A man in a feather war bonnet dances across from us in the parking lot. His outfit was bright orange, with white fringe trembling along the seams of the pants and sleeves, and a woman in the same clothes sat cross-legged on the pavement playing a tom-tom while he danced. People with cameras gathered and side-stepped around one another to snap their shots" (17). To this return to her "homeland" Great Mam asserts a quietly proud courage to refuse a place that is supposed to be home and isn't:

> "I guess things have changed pretty much since you moved away, huh, Great Mam?" I asked.
> She said, "I've never been here before." (18)

Great Mam's response echoes that of the young Palestinian boy's dream of the return to the homeland recounted below: the intrepid refusal of a home that is not home when the only alternative appears to be death in exile.[18]

These three fictional texts that invoke nationalism, gender, and citizenship would seem to confound some simple definition of being a citizen. For they, like many of the examples from the preceding chapters, speak, in nonexhortatory and implicit fashion, about mobility and displacement as both sorrowful and exhilarating, as mortally dangerous and as a way to "repossess our losses." They speak of the need for fierce activism and intervention, for clever storytelling in cognizance of the power and the controvertability of dominant narratives. They speak of the need for quiet listening to those who are not foregrounded or included, except in their relegation to the margins, in the great dialogues on states, rights, and citizenship. They speak of the need to remember that short-term intervention is not long-term vision of change. Both are simultaneously necessary, however contradictory that simultaneity might seem in the moment.

Two hundred years ago, before she lost her head to the guillotine, Olympe de Gouges suggested too the necessity of radically broadening the framework under which liberty, equality, sorority, and fraternity were to be exercised. Some fifty years after that, Marx scathingly analyzed the not-yet-secular state and civil society as he outlined the considerable difference between political emancipation and human emancipation. In the mid–twentieth century, Fernando Ortiz's formulation of transculturation points to the ways in which subordinate or marginalized or subaltern peoples wield power in their refashioning of that which is "given" (often coercively or at least hegemonically) from the dominant or metropolitan culture. And the late-twentieth-century fictions of Etel Adnan, Andrée Chedid, and Barbara Kingsolver address, if more implicitly, the questions of nationalism, citizenship, mobility, and gender. What do *we* know then? What story can *we* tell? Will *we* remember? Can we hear "what passes between us now in a silence on this side of the flames"?

"Remember that story . . ."

The stories here, as with the historical and cultural and literary examples of the preceding pages, are of the always profoundly contradictory and at best simply inaccurate claims to the ethnic or cultural or even linguistic homogeneity of the nation, to "natural" belonging as part of the nation, to that nation (and/or the land on which it is predicated) as gendered female: a metaphoric woman, pure (thus, potentially impure) and inviolable (thus, potentially violated). The stories here are also of (nation-)state-sponsored efforts to eradicate a people—literally, culturally, economically, socially, even historically; they are of enemies on the far side of national boundaries that are not faceless, monolithic, and utterly implacable and of enemies on the near side of national boundaries that are "brothers" and "sisters." These stories are foregrounded in specific historical and cultural instances. But they are nonetheless shared to a greater or lesser degree by Greek, Cypriot, and Palestinian nationalisms-in-crisis. This is not the result of some natural affinity or direct influence among these three instances. Rather, these nationalisms-in-crisis illustrate the complex contradictions and configurations of nationalism in general. And they illustrate, sometimes with stunningly quiet force, the silences, the dangers, and the promises of the nation and its state. But perhaps like the hope at the bottom of Pandora's box,[19] there is something else there—an otherwise—amidst (or under) the swarm of tribulations, disease, violence, and thwarted dreams. Only perhaps.

In the high-ceilinged room of glass and steel, the mechanically regulated metal window louvres opened and closed to a rhythm of their own. Around the huge table in the center of the room, the discussion was of "the internalization of systems of domination." By way of illustration, one of the men present, a distinguished writer and critic, told the story of his participation in a film project for which Palestinian children in refugee camps in Lebanon were asked about their dreams of return to Palestine. One young boy of ten or eleven told of his dream of riding with his fellow refugee camp residents on a bus back to Palestine: "The bus from the Lebanese refugee camp reaches Palestine; it stops at a central square in a large town. The people on the bus from Lebanon are called one by one to board the other buses waiting in the square for the trip back to the various villages, towns, and cities from which they were forced some fifty years earlier. The Palestinian boy is distressed as he sees the friends, neighbors, and acquaintances of a young lifetime leave the bus. Why do we have to leave each other? Why can't we live together as we did in Lebanon?" In the huge room with the mechanically louvred windows, heads nodded somberly. The poor young boy preferred the community of a refugee camp to returning home? Prisoners get used to—even don't want to leave—their prisons. That was it; the young boy was used to the refugee camp. More nodding. Solemn smiles. The young boy's dream was not the only one in the room.

In the very last section ("Certainty, Unfinished World, Homeland") of the concluding chapter of Ernst Bloch's massive compilation of hope's traces in the world as he knew it, *The Principle of Hope,* in which he returns to the figure of Karl Marx ("Karl Marx and Humanity"), Bloch reiterates: "The tomorrow in today is alive; people are always asking about it. The faces which turned in the utopian direction have of course been different in every age . . . but all are set up around that which speaks for itself by still remaining silent" (1374–75). Bloch's attempt to trace "hope"—as, in its various manifestations, insistently if still silently pointing to a better or "right" world—ranges famously through a diverse, even disparate, collection of textual and visual traces. His attempt is most interesting, not for its pursuit of the *telos* of hope, for Bloch resolutely holds that it is resistant to prediction. Rather, Bloch's tracing of hope(s) suggestively points to the constantly multiple, fluid, and symptomatic flashes of a *Vor-Schein* ("anticipatory illumination," in Jack Zipes's felicitous translation), of a "not-yet."

But that not-yet is one that speaks for itself by not speaking—or, by not *exactly* speaking. For its silent abiding is almost but not quite visible, almost but not quite audible. Thus (in something resembling a poststructuralist reading avant la lettre), *The Principle of Hope* points to what is *not* utterable or audible or demonstrable or visible as just as significant and as demanding of a reader/listener as that which *is* spoken, heard, seen. This insistence on the importance of the unspoken or unperformed suggests, then, a virtual imperative for an implied reader who listens, watches, notices.[20] This charge of the not-yet for an implicit audience itself underscores what Fredric Jameson demonstrates as the necessary differentiation of Bloch's "*philosophical* system" from its "*hermeneutic* use."[21] For the former, Jameson reminds us, "there is a right and a wrong way of presenting human reality"; "the judgments of truth and falsehood still exist as valid conceptual categories" (*Marxism and Form,* 125). But, for the latter, those judgments of truth and falsehood and "right and wrong" presentation (and representation) are conceptual distinctions intimately implicated in one another. The "wrong" is a distorted or masked attempt to configure the "right." Within the "false" is an attempt to answer "truly." Parenthetically, this postulation need not necessarily predicate itself on a single and monolithic "true" or "right"—even though, for Bloch, it can sometimes seem to do so. And also, the "wrong" way of telling a story or the systemic judgment of something as "false" carries a charge, then, to a careful reader/listener/participant to attend to the flashes within it of the "right" or "true." In this scheme of things, the careful reader/listener is a postulated necessity. And, there is no easy dismissal of "low" or popular culture, of the unorthodox, of the politically incorrect, of the false.[22] And so the text—whether a daydream, a fascist propaganda sheet, a fairy tale, an advertisement, or an expressionist painting—can function (for its audience and/or its producer) as a figure of desire for something beyond itself, a something else that looks not back to a past but forward to a not quite foreseeable future, the *Vor-Schein.*

Now at first, the story of the young Palestinian boy's distant dream and its retelling as "the internalization of systems of domination" might seem far from the "hope" of Ernst Bloch. For a young refugee boy's imaginary return to Palestine is an instance of personal narrative quite distinct from those favorite literary and philosophical texts that so often constitute the touchstones for Bloch's massive philosophical and hermeneutic effort. But the young boy's dream is in fact not so far from Bloch's citation of the *Vor-Schein* of daydreams, of stories, of tales. Nor is it any less significant a participant in the im/possible imagining of a future. It is a tiny refraction of or trope for a million texts in this one fragile one, a young boy's dream of return to Palestine.

And then again, the citation of Bloch, from "What's Missing," a dialogue between him and Theodor Adorno, might seem to abruptly shift the ground of the Palestinian boy's dream from the particular and historically rooted to the general and abstract. But if Bloch's work counsels anything, it is the workings of the (more) general in the detail of the particular. The specific historical dream of the young boy for a return to Palestine is, without negating or sublimating his specific dream, simultaneously the longing for a return *home.* And he longs for that return to a place he does not know and cannot imagine. Nor can he accept the already historically constituted definition of home as that space from which his family was driven before his birth. The young Palestinian boy's dream of home approaches that place toward which Bloch points in the closing of his *Princi-ple of Hope*. It is a home and a childhood where no one has yet been: "*True genesis is not at the beginning but at the end,* and it starts to begin only when society and existence become radical, i.e., grasp their roots. But the root of history is the working, creating human being who reshapes and overhauls the given facts. Once he has grasped himself and established what is his, without expropriation and alienation, in real democracy, there arises in the world something which shines into the childhood of all and in which no one has yet been: homeland" (1375–76, emphasis in the origi-nal). That that home is one the young boy never knew, could not know given the circumstances of his life (and the lives of many like him) in a refugee camp in Lebanon, does not mitigate his yearning. (The camps are literally mapped by that yearning with place-names from Palestine.) In fact, the young boy's dream re-presents in a particular fashion that longing of which Bloch writes. In an arguably small and particular way, the spe-cific dilemma and promise—the hope—of the young boy's dream and its retellings suggest something of what seems most pertinent in Bloch's no-tion of utopia and hope. And it suggests the necessity of "reutilizing" Bloch's own keen insistence that the future toward which "hope" points is precisely that which is not a mappable space or a regulatable time. It is there, latent—not yet conscious (as opposed to *unconscious*), awaiting recognition not as itself, the "future(s)," but as *Vor-Schein*. In fact, the "new" of the not-yet will be precisely that which we did not, indeed, could not possibly, foresee.[23]

Even though we might well not concur with Bloch's insistence that, "in the long run, everything that meets us, everything we notice particularly, is one and the same,"[24] his resolute insistence on pointing to the anticipa-tory flashes of hope in the present is important. And, in theory at least, there is no necessary or irrevocable link between the totalization of every-thing as "one and the same" and the insistence on the fluid, multiple, and symptomatic flashes of the not-yet. Precisely in the spirit of Bloch's own notion of "reutilization" (*Umfunktionierung*), his theorizing of the work-ings of hope is scarcely exempt from, in fact could lend itself to, some such "reutilization." So then, for all the biographical and intellectual contradic-tions of Bloch and his work,[25] for all the overwhelming weight of his insistence on a totality working its way toward an (unforeseeable) end, for all the sometimes slow and burdensome pace of his argumentative prose, juxtaposing the young Palestinian boy's thrice-removed dream to Bloch's "principle of hope" is a startling reminder of the disruptive and illumina-tive power of imagining the future.

The future of the "homeland" has particular poignance and concrete meaning for any diaspora. The historical circumstances of the Palestinians for at least the past fifty years—as exiles, some in their own land; as a forcibly displaced people; as refugees in other countries; and as potential returnees—make the call of the homeland especially compelling. So too, they make compelling the specificity of a spatially and temporally *locatable* return. This rather literal notion of a locatable homeland is not utterly foreign to Bloch's principle of hope.[26] But what is interesting in the simultaneous juxtaposition of Bloch's concept of the homeland and the young boy's dream and its retelling is the presence of two different and opposed homeland communities in the boy's dream and the extent to which their mutual presence suggests "that which speaks for itself by remaining silent." And what is silent is only noticeable in the interstices of what is spoken.

The two kinds of community in the homeland in the young Palestinian boy's dream point to what is left unquestioned at its second retelling. Spatially, both communities are somewhere on the ground of historic Palestine. Temporally, they are in a future where we are not (yet). But the organization of homeland and community in the distant time and nearby place is a strikingly contested one in the boy's dream. The second context in which the dream was recounted (perhaps even the first) was one that would seem to privilege return to the "homeland" as return to the community of a preexilic past. In the boy's dream, this is accounted for in the return of the riders on the bus from the Lebanese refugee camp to the original village or town or city from which their families were driven. The years of the refugee camps are bracketed to return to "home" as and where it *was*. But the second version of the homeland—the young boy's "childish" and plaintive question of what happens to the community of the refugee camp—is one in which the years of diaspora and refugee camps are figured into rather than rendered extraneous to or excess for the homeland. The privilege of (chronological) precedence is not automatically assumed. The more and less distant pasts—that of preexile Palestine and that of exile in the refugee camps—coexist uneasily in relation to a dream of the future. But from that future the years of the refugee camp are not foreclosed; they are there in the young boy's plaintive question, in his distress as the occupants of the bus from the refugee camp in Lebanon leave one by one to go elsewhere, to return home. Yet neither of these two notions of the homeland can quite accommodate the dream of the young boy. "I have never been here before," Great Mam tells her great-granddaughter. I have never been here before; this is not home, says the dream of the young Palestinian boy.

Of course, the young boy, telling his dream to the distinguished writer and critic who visits the refugee camp, is too young to possibly know firsthand the village or town of his family. His life in the refugee camp is, obviously enough, his only experience of home or community. To that extent, the writer who solicits his dream and the others in the high-ceilinged room who listen to the writer retelling the dream are at least partly accurate in their assertion that the young boy is attached to his "prison." For he knows nothing else; he is attached to what he knows and catches dream glimpses of the future through what he already knows. As do we all. But the glimpses of the future afforded in his dream are finally *neither* in that of the reestablishment of preexile communities *nor* in that of the preservation of refugee camp communities. They are, instead, in the silence between the two. They are in that which neither the second nor the first retelling of the dream can seem to accommodate. That is a community not-yet, the dimensions of which are not ascertainable but that cannot afford to abandon *either* kind (or time) of community—neither that of pre-1948 (or -1967) Palestine *nor* that of the intervening years of exile and diaspora. Nor can it afford to abandon by foreclosure or ignorance communities otherwise and elsewhere not yet figured here.

The discussion around the huge table in the high-ceilinged room, in contrast to and framing (at least in that retelling) the dreams of the young boy, was more world-weary and vastly (and painfully) more battle-weary. Mostly men and a few women, mostly eyewitnesses to and survivors of the 1982 battle of Beirut and of the camps, mostly committed and distinguished spokespersons for their people(s), the discussion in the high-ceilinged room, like the young Palestinian boy's dream, suggested other "anticipatory illuminations" of possible futures. Not in the characterization of the young boy's dream as "the internalization of systems of domination." Nor in the implicit projection of pre-1948 (or -1967) communities as authoritative. In the young boy's dream at its first and second (here, third) recounting, in the other stories told around the table in the high-ceilinged room, the possible futures persist in their silence. The overwhelming, vociferous weight of multiple pasts—of 1936–1939 (the Arab strike and revolt in Palestine), 1948 (the founding of the State of Israel and the subsequent fighting between the armies of the Arab states and Israel), 1967 (the Six-Day War between Israel and Egypt, Syria, and Jordan), 1973 (Egypt and Syria's war against Israel), 1982 (the second Israeli invasion of Lebanon, the first and more limited being in 1978), 1987 (the beginning of the intifada)—compel attention. Indeed, to ignore those pasts and their tragedies is, as Marx citing an unlocatable Hegel familiarly reminds us, to witness their return (as farce). But in the fervent attempts to imagine the future, in the discussions of necessary pragmatism, of very real past and present injustice, of constitutive law and the state (and, sometimes at least, of society), the young Palestinian boy's dream seems a trenchant if fragile reminder of the extent to which we can imagine or catch glimpses of but not know or altogether plot the future—nor can we predict its outcome.

Bloch's work, like the young boy's dream, is a reminder, too, to attend to the "anticipatory illuminations" of the futures not only in what we feel certain will be the case, though sometimes figured there too, but also in the complex configurations of daydreams and literary imaginings, in declarations of independence and bulletins of the uprising, in the banners and graffiti, in the organization of social movements and popular committees. Not that these are proverbial open books, waiting to be read and marshaled in the calculation of an equation: *this* equals, or will be made to equal, *that*. As the massive compilation of readings and theorizing in *The Principle of Hope* suggests, reading—or listening—is no such uncomplicated endeavor of constructing equivalencies. For, to forget the silence of the future(s) for which the Palestinian boy's dream, like much of Bloch's work, struggles to hold open a space veers toward the valorization of what Jacques Rancière has, in another context, called "the legal, the necessary, and the legitimate," the contraction of utopia and hope or desire to the "utopia of absolute guarantee."[27] Or, to reiterate the trope used above, it is to force the careful reading/listening/watching that Bloch's work encourages into a simple calculation of equivalencies. That is Rancière's notion of the lethal construction he calls "overlegitimated power." And the utter violence wrought in the name of those equivalencies, that overlegitimation, that uncomplicated and uncontradictory reading of an "open book," is what paved the way to the refugee camp for the young Palestinian boy in the first place.

If the homeland, then, is not just an uncomplicated return to communities of the past, neither is it the "internalization of systems of domination" nor the perpetuation of present communities. In that we attempt to travel there, rather than to construct it as Rancière's "utopia of absolute guarantee," it "arises out of the sea of the possible . . . but with new contents." The young Palestinian boy's dream, in the future toward which it turns but of which it cannot directly speak or clearly see, suggests something perhaps not so dissimilar from the hope of Ernst Bloch: "True genesis is not at the beginning but at the end." At an end in which it is possible to say, as Great Mam tells her great-granddaughter, "I have never been here before." So too, the young Palestinian boy says in his dream, I have never been here before; this is not home. Not yet the knowledge of the "home-land," much less a return to what is not known. In fact, there might be no such place in no such time. Yet, in the struggle to listen for, to make out anticipatory flashes of, to recognize the absence of the "homeland," is also the struggle to create a metaphoric and perhaps also a literal homeland. "Here we are, near there."

Notes

Introduction: Culturing the Nation

1 Translation altered.

2 Presentation following the 3 April 1995 showing in Madison, Wisconsin, of his documentary "Pitra, Putra, Aur Dharmyuddha" (Father, son, and holy war; 1994).

3 The Turkish military authorities occupying the north of Cyprus agreed, under pressure from the United Nations, to allow enclaved Greek Cypriots (though not Turkish Cypriots) a five-day leave each month to travel to the unoccupied south of Cyprus to see their families, attend to business affairs, and so forth. In fact, though, as my visitor reiterated, that monthly leave was subject to frequent and unexplained cancellation. This was the first time the old woman had been able to cross the "green line"—the boundary between occupied and unoccupied Cyprus—for five months.

4 The shift from a textual project—rereading literary and nonliterary texts of nationalism-in-crisis for mainland Greece (1922), Cyprus (1974), and Palestinian culture and society (1982)—to a project that also attends to oral histories and testimonials marks one of the lessons learned from the women who told me their stories of being refugees, who often quite bluntly broached the question of moving from being a reader/audience to a narrator.

5 For nationalism is constructed precisely as a narrative. (For an earlier formulation of this position, see my "Telling Spaces.") And within that narrative framework, nationalism proposes or proffers (and enforces) both a rhetoric and a grammar.

6 Gayatri Spivak's astute discussion of the double meaning of "representation" in her consideration of Marx's *Eighteenth Brumaire* and the difference between representation as *vertreten* and as *darstellen* (276–79) is pertinent here. See "Can the Subaltern Speak?"

7 In this, the implications of the old Cypriot woman's story come very close to the implications of the poems written by Mahmud Darwish after the Israeli invasion of Lebanon, for a discussion of which, see chap. 3.

8 I distinguish this proposition of nationalism as narrative from that of nationalism as a *discourse*. Although the latter, analytical specification is indisputable and discourse analysis of nationalism has generated much important work, it still does not necessarily entail an understanding of the narrative organization of nationalism.

9 The American Revolution of 1776 and the French Revolution of 1792 are often cited, both by historians and by later nationalists, as the two earliest exemplars of nationalist revolution as the basis for the constitution of a modern nation-state and its citizens. A noteworthy later, and instructively paradoxical, instance that is often ignored is the attempt to transform the Ottoman Empire into the modern Ottoman state in the first years of the twentieth century. These pluralist experiments (though often not pluralist enough, as Olympe de Gouges was quick to point out concerning the French Revolu-

tion, or as hundreds of thousands of women, indigenous peoples, and African slaves in the newly formed United States bear witness to). By the Treaty of Versailles, the notion of a people defined by a common language and culture was dominant in defining a nation, material reality to the contrary notwithstanding.

10 Siba Grovogui's *Sovereigns, Quasi-Sovereigns, and Africans: Race and Self-Determination in International Law* offers an astute analysis of this concept and of its limitations.

11 See, for example, Miroslav Hroch's "From National Movement to the Fully Formed Nation: The Nation-Building Process in Europe."

12 To understand nationalism-as-a-narrative construct is perhaps also to better comprehend how it is nearly impossible, historically or structurally, for it to be an "autonomous discourse." Such a desire for discursive autonomy simultaneously documenting its impossibility seems to inform Partha Chatterjee's important *Nationalist Thought and the Colonial World: An Autonomous Discourse?* In that work, Chatterjee persuasively points out the dependence of nationalism on discourses of modernity, capitalism, and colonialism. It is striking that, though his textual examples overwhelmingly illustrate the foundational importance to nationalist discourse in India of specific formulations of gender and sexuality, his analysis and theoretical formulation manage to ignore that aspect of things. Subsequent to *Nationalist Thought and the Colonial World,* Chatterjee's work seeks to address this earlier oversight.

13 At the tenth annual national convention of the American-Arab Anti-Discrimination Committee (22–25 April 1993) in Washington, DC. *ADC Times* 14, no. 3 (May–June 1993) carries coverage of Moughrabi's (and others') talks; see esp. p. 17.

14 This is not simply the predicament of "newer" states and their peoples. The culture wars in the United States, the fierce debates on a presumably requisite "cultural literacy," and the currency of English-only resolutions and propositions in various parts of the United States are examples enough of the extent to which a single-national-culture-as-unifying-force is still being argued.

15 See the brief discussion in chapter 4 of the bold recognition of this dependency very early on in the French Revolution and its aftermath by women such as Olympe de Gouges.

16 Although there have undoubtedly been both gains and losses for women in the regime of nationalism and the nation-state, those juridical or political gains and losses overall are less my focus here than their figural reformulation in crisis.

17 This insistence on redefining the organizing principles of the refectory table or of the centrality of that table at all is the note on which Grovogui's *Sovereigns, Quasi-Sovereigns, and Africans* ends as well. See note 10 above.

1 National Homogeneity and Population Exchanges

1 "E Mikroasiatiki katastrophe": literally, as here, the Asia Minor Catastrophe but often referred to as simply "e katastrophe," the Catastrophe—singular, unquestionable in its reference.

2 But, in fact, the massive doors of the main entrance, which one approaches by way of

an almost overgrown garden and large plaza with numerous sculptures and commemorative plaques, are scarcely ever open or used. The de facto entrance to the Center is a small, unassuming door around the side of the building.

3   One of the most popular of these tells of Constantinos XI Palaiologos, the last Byzantine emperor, who, about to be struck down by a "Turk," was rescued by an angel, taken to a cave near one of the gates of the city (the "golden door," *krysoporta*), and turned into marble. There he awaits his reawakening by the angel, when he will rise, free the city (Constantinople), and send the Turks back to their presumable place of origin, the "red apple tree" (*kokkini milia*).

4   And as such it was eagerly, and occasionally warily, welcomed by the western European powers, anxious promulgators and supervisors of the dismantling of the Ottoman Empire.

5   An often quoted passage of Kolletis's address to the Assembly reads, in retrospect, almost ominously: "The Greek kingdom is not the whole of Greece, but only a part, the smallest and poorest part. A native is not only someone who lives within this kingdom but also one who lives in Ioannina, in Thessaly, in Serres, in Adrianople, in Constantinople, . . . and in any land associated with Greek history or the Greek race." (See, for example, Clogg, *A Concise History of Greece,* 48.) Because Greeks were not compactly settled but widely scattered throughout the Balkans and the Middle East, Kolletis's "Greek kingdom" was potentially vast—and coincident, of course, with the "kingdoms" of numerous others as well.

6   Or it is predictable.

7   This is not as implausible a desire as it might at first appear. Some fifteen years earlier, Japan had, after all, succeeded with considerable acclaim by at least some Western powers in realizing the conspicuous connection between nationalism and imperialism in its territorial conquests from the Russo-Japanese War.

8   In his otherwise noteworthy and often exemplary *Disaster and Fiction: Modern Greek Fiction and the Asia Minor Disaster of 1922,* Thomas Doulis rather too quickly dismisses the international context of the 1919–1922 war and its aftermath and, in so doing, implicitly dismisses the broader significance of the cultural response to that period that is the object of his own study. That suggestion implicitly reinforces the assumption that "third" world or "minor" cultures and societies are properly and in fact of only marginal concern to an elsewhere of a broader cultural and political sphere where truly momentous and internationally significant events happen.

9   Quoted in its entirety in Dido Soteriou, *E Mikrasiatiki katastrophe kai i stratigiki tou imperialismou stin Anatoliki Mesogeio,* 17–18.

10   See Michael Llewellyn Smith's *Ionian Vision: Greece in Asia Minor 1919–1922,* esp. chap. 4, "The Paris Peace Conference." Llewellyn Smith's account of the almost foolhardy and certainly careless decisions taken at that "peace conference," based on accounts of the European participants themselves, makes the slenderness of the threads on which Venizelos hung his expansionist plans for Greece more apparent than even Venizelos could have realized. See also Nikos Psyroukis's incisive and extensively documented *E Mikrasiatiki katastrofe: E Engus Anatoli meta ton proto Pankosmio Polemo (1918–1923)* (The Asia Minor Catastrophe: The Near East after WW I [1918–1923]).

11 The novelist and essayist Dido Soteriou in her otherwise highly critical account of Greece's expansionist endeavor in Asia Minor, *E Mikrasiatiki katastrophe kai i stratigiki toy imperialismou stin Anatoliki Mesogeio* (The Asia Minor catastrophe and the strategy of imperialism in the Eastern Mediterranean), melodramatically insists: "Who could demand logic of the Asia Minor Greeks at that moment? Who could reproach them for their intoxication from the dizzying wine of freedom? . . . How could the Greek of Asia Minor be aware of the deliberate ambiguities, the questions, and the unease which closed that first announcement of joy?" (18–19).

12 Thus, Eric Hobsbawm's claim, in his *Nations and Nationalisms Since 1780,* that the "ethnic" or "ethnicity" enters European discourse of the nation-state only in the 1960s is, in the case of Greek nationalism and its language, not quite the case. And, given the fervent German and larger European reappropriation of classical Greece in the late eighteenth and early nineteenth centuries, the notion of the "ethnic" might be in circulation there as well.

13 Clogg, *A Concise History of Greece,* 94.

14 The subsequent plebiscite of December 1920, in which the monarchy (King Constantine) was returned to power in Greece (against the wishes of the Great Powers), was also certainly an assertion of "national independence" over against what was often popularly referred to at the time as Venizelos's capitulation to the Entente and their "foreign" interventions in Greek affairs.

15 There were at least fifty thousand Armenians, for example, among the refugees who resettled in Greece.

16 Ironically, given the impact of the forced exchange, it was Venizelos himself who had first outlined such a plan, though not one so patently compulsory as the Convention of Lausanne, and who made the argument for the desirability of homogeneous population zones. See Llewellyn Smith, esp. 71–74, for a concise account of Venizelos's views and arguments to the Great Powers on the issue of population exchange and ethnic homogeneity. Not surprisingly, the source of the insistence on the explicitly compulsory nature of the population exchanges is identified with different historical figures depending on which historical account or personal memoir you read.

17 As, indeed, it would also seem to have been for the transformation of the multiethnic, multicultural Ottoman State (formerly Empire) into the Turkish Republic.

18 The text of the Lausanne Treaty and its conventions are reproduced in Dimitri Pentzopoulos, *The Balkan Exchange of Minorities and Its Impact on Greece.*

19 With the more recent crises in the Balkans and Eastern Europe in general, the referents for the category of "refugees" has, however, radically expanded.

20 Where literal isolation was not an issue, social segregation often was. See, for example, Dimitri Pentzopoulos, *The Balkan Exchange of Minorities and Its Impact on Greece,* 209–12, or, even earlier and at greater length, A. Deimizis's *Situation sociale créé en Grèce à la suite de l'Echange de Populations,* 18–20. Both writers characteristically note the charged significance for mainland Greeks of the social and cultural mores of the women refugees from Asia Minor (from the more cosmopolitan coastal regions in particular).

21 They were "Protocol Relating to the Settlement of Refugees in Greece and the Creation for This Purpose of a Refugees Settlement Commission" and an appendix to

that Protocol, "The Organic Statutes of the Greek Refugees Settlement Commission," both dated 29 September 1923, copies in the archives of the Estia Neas Smyrnis.

22 See Mark Mazower's *Greece and the Inter-War Economic Crisis,* especially his succinct and excellent discussion of land reform and agricultural development in chap. 4, "Reconstructing the Bourgeois Order, 1922–1929," 75–91.

23 See Pentzopoulos's discussion of "Relations between the Natives and the Newcomers" in *The Balkan Exchange of Minorities and Its Impact on Greece,* 209–12.

24 As established in 1923 and until its dissolution in 1930, the Refugee Settlement Commission was composed of two representatives appointed by the Greek government, an American chair appointed by the U.S. government, and a British representative appointed by that government. The RSC was directly accountable to the League of Nations, providing them with quarterly progress reports.

25 See, for example, Pentzopoulos's citation and general endorsement of some of these observers' comments (191). Also see the vaguely allegorical admonition of the first U.S. chair of the RSC, Henry Morgenthau, to the Greeks in a public speech in Athens upon his being awarded honorary citizenship of that city 2 February 1924. In his memoirs of his years in Greece, *I Was Sent to Athens,* Morgenthau reports on his acceptance of honorary Athenian citizenship and use of that occasion to caution the Greeks on their upcoming election: "I told them that the left road was the Russian Road, and was occupied by the Bolsheviks, Mexicans, and Turks, and as they could see it was in very bad shape and quite unsafe for travelers, and it seemed to end in a Morass of Disaster" (155).

26 Pentzopoulos's *The Balkan Exchange of Minorities* is a sometimes unwitting illustration of the tensions between "native and newcomer," even when that topic is not the explicit one. See his introduction (esp. 19) and "Conclusions" and chaps. 3 and 4, "The Political Impact" and "The Social and Cultural Impact."

27 Kendro Mikrasiatikon Spoudon (Center for Asia Minor Studies), *E Exodos* (The exodus), 2:I.4.5, 214; 2:I.4.6b 218.

28 This specific (but not atypical) litany is from a letters to the editor section of *E Pamprosfugiki* (Panrefugee), 11 May 1924.

29 Poems and serialized novels were staple features of virtually all newspapers of the day.

30 Thus, for example, An. Asimakopoulou, *Mari Xanoum: E perifimi eromeni tou fexim pasa* (Mari Hanoum: The famous mistress of Pasha Fehim) *E Pamprosfugiki* of 1924–1925.

31 Kendro Mikrasiatikon Spoudon, *E Exodos,* 1:I.1.6a, 29. Quotations that follow are also from this source. Manaeloglou's testimonial contains an astute commentary on class relations in her village in her account of the authorities' efforts to raise money for one of the Greek-women-become-Turkish so that she could return to Greece with some money in her possession. "Ten rich families" in the village are approached for charitable contributions for the woman; they refuse. "Fifty poor families" in the village, however, "all gave something." At this display of generosity, the rich are shamed and decide to contribute money for the woman. So the money of the poor was returned (29).

32 There are similar implications of being a "milk-mother" (رضاع) in the Arabic context,

established by nursing another woman's child, similarly regardless of the "ethnic" or national identification of that child. So, for example, there are "unthinkable" accounts of Palestinian and Israeli women nursing one another's children, both fully cognizant of the obligations and responsibilities that such an action involves.

33   The contradictions of ordering and categorizing are illustrated even in the collection of testimonials in which Soteriou's is located. The headnote for testimonials from her village—place of origin in Turkey being the organizing principle for the two-volume collection as a whole—includes the statement that Sivrihisar, "consonant with the information of the KMS [Kendro Mikroastikon Spoudon, Center for Asia Minor Studies], had relations and trade only with Greek villages." Soteriou's account of trade with the Turkish villagers of Melendiz, Azatala, and Sorsovou clearly counters the headnote. Even the effort to "bear witness to" and "preserve" the culture and history of Asia Minor Greeks is beset with some of the same problems as the document (the Treaty of Lausanne and its conventions) that effectively ordered and separated them from Asia Minor.

34   See, for example, Giannis Kapsis's selection of refugee depositions (collected from among those scattered in the archives of various Greek ministries), *1922, E mavri biblos* (1922, The black book).

35   In an interview broadcast on Cypriot television in October 1989. In the Cypriot context of the continuing occupation of 40 percent of Cyprus by the mainland Turkish military and the proclamation of a separate Turkish Cypriot state on that occupied land, Iordanidou's story of intercommunal relations and official proclamations has an additional and trenchant significance. Iordanidou offered this story as a perhaps ingenuous explanation of her decision, upon retirement in her mid-sixties, to begin writing novels. For, by her account, she could not find novels that she wanted to read, novels that told the stories she knew. So she decided to write them herself.

36   Koumoglou's deposition, taken immediately upon his arrival in Greece, is reprinted in Kapsis's *1922, E mavri biblos,* 24.

37   In the Smyrna/Izmir edition of the Greek-language newspaper, *Amaltheia (Smyrnis),* based in Constantinople/Istanbul, 22 December, p. 1.

38   Richard Clogg, "Anadolu Hiristiyan Karindaşlarimiz: The Turkish-Speaking Greeks of Asia Minor," 83.

39   Dido Sotiriou, *Oi nekroi perimenoun* (The Dead Are Waiting) (Athens: Kedros, 1959).

40   These were the *amele tambourou* or forced labor battalions masterminded by Liman von Sanders and used by the Ottoman state as a means to control and relocate minority populations preceding and especially during WWI.

41   In fact, treason against the Ottoman state was the charge under which Anatolian Greeks, suspected of serving or actually having served in the Greek forces, were executed by Turkish regular and irregular forces after the Greek defeat.

42   Venizelos and Constantine represent the two dominant and opposed figures and positions in Greek politics of the time. The former was a "liberal" who aligned himself with the major European imperialist powers of the day, France and especially Britain. Constantine represented the monarchist forces: "conservative," allied with Germany, purportedly opposed to the expansionist politics of Venizelos. When

the monarchists were voted into power in 1920, defeating Venizelos, it was on a platform of ending the war and bringing the Greek troops home immediately. They did neither.

43   The phrase is literally "what we're engaged in is the dance of Zalongo," a reference to a valorized incident during the Greek War of Independence against the Ottoman Empire in the first decades of the nineteenth century when Epiriot women and children from the besieged village of Zalongo danced off the edge of a cliff rather than be captured by Ottoman forces. In addition to the citation of an incident famously appropriated by nationalist rhetoric, the gender reversal in this passage is noteworthy. The exhausted and imminently defeated Greek soldiers in Asia Minor are constructed as analogous to the besieged women and children of Zalongo.

44   See the introduction and first essays in *Mistrusting Refugees,* ed. Daniel and Knudsen, for a qualified assertion of trust and "the refugee experience" and the subsequent essay by Voutira and Harrell-Bond, which explicitly challenges the centrality of the concept of trust and its violation.

2   The Gendered Purity of the Nation

1   I am grateful to Jeff Shalan for bringing this article to my attention.

2   EOKA-B was (the use of the past tense here is hopefully accurate) the latter-day manifestation of the Cypriot "national liberation organization" of the 1950s against British colonial rule and for union with Greece. That organization, formed in January 1955, was named Ethniki Organosis Kypriakon Agoniston (National Organization of Cypriot Fighters). It was "almost entirely a right-wing nationalist-led movement" (Panteli, 165) of Greek Cypriots; Turkish Cypriots and leftists were excluded. But because of its anticolonial stance, it had wider popular support in the struggle against British rule on the island. The founder of EOKA was the Cypriot George "Dighenis" Grivas, a fanatic anticommunist and extreme right-wing military officer who had been trained by and served in the mainland Greek military. So it should have come as no surprise that the target of EOKA military actions was not only the British colonial power but also other Cypriots—most especially, communists, socialists, and their liberal sympathizers of whatever ethnicity, Turkish Cypriot policemen recruited by the British for their Special Branch, and Greek Cypriots in the employ of the British. Ironically, EOKA had the cooperation of Archbishop Makarios at the time. Later, as president of Cyprus, he was to become the hated target of EOKA-B. Still fervently advocating union with Greece as the only guarantee against "foreign" communism in Cyprus, EOKA-B was formed in 1967 by the same infamous General Grivas. From its founding, EOKA-B sponsored countless and largely indiscriminate acts of sabotage and terror in opposition to what it saw as the failure of the Cypriot government and of Greek Cypriots to insist on union with Greece—and implicitly at least, the partition of the island.

3   For an astute and succinct account of the foreign and internal machinations against the government of "independent" Cyprus and against Makarios personally, see Christopher Hitchens, *Cyprus,* esp. chap. 3, "The Dragon's Teeth," in which he also details the intense involvement of the U.S. government and of its famous "peacemaker," Henry Kissinger.

4   Omorphita was a largely Turkish Cypriot district of the capital city of Nicosia. In late December 1963, "intercommunal violence" broke out in the capital city following on the Akritas Plan—a secret program formulated earlier in 1963 to use intercommunal violence and subsequent pressure on the UN to remove treaty restrictions on Cypriot union with Greece—and on the Turkish government's official refusal of a thirteen-point proposal for constitutional reform submitted by President Makarios to the leader of the Turkish Cypriot community. In accordance with the Cypriot Constitution and the Treaties of Guarantee and Alliance that founded the Cypriot state, Makarios also submitted his proposal for informational purposes to the governments of England, Greece, and Turkey. His proposal ensued from months of UN-negotiated "proximity talks" between Turkish Cypriot and Greek Cypriot leaders and representatives of England, Greece, and Turkey. In the wake of the quelling of that violence, Nikos Sampson and his gang engaged in horrendous atrocities against the unarmed Turkish Cypriot population. Twenty-five years later, scorched ruins in Omorphita still stood witness to the genocidal ferocity of Sampson's assault.

5   This is literally the case: Makarios was elected *only* by Greek Cypriots. According to the Cypriot Constitution, and reminiscent of the equally disastrous confessionally defined constitution promulgated by France in Lebanon, the president of Cyprus was always to be a Greek Cypriot, the vice president a Turkish Cypriot. And they were each elected *separately* by the Greek Cypriot and Turkish Cypriot communities respectively (Constitution of Cyprus, Articles 1 and 39).

6   As in the past-tense reference to EOKA-B above, I would hope that the past tense is appropriate here as well.

7   This is precisely the opening context of the short story, "Oi stoles" (The uniforms), by Panos Ioannidis, discussed below.

8   In an interview with Michael Cacoyannis in the latter's *Attila '74: A Testimony on Film* (1975).

9   Odious as the claims of the fascist junta in Greece at the time of their promotion of and collusion in the far right-wing coup in Cyprus and profoundly dubious as the claims of the (ironically, social democratic) government in Turkey on the occasion of their invasion of the island, both the Turkish and Greek governments as well as that of England (as the former colonial power in Cyprus) had a "right of guarantee" in Cyprus as detailed in the documents that founded the Republic of Cyprus as an independent state. Effectively, Greece, Turkey, and England were granted the right to intervene in the internal and external affairs of Cyprus. Article 4 of the 1960 Treaty of Guarantee specifies that "each of the three guaranteeing Powers reserves the right to take action with the sole aim of re-establishing the state of affairs created by the present treaty." No minor comment on the issue of "postcolonial" sovereignty, this.

10 Quoted in Kostas Graikos, *Kypriaki istoria* (Cypriot history), B: 127.

11 They include, most importantly, Security Council Resolution 353 on 20 July 1974, calling for the restoration of constitutional order and the cessation of hostilities, and Resolution 354 on 22 July, calling for a cease-fire and the withdrawal of foreign troops from Cyprus.

12 The First Geneva Conference was held from 24 to 30 July 1974; the Second was

convened in early August but interrupted by deadlock and subsequently by the second phase of the Turkish invasion that began on 14 August 1974.

13   Although the British colonial policies with their emphasis on the distinction between and separation of ethnoreligious communities compelled a gradual differentiation of villages. The preponderant transformation from mixed villages to ethnoreligiously defined villages in Cyprus between 1881 and 1960 (the period of British rule) is striking.

14   In descending order of the size of their communities. The Maronite community was established (or at least, first recorded) in Cyprus from the 8th century A.D. They were largely from the areas of Syria and Lebanon and identified with the Maronite Catholic church. The recorded presence of the Armenian community in Cyprus dates to the 5th century A.D. The Latins, the smallest ethnic/confessional community in Cyprus, were originally French, Italians, and Dalmatians identified with the western Catholic church. The ethnoconfessional system which the British left in place in "independent" Cyprus designated divided rights, powers, and systems for each of the five communities (these three and the Turkish Cypriot and Greek Cypriot) on the basis of their communal affiliation rather than on some more comprehensive or inclusive paradigm of citizenship.

15   Moira Killoran's essay "Nationalisms and Embodied Memory in Northern Cyprus" is a suggestive consideration of the struggle for self-definition and historical memory between Turkish Cypriots and what she calls "Cypriot Turks." The former define themselves as Cypriots of Turkish origin, the latter as Turks residing in Cyprus. The dimensions of the struggle for which Killoran's essay accounts are textually evident in the newspapers and journals from northern Cyprus. An inclusive list of individual citations would be massive, but some representative examples are the series of four articles on the smuggling of Cypriot antiquities, "Perishing Cyprus" by Mehmet Yasin; the fierce debates in spring 1989 over the Turkish Cypriot leader Rauf Denktash's "humanitarian" offer to allow Bulgarian Muslims to settle in northern Cyprus (in *Ortam,* 17 and 20 June 1989, 22 January 1991); the emigration of Turkish Cypriots from northern Cyprus (in *Ortam,* 18 May 1989, 7 February 1994; *Yeniduzen,* 24 April 1989); and the increasing influx of settlers from Turkey (in *Yeniduzen* 12 and 14 February, 12 April, 21 May, 20 August 1990).

16   H. B. Archbishop Makarios, President of Cyprus, address, 29th UN General Assembly, 1 October 1974.

17   A character in Christos Hatzipapas's novel *To chroma tou galaziou iakinthou* (The color of the blue hyacinth, 1989) proffers a scathingly ironic account of Klerides's "generosity": "Can you believe it?—the nerve of that man [Klerides], god damn him . . . Listen to what he came up with. To hold elections, he says, and if the people want him [Makarios] then he [Klerides] won't have any objections to his return. Who, my friend? Makarios. Why, mister, did any of you ask permission when you staged the coup? Did 'the people' overthrow Makarios or the junta's men? . . . Listen to that, to hold elections, so that the [already] elected leader can return" (224).

18   For a complete text of Johnson's letter to Inonu, see "Correspondence between President Johnson and Prime Minister Inonu, June 1964."

19 Makarios's slip in reference suggests in retrospect, however, what he could not have foreseen then. For what subsequently ensued was precisely the massive establishment of "Turkish populations" from mainland Turkey and of Muslim refugees from Bulgaria in northern Cyprus, resulting in the marginalization and subsumption of Turkish Cypriots.

20 See references above for accounts of Greek Cypriot (and mainland Greek) right-wing activities in Cyprus that predate by far the 1967 junta in Greece. For an informed English-language account of Turkish Cypriot (and mainland Turkish) right-wing activities in Cyprus that predate the Turkish invasion in Cyprus, see C. P. Ioannides's well-documented book *In Turkey's Image: The Transformation of Occupied Cyprus into a Turkish Province.* Although the title of his book would seem to suggest a primary concern with post-1974 Cyprus, in chapters 4 through 7, Ioannides provides a substantial account of the dynamics of right-wing Turkish Cypriot and Turkish activities—this in spite of his rather prejudicial rationalization of Greek Cypriot and Greek right-wing activities.

21 In fact, the mayors of the two halves of the capital city—Lellos Demetriades and Mustafa Akinci, of the southern and northern halves of the city, respectively—received the Habitat Award in October 1989 in recognition of their intercommunal cooperation to preserve and develop the city, which included the renovation of the medieval walls of the old city, across the military barricades of the "green line" that divide the city.

22 The organization sponsoring the discussion was the Koine Kinesi Elenokyprion-Tourkokyprion yia Omospondi kai Anexartiti Kypro (Joint Movement for a Federated and Independent Cyprus).

23 He subsequently founded a new Turkish Cypriot party, the New Cyprus Party, of which he was the articulate and outspoken leader.

24 From the author's notes and audio tapes of the 14 December 1989 meeting. See Mehmet Yasin's four-part article "Perishing Cyprus" for similar sentiments. Yasin too locates all contemporary Cypriots, regardless of ethnoreligious derivation, as heirs of Cypriot culture and history from 7000 B.C. The familiar nationalist claim to an unbroken past that bears directly on the present is even more explicit there: "At the threshold of the twenty-first century we are also living through the remote, very remote centuries. Yet we do not realize this." In the context of the sharply communalist nationalism that has marked modern Cyprus, claims such as those of Yasin and Durduran to an intercommunal nationalist inheritance of history and culture are remarkable for their inclusiveness.

25 While the events of this meeting were covered in both local and international newspapers and some of that newspaper coverage is cited here, the primary basis for what follows is my own eyewitness account.

26 "Can We Escape the Past?," *Cyprus Weekly* 527, 15–21 December 1989: 1.

27 They included the demilitarization of Cyprus and the departure of foreign troops, the de Cuellar proposal on a federated republic, the protection of the cultural heritage of Cyprus, and the increased emigration of Turkish Cypriots from the occupied north.

28 "Alpay Durduran: 'Na nikisoume to sovinismo yia na enosoume tin patrida mas' " (Alpay Durduran: "We must be victorious against chauvinism to reunite our father-

land"), *Xaravghi* (Daybreak) 34, no. 11475 (15 December 1989): 1. The same day, *Xaravghi* ran the text of Niazi Kizilgiourek's speech of 14 December 1989 with the title "Pros mia enomeni Kypro" (Towards a united Cyprus), p. 5.

29   For an account of Turkish Cypriot newspaper coverage of the event see "Stoxos soviniston o A. Durduran" (A. Durduran, the target of chauvinism), *Haravghi* 17 December 1989, 24.

30   In *Haravaghi* 15 December 1989, 34. See note 29 above.

31   Literally, *prosfugia* is the condition or state of being a refugee. Katselli, like her narrator, is still in Cyprus but not in her home city of Kyrenia, which is occupied by the Turkish military and to which she is not allowed to return.

32   Curiously, the Ioannides translation omits several significant words and passages and eliminates the final section (39) of the novel altogether. In that last section, one of the nineteen readers utterly rejects the manuscript and returns it in disgust to the narrator/author, challenging him to find a more appropriate way to confront the uprooting of the Cypriot people. The omission of that conclusion is even more baffling than the selective deletion of passages earlier in the novel, because the conclusion so clearly gestures back to and is a critical comment on the overall shape of the novel.

33   The "D.G.C."/"X.E.K." of the opening invocation.

34   If the narrator's response to the story of the blue whales' demise is a rehearsal for the response of the narratee or implied reader to *his* narrative, the implications are indeed grimly limited.

35   This acronym is finally specified on his refugee identity card as standing for "displaced [or, more literally, "unhoused": *xespitomeno*] Greek Cypriot."

36   And in this, reminiscent of Makarios's 1 October 1974 address to the United Nations in which he refers to Cyprus before the invasion as "a happy and flourishing island."

37   To this last question about whether or not the human race is worthy of survival he asks the reader to respond by writing yes or no in a small box, the permissible range for reader response here apparently fiercely restricted.

38   Her text is postulated as the "feminine" antithesis of his: "her experiences of the Turkish invasion of Cyprus and displacement" (*xespitomo*, unhousing), which he hastens to characterize as inadequate and unsatisfactory. After reproducing its opening lines, he edits her "small book" with the comment, "Like the woman that she is, she babbles on about insignificant things." He concludes the fragments excerpted from her text with the statement, "I found this book of my cousin's lukewarm and many other refugee acquaintances of mine agree" (39–40).

39   This moment is almost obsessively foreshadowed in an earlier moment of narrative disjuncture—again, specifically a refusal to narrate—in the conclusion to section 12. This is the point at which the narrator grudgingly acquiesces to the insistent requests of his cousin to insert *her* literary narratives into *his* text. In this interruption of his narrative, something of the threat of the displaced/unhoused woman and her narratives is rather explicitly indicated. And then there are the persistent criticisms of the narrator's writing by his wife, a similarly "unhoused" woman. Her criticism of him is also an attempt by her to read his story differently, and even to change its direction. Thus, the response of the narrator's nineteenth reader—yet another "unhoused"

woman who, in the closing lines of the novel, disrupts his narrative both by reading it differently and by forcibly returning it to him—is the final in a series of disruptions of his narrative by "unhoused" women. Their threat is omnipresent.

40   The protestations of and demonstrations by the nonrefugee poor that their needs have been and continue to be ignored in favor of virtually exclusive aid for the refugees casts an interesting light on this assertion by the narrator. See, for example, Tassos Tsapparellas, "Unacceptable Living Conditions," *Haravghi* 15 October 1989, 10.

41   This constitutes a parallel in closing to the television documentary on the blue whale that provides the title and opening trope for the novel.

42   This is, of course, the narrator's earlier characterization of his cousin's writing as "lukewarm."

43   It is this section of the novel that is not included in the English translation.

44   See Peter Loizos, *The Heart Grown Bitter: A Chronicle of Cypriot War Refugees,* esp. 133, for an account of the elision that the currency of this phrase makes possible.

45   This implicit analogy between the order imposed by the coup and the order imposed by the narrator on his books during that coup is accentuated by the fact that the word in Greek is *diorthoso,* literally, "I correct/rectify/remedy" the implicit disorder of my bookshelves. In a remarkably coincident fashion, the coup proposed to correct or remedy or rectify the putative disorder of Cyprus under President Makarios.

46   Literally, "to the perceptible [*noete*] side" or "to my own perception of my soul."

47   The idiomatic phrase is literally *eisai yia desimo* (you should be tied up). In the penultimate line of the novel/manuscript, the image of this idiom is reflected in the narrator's reference to his vehemently rejected manuscript as *desmi,* a bound bundle or packet of papers. Perhaps his manuscript is gendered female and "crazy"—"fit to be tied" in the English idiom—like the nineteenth reader and the other women of his text.

48   Literally, her name means "good luck."

49   The sunlight in her story here is in contradistinction to the moonlight that she notices illuminating the hands of the Turkish soldier.

50   Here, as throughout this chapter and the ones that precede and follow it, there may be a temptation to understand some of the cultural responses to the crises of nationalism as an echo of a kind of "orientalism," even if one considerably reshaped by its context. Although this "echo" *is* audible, orientalism seems a far less interesting and productive way to understand what occurs.

51   There was, for example, a card and wall poster that circulated in Cyprus as late as 1989–1990 that pictured a gold wreath behind a blue and white flag. The flag is not that of Cyprus but of Greece. And the message printed across the flag reads (a holiday salutation, among other things): "And on earth peace." In smaller lettering underneath the flag are the disturbingly *un*ironic words: "Cyprus—Free—Greek."

52   Some fifteen years later, the ambiguity of that bill gave rise to debate as to whether or not abortions are, in fact, legal in Cyprus. See, for example, "Abortion on the Increase," *Cyprus Weekly* 1–7 December 1989, 6.

53   " . . . the story had begun and it had to end," Evtuxia observes.

54   The female body as the site of such transgression is, in the post-1974 Cypriot cultural and social context, scarcely peculiar to Abraamidou's short story. Rather than an

isolated literary phenomenon, this configuration assumed the proportions of a dominant social trope—as the fiction of Panos Ioannidis, especially "The 'Uniforms' " (Oi
stoles) and "The Invisible Side" (E atheate opsi), or Christos Xatzipapa's novel *The
Color of the Blue Hyacinth* (*To chroma tou galaziou iakinthou*), discussed below,
make even clearer.

55   Mehmet Yasin, "The Myth of Our Own Cat."

56   The (mainland) Turkish flag and the photograph of the old man's son, murdered
some ten years earlier in what is rather euphemistically called "intercommunal violence," is already sufficient indication of the extent to which the putative "outside"
is "inside."

57   This is a reference to the bloody Greek Cypriot attacks on two Turkish Cypriot villages, Kofinou and Ayios Theodoros, in November 1967 ordered by General Grivas.
In those infamous incidents, many of the residents as well as Turkish Cypriots from
other villages and cities who came to the defense of the two villages or who sought
revenge for the killings were also murdered. It is presumably in this series of battles
that the Old Turkish Cypriot's son was killed. "The 'Uniforms' " explicitly refers to
his death as the young Turkish Cypriot woman dons the clothes of her dead mother
and, in doing so, remembers her mother's death from asthma and from the anguish of
seeing her son "brought back to her in pieces from the explosion, a bundle wrapped
in a blood red flag" (17). It is the same massacre at Kofinou and Greek Cypriot
reluctance to acknowledge the atrocities committed against Turkish Cypriots that the
Greek Cypriot ex-National Guardsman recalled in the public intercommunal meeting of 14 December 1989.

58   His name is literally (and ironically) "freedom enlightened."

59   This, in turn, obliquely suggests the moon of the Turkish and Turkish Cypriot flags.
They too are the other and "invisible side" of things; the Turkish Cypriots are the
"unseen side" of Cypriot society, of a narrow Greek Cypriot nationalism.

60   The sexual implications of the imminent amputation of his "lower limbs" is fairly
explicitly rendered in the novel; in other words, in this fictional narrative too the
violations of the summer of 1974 result in a threat of (male) impotency.

61   In this, Xatzipapas's novel is reminiscent of the novel *The Events Surrounding the
Strange Disappearance of Said the Pessoptimist* (1974), by the Palestinian Israeli
Imil Habibi. In that work too, in addition to the fantastic events of the novel, there is a
virtual retelling of Palestinian history—footnoted, documented, nonfantastic.

62   For this latter situation in particular, the predicament of *pseftohyres* or "false wid-
ows" (i.e., women whose fiancés or husbands remained missing after the coup and
invasion) and their virtual effacement from Cypriot society because of their missing
male members, see Maria Roussou's excellent essay "War in Cyprus: Patriarchy and
the Penelope Myth."

63   In English, "agency" might be a more appropriate, though freer, translation.

64   This dangerous ignorance is the pretext of another Cypriot novel, Eve Meleagrou's
Protelevtaia epochi (The next to the last season), which opens with a section ironically entitled "Apodrasi" or "Way Out" (ironic because, dated "spring of 1973,"
there is already no "escape" from the events that will follow). There, two of the
novel's characters watch a television news program, which is reporting on the new

(mainland) Greek military commander on Cyprus, in amazement at the program's (and the Cypriot state's) avoidance of the grave events occurring immediately around them: "the perpetual ostrich-like politics of the State, to cover up everything, so that people don't learn anything, so that they aren't upset . . . as if the people were all underage and need protection" (14).

3 Between Here and There

1   For a thoughtful and astute account of the "War of the Camps" focused on the people of Shatila in particular, see Rosemary Sayigh's *Too Many Enemies: The Palestinian Experience in Lebanon.*

2   Surely the Palestinian uprising in the Israeli Occupied Territories of late 1987 was one momentous culmination of the diverse range of responses, from both inside and outside of historic Palestine, to the summer of 1982 and the devastation of the Israeli invasion.

3   That is, until fall of 1970, with the "Black September" events and the subsequent expulsion of Palestinian forces from Jordan and with the November 1970 coup in Syria.

4   In *The Palestine Liberation Organisation: People, Power and Politics,* Helena Cobban offers a succinct summation of the effects of the defeat of Egypt, Syria, and Jordan by Israel: "In all these countries, the military defeat at the hands of Israel had sent their governments' negotiating power *vis-à-vis* the [Palestinian] guerrillas plummeting to near zero" (36).

5   Lebanese mass support for the Palestinian actions—the camp uprisings in fall of 1969 against the violent harassment of Palestinians by the Lebanese state and particularly its hated Deuxième Bureau, the intelligence section of the Lebanese army—was crucial. Those actions culminated in the gains for Palestinians in Lebanon of the Cairo Accords.

6   See Cobban, *The Palestinian Liberation Organisation: People, Power and Politics,* for a good English-language account of the PLO and its development to 1983.

7   That is, in the sixteen refugee camps officially established as such by United Nations Relief Works Association (UNRWA). Settlements of Palestinians elsewhere, though in camplike conditions, were not formally included. In return, the PLO agreed to coordinate its activities based in Lebanon with the Lebanese army and to respect Lebanese "sovereignty and security."

8   See Helena Cobban, pp. 60–63 and footnote 9 on p. 279, for a succinct account of this affirmation of the PLO at the Seventh Arab Summit in Rabat (28 October 1974).

9   The Camp David Accords were signed by Egypt, Israel, and the United States on 17 September 1978.

10 The results of the 1976 elections also clearly signaled the waning among Palestinians in the Territories and in Israel of the "Jordanian option," the notion that some kind of homeland for Palestinians would be created in and near Jordan and governed by the Hashemite ruler. For the success of the pro-PLO candidates marked the defeat of the pro-Jordanian local councils.

11 This turn was made even more explicit at the Palestine National Council meeting in Cairo in 1977 when an official position that "negotiation is struggle" was adopted.

12 On the same day, 13 April 1975, unidentified assailants reportedly fired on Pierre Gemayel, the head of the right-wing, Maronite-dominated Phalangist Party. The attack on the busload of Palestinians returning from a rally and the massacre of twenty-seven of them was supposedly a retaliation for the "attack" on Gemayel.

13 See also Rex Brynen's "PLO Policy in Lebanon: Legacies and Lessons" for a brief but astute account of PLO excesses and less than strategic political choices, including its reliance on "military predominance" in Lebanon rather than on "building on the mass base that had allowed the Palestinian movement to survive multiple challenges" (57).

14 Kamal Jumblatt was killed in March 1977 in circumstances that suggested a right-wing Christian assassination.

15 In fact, the PLO Executive Committee, as the Arab world remained divided on the Fahd Plan. When Syria's President Assad boycotted the Arab Summit meeting (on 25 November in Fez, Morocco), at which the discussion and possible adoption of the plan was to have taken place, it was apparent that there would be no united stand on the issue. Egypt's President Sadat had been assassinated in the meantime (early October 1981), but his successor, Hosni Mubarak, quickly made clear that he would stick to the letter of the Camp David Accords; that is, he would not consider supporting the Fahd Plan. Thus, Prince Fahd formally withdrew his plan. The PLO's disagreement over, or at least its inconclusive response to, the Fahd Plan was never resolved.

16 *Facts on File* (1982), 121.

17 Special U.S. envoy Phillip Habib brokered the first cease-fire ever explicitly reached between Israel and the PLO. In doing so, Habib engaged in direct (if not quite open) negotiations with the PLO, a matter of no little significance given the adamant U.S. refusal, since 1975, to negotiate directly with the PLO. The PLO agreed to—and maintained—an earlier cease-fire with Israel for three years, from 1978 until the massive Israeli air strike of July 1981 against heavily Palestinian-populated areas of Beirut. But it had done so in response to United Nations and indirect U.S. requests, not in an almost one-on-one arrangement with the State of Israel.

18 Milson's appointment and the cultural rhetoric of his colonial administration suggest the example, whether perversely or utterly in keeping, of "gainful" political service in which professors of literature can engage.

19 See Judith Tucker's "The War of Numbers" and its account of the battle over Palestinian and Lebanese casualties of the Israeli invasion.

20 The lengthy press release of February 1983 of the Israeli Committee for Solidarity with Birzeit University (a Palestinian university on the West Bank) and the Committee against the War in Lebanon, Israel (CAWL) gives a succinct account of the solidarity efforts and opposition to the war in Lebanon by one of the more politically astute Israeli groups at the time.

21 See, for example, the statement by Palestinian mayors of the West Bank and Gaza (printed in the Jerusalem newspaper *Al-Fajr,* 6 July 1982) which was sent to the

heads of ten European states, the prime minister of Canada, the UN, the Australian
Embassy in Tel Aviv, and, of course, to then-U.S. President Ronald Reagan.

22 To list the dates and contents of UN Security Council resolutions seems an ironic
comment on their effectiveness.

23 Quoted in Alain Gresh, "Palestinian Communists and the Intifadah."

24 Emile Sahliyeh, *In Search of Leadership: West Bank Politics Since 1967*, 166.

25 See, for example, Jean Genet, "Four Hours in Shatila"; Jean Makdisi, *Beirut Fragments;* Fawwaz Traboulsi, "Beirut-Guernica: A City and a Painting"; and Mahmud
Darwish's simultaneously stunning and horrifying *Dākira lil-nisyān*.

26 "They'd love to see me dead," writes Mahmud Darwish in an eponymously titled
poem, "so they could say: he was one of us, he belonged to us" (in *Dahāyā al-karīta*
[Victims of a map]). For, alive and writing, the poet in the poem cannot be so easily
appropriated. He "sends shoes to the soul" ("so it can travel on the land") and "writes
a white poem when the earth is black" ("because thirty seas flow in my heart"). So,
the poem concludes, "they laughed and stole from my house only the words that I
was going to say to the wife of my heart." This sardonic commentary on the "useful-
ness" and "faithfulness" to the real of poetry and the poet is certainly not limited to
the Palestinian context.

27 The poems by Darwish discussed here were written in November 1982 but published
for the first time in book form in *Dahāyā al-karīta* (Victims of a map). I have consulted that volume's elegant translations of Darwish's poems with pleasure. The
distinctly less elegant but more literal translations here are my own.

28 A lecture delivered at the Sorbonne on 11 March 1882. An excellent translation of
Renan's essay by Martin Thom is available in *Nation and Narration*, ed. Homi
Bhabha and is reprinted in *The Nationalism Reader*, ed. Dahbour and Ishay.

29 This impossibly "nonspatial" place is an ironic turn on the very word for place itself
(*makān*): in this instance, literally the place where one stands, where one is or exists
(*kāna*). Most literally and tangibly, the space of Lebanon has been destroyed; there is
no place for Palestinians or the PLO in Lebanon. But this tangible and literal meaning
of *makān* does not exhaust the poetic sense of its use and reiteration.

30 Mahmud Darwish, "Nasāfiru k'alnnās" ("We travel like [all] people"): "Linā baladun
min kalāmin."

31 Ibid.

32 "Nasayaru ili baladin" ("We travel to a country").

33 It is not quite boundaries themselves that are the issue. Poems, after all, have boundaries—beginnings and endings; they operate under the organizing rule of dominant
signs and images. States, too, organize boundaries of beginnings and endings and
operate under the rule of dominant signs and images. And states do so with rather
more material force to both persuade and coerce acceptance of those organized beginnings and endings and of the incontrovertibility of its dominant signs and images. Still, the poetic suggestion of holding open possibility offers a scandalous but
perhaps nonetheless potentially productive question for other kinds of organization
and rule.

34 This is already an implicit suggestion of Darwish's early poem, "Blessed is that which
has not come," with its poignant invocation of a "wedding [and a courtyard and a

night and a longing] without end." But what if there is fulfillment without an end to desire, satisfaction without an end to longing? What if the lover reaches her beloved on the wedding night and consummates her union without desire thereby being finally satisfied—as Michel Khleifi's film *Wedding in Galilee* rather explicitly suggests?

35 *"Al-awda*/the return conjures up the past. It is a Sufi concept. *Al-dhahab*/the journey, however, is a revolutionary endeavor. This is the difference between Andalusia and Palestine, between the Zionist enterprise and the Palestinian enterprise" (interview in *Le Monde* [1 January 1983]; quoted in Barbara Harlow, "Palestine or Andalusia: The Literary Response to the Israeli Invasion of Lebanon," 43).

36 This debate takes place not only between Israelis and Palestinians or between the Israeli state and the Palestine National Authority but also within the PNA, among the various organizations under the umbrella of the PLO, and among the Palestinians in and outside of historic Palestine. See the brief report by Ingrid Jaradat Gassner and her interview of Saleh Abed Rabbo in *News from Within.*

37 For a literal example, see Edward Said's account in *"Intifada* and Independence" of the writing of the Palestinian Declaration of Independence at which Mahmud Darwish's suggestions for the wording of the Declaration were rejected as "poetic" rather than substantive—in spite of Darwish's insistence on their substantive relevance to the document.

38 It was subsequently reproduced in a memorial retrospective of al-'Ali's work in the Palestinian journal, *al-Fikr al demoqratiyya*, no. 1 (1988). Al-'Ali was shot by a gunman in London in late July 1987 and, after five weeks in a coma, died in August the same year.

39 See the excellent and exceedingly suggestive work of Boaventura de Sousa Santos, whose *Toward a New Common Sense: Law, Science, and Politics in the Paradigmatic Transition* I had the provocative pleasure to discover after I had written these lines.

40 The predominance of particular conceptions of interior and exterior in other Palestinian texts and situations is also discussed in my "Telling Spaces: Palestinian Women and the Engendering of National Narratives."

41 There is another notable way in which *Wedding in Galilee* confounds time, as Ella Shohat points out in her characteristically insightful and astute review of the film. That is, in the situation of the events of the film in an ambiguous present/space—a wedding in Galilee, within the boundaries of the state of Israel—for which, historically, military rule in the post-1967 period was lifted. It was extended, of course, to the now Israeli-occupied West Bank and Gaza. A further folding—forward, in this instance—of linear historical time occurs in the military governor's reference to the Israeli invasion of Lebanon (1982) at the wedding of Daoud's son. Though the film was, in fact, filmed in Palestinian villages both within Israel and in the West Bank, its titular designation and selected internal references are presumably to location in a post-1967 Palestinian village in the state of Israel. But there is a distinct sense in which this wedding in Galilee takes place in many (Palestinian) places, at many times, drawing from many "traditions" and customs. This folding in of diverse historical times and places serves to suggest a larger Palestinian community that is linked (if not united) in spite of temporal and spatial insides and outsides, in spite of Muslim and Christian traditions (i.e., as in the wedding). But a no less daring folding

in occurs in the visual knowledge to which only an Israeli soldier (and the film's audience) is witness.

42 There is a popular joke from this period, suggested by the image of Israelis firing into the air. One person says to another, "Did you know that Palestinians can fly?" "How is that?" asks the second person. "Well," says the first person, "every time there are reports of Israelis firing their guns into the air, more Palestinians die."

4 Thinking Citizens Again

1 For a formulation of "relational literacy" over against "mastery," see my "The Multi-, the Pluri-, the Trans-, and the Meta-: A Few Thoughts on the Comparative and 'Relational Literacy.'"

2 Not unlike that "fullness of time" of which the proclamation of (an absent) Venizelos spoke as mainland Greek troops invaded Asia Minor.

3 Fredric Jameson, "The Dialectic of Utopia and Ideology," 283.

4 In spite of the acrid accusations against the perversity of humanities scholars who misunderstand and misuse "science" and its concepts, let me cite anyway Stephen Jay Gould's wonderful essay on contingency and evolution: "George Canning's Left Buttock and the Origin of the Species."

5 Of course, the extent to which at least a sociocultural "modern" is defined by a predication on that distant and inaccessible "past" as well as by a presumably radical departure from it is striking.

6 Julia Kristeva, "Women's Time," p. 199.

7 Kristeva's statement continues: "of separation and articulation of differences which in this way produces communicable meaning" (199). De Gouges might well have refused this qualification of a "sacrificial relationship" as a prerequisite for the production of "communicable meaning." She was far too committed to the at least potential power of reason. See "Les droits de la femme."

8 Mary Wollestonecraft is a well-known English example. But there were many other women in both France and the United States who brought the question of women-as-citizen to the fore.

9 Etienne Balibar, "The Nation Form" (89), in Balibar and Wallerstein, *Race, Nation, Class: Ambiguous Identities*.

10 That every modern state is also the product of the regulation of sexuality, gender, and the putatively "private" realm of the family is also apparent in de Gouges's offering of a model marriage contract that accords equal rights to both partners in her postscript to "Les droits de la Femme."

11 "Transculturation" was coined by the Cuban sociologist Fernando Ortiz in the 1940s and later centrally incorporated in the work of the Uruguayan literary critic Angel Rama; Mary Louise Pratt accounts for the trajectory of the term in a thoughtful exploration of its workings in her *Imperial Eyes: Travel Writing and Transculturation*.

12 In this context, transculturation as a cultural effort and process of selective reproduction and transformation is more than a little reminiscent of the much-quoted reference to the effort and process of making history that opens Marx's *Eighteenth Brumaire*. History, in Marx's fierce effort to analyze a particular moment of it, is

something formulated "not as they please, not under self-chosen circumstances, but under those already existing, given and transmitted (from the past)" (245). This is not to suggest, however, that the possibilities, force, and limitations of that "construction" process are equally dispersed among the peoples of the world. Colonial or now neo-imperial power is in the hands of a distinct few. But even those few cannot make history "just as they please." And the potentially radical force of transculturation itself is not effaced by the fact that it is effected by the marginal or subordinate or subaltern peoples.

13   A striking but largely unnoticed passage in Benedict Anderson's often-cited *Imagined Communities* is his reference to the end of religious and monarchic reigns and dynasties and their concomitant communities as the antecedent to the rise of the national community.

14   In "Borders, Boundaries, Taxes, and State in the Medieval Islamic World," Ellis Goldberg offers a provocatively suggestive commentary by implication from beyond the borders of Europe and of the modern period on the notion that at least a particular group of people—merchants—not within their "proper borders" are in the diaspora. In "Revenue Production," a paper presented at a Social Sciences Research Council conference, Goldberg astutely reexamines historical accounts of the conduct of merchants in the medieval Islamic city as they moved from one city to another to escape unjust taxation or an unjust ruler and as they banded together within a single city to replace said unjust rulers by inviting another one in. There was no sense of "proper place" as national people as there was no sense of "citizenship" bound to that place or ruler. (This is not to say there was no sense of community membership; it just was not bound by place or ruler.) It should be added that the ruler or king in the medieval Muslim world was a rather more secular figure than his counterpart in Europe of the time.

15   Ernst Renan, "What Is a Nation?" (1882).

16   Enloe concludes her essay "It Takes Two" with "Listening is a political act" (27).

17   I am immensely grateful to the organizers of and participants in the Third European Feminist Studies Conference, "Shifting Bounds, Shifting Bonds," held in Coimbra, Portugal, in the summer of 1997, for their suggestive title—to which there is an oblique reference here—but more especially for the opportunity to present an earlier version of a portion of this chapter and to engage in discussion with the amazing scholars and activists who were assembled there.

18   And in this, it recalls the poignant poem by Samih al-Qasim, "The Will of a Man Dying in Exile":
> Light the fire so that I can see in the mirror of flames
> the courtyard of the house and the bridge
> and the golden meadows
> light the fire so I can see my tears . . .

19   I am grateful to Odysseas Ladopoulos for reminding me of this story.

20   This is one of the instances—in Bloch's insistence on the necessity of a critical hermeneutic process for more than the analyst—in which Bloch's debt to and substantial revision of the work of Freud is striking. This qualification of the acts of being an audience also suggests an inflection of Enloe's "listening . . . [as] a political act,"

because that act of listening, as Enloe would no doubt agree, is never an uninterested or innocent one.

21   See Fredric Jameson, "Ernst Bloch and the Future," esp. 124–25. But also, Jameson's resonant discussion of utopia and ideology (in *The Political Unconscious*, for example) as his critical readings of popular culture elsewhere, seem substantially informed by his earlier work on Bloch.

22   This is, perhaps, one reason why Bloch's work is so encyclopedic.

23   Fredric Jameson's parallel of the future in Proust's *A la recherche du temps perdu* to that of Bloch's *The Principle of Hope*, and his work in general, is instructive here. In a wonderful commentary, Jameson cites Proust's Marcel endlessly composing to himself the letter he wants to receive from his beloved Gilberte until, suddenly, he realizes that he can never receive the letter that he is composing precisely because he *is* composing it. And so he gives up composing letters altogether so as not to foreclose the possibility of actually receiving one: "As in Bloch, the future always turns out in Proust to be that which is more, or other, than what was expected, even if what had been expected was . . . dissatisfaction itself" ("Ernst Bloch and the Future," *Marxism and Form*, 151). See Bloch's *The Principle of Hope*, 2:621, for one of the many instances in which he points out, here in a discussion of Marx, that "actual descriptions of the future are deliberately missing" in a "keeping open" of future possibilities.

24   Ernst Bloch, *Spuren*, 16; quoted in Jameson, "Ernst Bloch and the Future," *Marxism and Form*, 125.

25   For a discussion of Ernst Bloch as "scandal and embarrassment to most of his contemporaries in both heterodox and orthodox Marxist circles" (174), as "a fossilized remnant of Western Marxism's earlier years" (195), that is nonetheless an astute reading of Bloch's work in many ways, see Martin Jay's "Ernst Bloch and the Extension of Marxist Holism to Nature."

26   For a most explicit example, see his discussion of Zionism in *The Principle of Hope*, 2:598–610, where he focuses on the Zionist construction of the Israeli nation-state as homeland. But there is a suggestive tension throughout the work as a whole between the metaphoric and the literal homeland, though Bloch clearly comes down on the side of an as yet unrealized socialist "homeland" predicated on an end to exploitation and alienation and for which the literal nation-state of Israel, for example, is not sufficient.

27   Jacques Rancière, "Overlegitimation," 252–58.

Bibliography

Archives

Estia Neas Smyrnis, Athens, Greece.
Ministry of the Interior, Press and Information Office, Nicosia, Cyprus.
National Library of Greece, Athens, Greece.
Palestine Research Center, Department of Information and Culture, Nicosia, Cyprus.

Newspapers and Journals

al-Fajr (Jerusalem, Israel)
al-Fiqr al-Dimuqrāti (Nicosia, Cyprus)
Al-Ittiḥād (Haifa, Israel)
al-Karmel (Nicosia, Cyprus)
Al-Nahār (Beirut, Lebanon)
Al-Ōfoq (Nicosia, Cyprus)
Amaltheia Smyrnis (Smyrna/Constantinople)
Anti (Athens, Greece)
Arab Studies Quarterly (Washington, D.C.)
Cyprus Today (Nicosia, Cyprus)
Cyprus Weekly (Nicosia, Cyprus)
Fileleftheros Kosmos (Nicosia, Cyprus)
Jerusalem Post
Journal of Palestine Studies (Nicosia, Cyprus)
Khamsin (London; publication ceased)
Maxi (Nicosia, Cyprus)
MERIP/MER (Middle East Report; Washington, D.C.)
Nea Epochi (Nicosia, Cyprus)
Neos Kosmos (Athens, Greece)
News from Within (Jerusalem, Israel)
Ortam (Istanbul, Turkey)
Palestine Focus (publication ceased)
Pamprosfugiki (Athens, Greece)
Proodos (Constantinople/Istanbul, Turkey)
Prosfugiki Phoni (Athens, Greece)
Prosfugikos Kosmos (Athens, Greece)
Race and Class (London, England)
Xaravghi (Nicosia, Cyprus)
Yeniduzen (Nicosia, Cyprus)

Published Sources

Abraamidou, Maria. "Paralogismos" (Paralogic). In *O Televtaios khorismos* (The final separation). Levkosia: Kypros Printing, 1979.

Aburish, Saïd K. *Cry Palestine: Inside the West Bank.* Boulder, CO: Westview Press, 1993.

Adali, Emine. "Tourkokypriaki logotechnia" (Turkish-Cypriot literature). *Nea Epochi* 174 (January–February 1989): 60–63.

Adnan, Etel. *Of Cities and Women* (Letters to Fawwaz). Sausalito, CA: Post-Apollo Press, 1993.

Adonis, "Mirror for the Twentieth Century." In *Victims of a Map* (Ḍaḥāyā al-ḵarīta). Ed. and trans. Abdullah al-Udhari. London: al-Saqi Books, 1984.

Alcalay, Ammiel. *After Arabs and Jews: Remaking Levantine Culture.* Minneapolis: University of Minnesota Press, 1993.

Anderson, Benedict. *Imagined Communities.* New York: Verso, 1983.

Angelomatis, Xpistos E. *Xpovikon megalis tpagodias: To epos tis Mikras Asias* (The chronicle of a great tragedy in Asia Minor). Athens: Kollarou, 1963.

Asimakopoulou, An. *Mari Xanoum: E perifimi eromeni tou Fexim Pasa* (Mari Hanoum: The famous mistress of Fehim Pasha). In *E Pamprosfugiki* (The Pan-Refugee). Ed. G. Violakis. Athens: (serialized) 1924–1925.

Attila 1974: A Testimony on Film. Dir. Michael Cacoyannis. London, 1975.

Aziz, Ibrahim. *Bolunur mu hic/De moirazetai* (It is not divisible: Poems). Nicosia, Cyprus: Vaso Press, 1986.

Bakhtin, M. M. *Speech Genres and Other Late Essays.* Eds. Caryl Emerson and Michael Holquist. Trans. Vern W. McGee. Austin: University of Texas Press, 1986.

Bakalbasis, Anastasis, Michail Argyropoulos, Eleftheris Pavlidis, and Frangiskos Sarandis. "Oi Prosfuges" (The Refugees). Speeches to Kentron Prosgygon (The Refugee Center). Athens, Greece. 18 March 1945.

Balibar, Etienne, and Immanuel Wallerstein. *Race, Nation, Class: Ambiguous Identities.* London: Verso, 1991.

Barbalet, J. M. *Citizenship.* Minneapolis: University of Minnesota Press, 1988.

Bellou, Soteria. "Sakatameni mou genia" (My maimed generation). Lyrics, Michalis Bourboulis, cond. Dimitris Lagios. *O 'Ai Laos.* Lyra 3761.

——. "Chronia perifronimena" (Years of contempt). Lyrics, Michalis Bourboulis, cond. Dimitris Lagios. *O 'Ai Laos.* Lyra 3761.

Benhabib, Seyla, and Drucilla Cornell, eds. *Feminism as Critique.* Minneapolis: University of Minnesota Press, 1987.

Bhabha, Homi, ed. *Nation and Narration.* New York: Routledge, 1990.

Bloch, Ernst. *The Principle of Hope.* 3 volumes. Trans. Neville Plaice, Stephen Plaice, and Paul Knight. Cambridge, MA: MIT Press, 1986. Originally published as *Das Prinzip Hoffnung.* Frankfurt am Main: Suhrkamp, 1959.

——. "Something's Missing." In *A Discussion between Ernst Bloch and Theodor W. Adorno on the Contradictions of Utopian Longing.* Trans. J. Zipes and F. Mecklenburg. Cambridge, MA: MIT Press, 1988.

Brynen, Rex. "PLO Policy in Lebanon: Legacies and Lessons." *Journal of Palestine Studies* 70 (winter 1989): 48–70.

Butler, Judith, and Joan Scott, eds. *Feminists Theorize the Political.* New York: Routledge, 1992.

Chatterjee, Partha. *Nationalist Thought and the Colonial World: An Autonomous Discourse?* London: Zed Books/United Nations University Press, 1986.

Chedid, Andrée. *The Return to Beirut.* Trans. Ros Schwartz. London: Serpent's Tail, 1989. Originally published as *La Maison sans racines.* Paris: Flammarion, 1985.

Clarke, Paul Barry. *Deep Citizenship.* London: Pluto Press, 1996.

Clogg, Richard. "*Anadolu Hiristiyan Karindaşlarimiz*: The Turkish-Speaking Greeks of Asia Minor." In *Hellenism and Neo-Hellenism,* ed. John Burke and Stathis Gauntlett. Melbourne: Australian National University, Humanities Research Centre Monograph no. 5, 1992. 65–91.

——. *A Concise History of Greece.* London: Cambridge University Press, 1992.

Cobban, Helena. *The Palestine Liberation Organisation: People, Power and Politics.* Cambridge, England: Cambridge University Press, 1984.

Committee for the Restoration of Human Rights throughout Cyprus. *Turkish Cypriots Call Denktash's Bluff.* Introduction by Umit Intaci. Levkosia: N.p., 1991.

Cooke, Miriam. *War's Other Voices: Women Writers on the Lebanese Civil War.* Cambridge, England: Cambridge University Press, 1988.

"Correspondence between President Johnson and Prime Minister Inonu." *Middle East Journal* 20, no. 3 (summer 1966): 386–93.

Cyprus in Brief. Nicosia: Press and Information Office, 1982.

Darwish, Mahmoud. Selected poems. In *Ḍaḥāyā al-ḳarīta (Victims of a Map).* Ed. and trans. Abdullah al-Udhari. London: Al-Saqi Books, 1984.

——. *Ḍhākira lil-nisyān.* Nicosia, Cyprus: al-Karmel, 1986. Translated by Ibrahim Muhawi under the title *Memory for Forgetfulness: August, Beirut, 1982.* Berkeley: University of California Press, 1995.

de Gouges, Olympe. "Les droits de la femme" (The Rights of Woman and the Citizen). In *Women in Revolutionary Pris, 1789–1795: Selected Documents,* trans. and eds. Daline Gay Levy, Harriet Branson Applewhite, and Mary Durham Johnson. Urbana: University of Illinois Press, 1979.

Deimizis, A. *Situation sociale créé en Grèce à la suite de l'Echange de Populations.* Paris, 1927.

Doukas, Stratis. *Istoria enos aixmalotou* (Story of a prisoner of war). Athens, 1929.

Doulis, Thomas. *Disaster and Fiction: Modern Greek Fiction and the Asia Minor Disaster of 1922.* Berkeley: University of California Press, 1977.

Drousiotis, Makarios. *Stis fylakes tou Denktash* (In Denktash's prisons). Levkosia: N.p., 1989.

'Ein Gil, Ehud. "The Twenty-First Year: New Ideas." In *Palestine: Profile of an Occupation.* London: Khamsin/Zed Press, 1989. 93–119.

Elshtain, Jean Bethke. *Democracy on Trial.* New York: Basic Books, 1995.

Enloe, Cynthia. *Bananas, Beaches, and Bases: Making Feminist Sense of International Politics.* Berkeley: University of California Press, 1990.

——. "It Takes Two." In *Let the Good Times Roll: Prostitution and the U.S. Military in Asia,* ed. Saundra Sturdevant and Brenda Stoltzfus. New York: The New Press, 1992.

Ertug, H. E. Osman. Lecture. University of Wisconsin–Madison, 8 November 1991.

Flores, Alexander. *The Palestinians in the Israeli-Arab Conflict: Social Conditions and Political Attitudes of the Palestinians in Israel, the Occupied Territories and the Diaspora.* Bonn, Germany: Forschungsinstitut der Deutchen Gessellschaft für Auswärtige Politik E.V., 1984.

Fotiadis, Dimitris. *Enthymimata* (Recollections). Athens: Kedros, 1981.

Gassner, Ingrid Jaradat. "Interview with Salek Abed Rabbo." *News from Within* (Jerusalem Alternative Information Center) 13, no. 7 (July 1997): 23–25.

Genet, Jean. "Four Hours in Shatila." *Journal of Palestine Studies* 47, 12:3 (spring 1983): 3–22.

Georgiadis, Nearkhos. *Rembetiko kai politiki* (The rembetiko [song] and politics). Athens: Synchroni Epokhi, 1993.

Giacaman, Rita, and Muna Odeh. "Palestinian Women's Movement in the Israeli-Occupied West Bank and Gaza Strip." In *Women of the Arab World: The Coming Challenge,* ed. Nahid Toubia. Atlantic Highlands, NJ: Zed Books, 1988.

Gizeli, Vika D. *Koinonikoi metaschematismoi kai proelevsi tis koinokikis katoikias stin Ellada (1920–1930)* (Social transformation and origins of social housing in Greece [1920–1930]). Athens: Epikairotita, 1984.

Goldberg, Ellis. "Borders, Boundaries, Taxes, and State in the Medieval Islamic World." Unpublished manuscript, n.d.

—. "Revenue Production." Paper presented at the Social Science Research Council Conference, University of Washington-Seattle, April 1990.

Gould, Stephen Jay. "George Canning's Left Buttock and the Origin of the Species." In *Bully for Brontosaurus: Reflections in Natural History.* New York: Norton, 1991. 21–31.

Graikos, Kostas. *Kypriaki istoria* (Cypriot history), vol. B. Levkosia: N.p., 1982.

Greece and Asia Minor, eds. John Iatrides, Giannes Koliopoulos, and John McGrew. Special issue of *Journal of Modern Greek Studies* 4, no. 2 (1986).

Gresh, Alain. "Palestinian Communists and the Intifadah." *Middle East Report* 157, 19:2 (March–April 1989): 34–36.

Grovogui, Siba. *Sovereigns, Quasi-Sovereigns, and Africans: Race and Self-Determination in International Law.* Minneapolis: University of Minnesota Press, 1996.

Habibi, Imil. *al-Waqā'a al-gharībah fī ikhtifā' Saīd Abī al-Nahs al-Mutashāil.* Tunis: Dār al-Janūb lil-Nashr, 1982. Trans. by Salma Khadra Jayyusi and Trevor Le Gassick as *The Secret Life of Saeed, the ill-fated pessoptimist: A Palestinian who became a citizen of Israel.* New York: Readers International, 1989.

Harlow, Barbara. "Palestine or Andalusia: The Literary Response to the Israeli Invasion of Lebanon." *Race and Class* 26, no. 2 (autumn 1984): 33–43.

Hatzimousis, Pavlos. *Bibliographia 1919–1978: Mikrasiatiki ekstrateia—itta profygia* (Bibliography 1919–1978: The Asia Minor Expedition—defeat displacement). Athens: Ermis, 1981.

Hatzipappas, Christos. *To chroma tou galaziou iakinthou* (The color of the blue hyacinth). Athens: Kastinioti, 1989.

Held, David. "Democracy, the Nation-State, and the Global System." In *Political Theory Today,* ed. David Held. Stanford: Stanford University Press 1991. 197–235.

Hiltermann, Joost R. *Behind the Intifada: Labor and Women's Movements in the Occupied Territories*. Princeton, NJ: Princeton University Press, 1991.

Hirschon-Fillipaki, Renée. "*Mnymi kai tavtotita: Oi Mikrasiates prosfyges tis Kokkinias*" (Memory and Identity: The Asia Minor refugees of Kokkinia). In *Anthropology and the Past: Contributions to the Social History of Modern Greece*, eds. Evthymios Papataxiarchis and Theodoros Paradellis. Athens: Alexandria Press, 1993.

Hitchens, Christopher. *Cyprus*. London: Quartet Books, 1984.

Hobsbawm, Eric. *The Age of Extremes: A History of the World, 1914–1991*. New York: Vintage, 1994.

——. *Nations and Nationalism Since 1780: Programme, Myth, Reality*. New York: Vintage, 1994.

Hobsbawm, Eric, and Terence Ranger, eds. *The Invention of Tradition*. New York: Cambridge University Press, 1984.

Horton, George. *The Blight of Asia: An Account of the Systematic Extermination of Christian Populations by Mohammedans and of the Culpability of Certain Great Powers with the True Story of the Burning of Smyrna*. Indianapolis: Bobbs-Merrill, 1926.

Hroch, Miroslav. "From National Movement to the Fully Formed Nation: The Nation-Building Process in Europe." *New Left Review* 198 (March–April 1993): 3–20.

——. *Social Preconditions of National Revival in Europe*. London: Cambridge University Press, 1985.

Ioannides, Christos P. *In Turkey's Image: The Transformation of Occupied Cyprus into a Turkish Province*. New Rochelle, NY: Aristide D. Caratzas, 1991.

Ioannidis, Panos. "Oi stoles" (The uniforms). In *E atheati opsi* (The invisible side). Levkosia: Kinyras, 1979. 9–18.

Iordanidou, Maria. *E avli mas* (Our yard). Athens: Estia, 1981.

——. *San ta trella poulia* (Like crazy birds). Athens: Estia, 1979.

Jameson, Fredric. "The Dialectic of Utopia and Ideology." In *The Political Unconscious*. Ithaca, NY: Cornell University Press, 1981.

——. "Ernst Bloch and the Future." In *Marxism and Form*. Princeton: Princeton University Press, 1971.

Jay, Martin. "Ernst Bloch and the Extension of Marxist Holism to Nature." In *Marxism and Totality*. Berkeley: University of California Press, 1984.

Kapsis, Yiannis. *1922: E Mavri Biblos* (1922: The Black Book). Athens: Nea Synora-A. A. Livanis, 1992.

——. *Xamenes Patrides* (Lost homelands). Athens: Nea Synora-A. A. Livanis, 1962.

Katselli, Rina. *Galazia falaina* (Blue whale). Levkosia: Chrysopolitissa, 1978.

——. *Prosfugas ston topo mou* (Refugee in my homeland). Leukosia: Chrisopolitissa, 1975.

Kendro Mikrasiatikon Spoudon (Center for Asia Minor Studies). *E Exodos* (The exodus), vols. 1 and 2. Athens, 1980 and 1982.

Khalidi, Rashid. *Palestinian Identity: The Construction of Modern National Consciousness*. New York: Columbia University Press, 1997.

——. "The Palestinian People: Twenty-two Years after 1967." In *Intifada: The Palestinian Uprising against Israeli Occupation,* eds. Zachary Lockman and Joel Beinin. Boston, MA: MERIP/South End Press, 1989.

——. *Under Siege: PLO Decisionmaking during the 1982 War.* New York: Columbia University Press, 1986.

Killoran, Moira. "Nationalisms and Embodied Memory in Northern Cyprus." *Cyprus and Its People: Nation, Identity and Experience in an Unimaginable Community (1955–1997,* ed. Vangelis Calotychos. Boulder, CO: Westview Press, 1998.

Kingsolver, Barbara. "Homeland." In *Homeland and Other Stories.* New York: Harper-Collins, 1989.

Kleanthis, Fanis N. *Etsi xasame ti mikrasia: istoriki erevna* (This is how we lost Asia Minor: A historical inquiry). Athens: Kollarou, 1983.

Kristeva, Julia. *Nations without Nationalism.* Trans. Leon Roudiez. New York: Columbia University Press, 1993. Originally published as *Lettre ouverte à Harlem Désir* (Paris: Editions Rivages, 1990).

——. *Strangers to Ourselves.* Trans. Leon Roudiez. New York: Columbia University Press, 1991. Originally published as *Étrangers à nous-mêmes* (Paris: Librairie Artheme Fayard, 1991).

——. "Women's Time." In *The Kristeva Reader,* ed. Toril Moi. New York: Columbia University Press, 1986.

Kruger, Barbara. "What's High, What's Low—and Who Cares?" *New York Times,* 9 September 1990, nat'l. ed., H43.

Kypros: Logotekhnia kai texni (Cyprus: Literature and Art). Special issue of *E Lexi* (The Word) 85–86 (1989).

Kypros '74: To allo propospo tis Aphroditis (Cyprus '74: The other face of Aphrodite). Athens: National Bank of Greece, 1975.

Lampsidis, Giorgos. *Oi prosfuges tou 1922* (The refugees of 1922). Athens: Elleniki phoni, 1982.

Landros, X. "70 Xronia Nostalgias" (70 years of nostalgia). In *Apoplous: Samiakon grammaton and tekhnon pereigisi* (Setting Sail: A tour of the letters and arts of Samos) 30, no. 9 (1992): 33–62.

Layoun, Mary N. "Telling Spaces." In *Nationalisms and Sexualities,* eds. Andrew Parker, Mary Russo, Doris Sommer, and Patricia Yeager. New York: Routledge, 1992.

——. "The Trans-, the Multi-, the Pluri-, and the Global: A Few Thoughts on the Comparative and 'Relational Literacy.' " *Passages* 1:2 (1999): 173–213.

League of Nations. *Greek Refugee Settlement Commission.* Geneva: League of Nations' Publications, 1926.

Liatsou, Dimitris. *Oi prosfuges tis mikrasias kai to rembetiko tragoudi* (The Asia Minor refugees and the rembetiki song). Athens: Basilopoulos, 1985.

——. *E mikrasiatiki katastrophe sti neo-Elleniki logotexnia* (The Asia Minor catastrophe in modern Greek literature). Athens: To Elleniko biblio, 1962.

Livieratos, Dimitris. *Koinonikoi agones stin Ellada 1923–1927* (Social struggles in Greece 1923–1927). Athens: Kommouna, 1985.

Llewellyn Smith, Michael. *Ionian Vision: Greece in Asia Minor 1919–1922.* London: Allen Lane Books, 1973.

Loizos, Peter. *The Heart Grown Bitter: A Chronicle of Cypriot War Refugees.* Cambridge, England: Cambridge University Press, 1981.

H. B. Archbishop Makarios, President of Cyprus. Address. 29th UN General Assembly, 1 October 1974.

Makdisi, Jean. *Beirut Fragments*. New York: Persea Books, 1990.

Malovrouva, Isabella Sikiaridi. *Mikrasia E Megali Ellada* (Asia Minor, Greater Greece). Athens: Estia Neas Smyrnis, 1982.

Marx, Karl. "On *Die Judengrage*" (On *The Jewish Question*), trans. Rodney Livingstone and Gregor Benton in *Karl Marx: Early Writings*. New York: Vintage Books, 1975.

——. *The Eighteenth Brumaire of Louis Napoleon*. In *On Revolution,* vol. 1 of *The Karl Marx Library,* trans. and ed. Saul K. Padover. New York: McGraw Hill, 1971.

——. *The German Ideology,* trans. W. Lough, C. Dutt, and C. P. Magill. New York: International Publishers, 1970.

Mazower, Mark. *Greece and the Inter-War Economic Crisis.* Oxford: Clarendon, 1991.

McNeil, William H. *Polyethnicity and National Unity in World History.* Toronto: University of Toronto Press, 1986.

Meleagrou, Eve. *Protelevtaia epochi* (The next to the last season). Athens: Kedros, 1981.

Merwin, W. S. "Cover Note." In *Travels.* New York: Knopf, 1994.

Mistrusting Refugees, eds. E. Valentine Daniel and John C. Knudsen. Berkeley: University of California Press, 1995.

Morgenthau, Henry, with French Strother. *I Was Sent to Athens.* New York: Doubleday, 1929.

Mosse, George. *Fallen Soldiers: Reshaping the Memory of the World Wars.* New York: Oxford University Press, 1990.

——. *Nationalism and Sexuality: Middle-Class Morality and Sexual Norms in Modern Europe.* Madison: University of Wisconsin Press, 1985.

Nairn, Tom. *The Break-Up of Britain: Crisis and Neo-Nationalism.* London: New Left Books, 1977.

Nejatigil, Zaim M. *The Turkish Republic of Northern Cyprus in Perspective.* Nicosia, Northern Cyprus: N.p., 1985.

Okigbo, Christopher. "Lament of the Silent Sisters." In *Labyrinths.* New York: African Publishing, 1971.

The Palestinian-Israeli Peace Agreement: A Documentary Record. Washington, D.C.: Institute for Palestine Studies, 1994.

Pallis, A. A. "E Antallagi ton Plithysmon apo apopsi nomiki kai istoriki kai e simasia tis yia ti diethni thesi tis Ellados" (The exchange of populations from a legal and historical viewpoint and the importance of it for the international position of Greece). Speech. Athens, 20 April 1933.

Panteli, Stavros. *The Making of Modern Cyprus: From Obscurity to Statehood.* New Barnet, England: Interworld Publications, 1990.

Papaioannou, Ezekias. *Enthumiseis apo ti zoi mou* (Memories from my life). Levkosia: Pyrsos, 1988.

Pentzopoulos, Dimitri. *The Balkan Exchange of Minorities and Its Impact on Greece.* The Hague: Mouton, 1962.

Peteet, Julie. *Gender in Crisis: Women and the Palestinian Resistance Movement.* New York: Columbia University Press, 1991.

Petran, Tabitha. *The Struggle over Lebanon*. New York: Monthly Review Books, 1987.

Politis, Kosmas. *Stou Hatzifrangou Ta sarandakhronia mias khamenis politeias* (At Hatzifragou: The forty years of a lost city). Athens: Karavia, 1963.

Pratt, Mary Louise. *Imperial Eyes: Travel Writing and Transculturation*. New York: Routledge, 1992.

Prosfuges kai oikonomia (Refugees and the economy). Special issue of *O Oikonomikos Takhydromos* (The economic courier), 26 April 1973.

Psyroukis, Nikos. *E Mikrasiatiki katastrophe: E Engus Anatoli meta ton proto Pankosmio Polemo (1918–1923)* (The Asia Minor disaster: The Near East after WWI [1918–1923]). Athens: Epikairotita, 1982.

al-Qasim, Samih. "The Will of a Man Dying in Exile." *Victims of a Map (Ḍaḥāyā al-ḵarīta)*. Ed. and trans. Abdullah al-Udhari. London: al-Saqi Books, 1984.

Rancière, Jacques. "Overlegitimation." *Social Text* 31, no. 31 (1992): 252–58.

Renan, Ernst. "What Is a Nation?" Reprinted in *The Nationalism Reader*, eds. Omar Dahbour and Micheline Ishay. Atlantic Highlands, NJ: Humanities Press International, 1995. 143–55.

Roussou, Maria. "War in Cyprus: Patriarchy and the Penelope Myth." In *Women and Political Conflict: Portraits of Struggle in Times of Crisis,* eds. Rosemary Ridd and Helen Callaway. New York: New York University Press, 1987.

Rubenberg, Cheryl A. "The Civilian Infrastructure of the Palestine Liberation Organization." *Journal of Palestine Studies* 47 (spring 1983): 54–78.

Said, Edward. *After the Last Sky.* New York: Pantheon, 1986.

——. "Intifada and Independence." *Social Text 22* (spring 1989): 23–29. Reprinted in *Intifada: The Palestinian Uprising against Israeli Occupation,* eds. Zachary Lockman and Joel Beinin. Boston: South End Press, 1989.

Sahliyeh, Emile. *In Search of Leadership: West Bank Politics Since 1967*. Washington, DC: Brookings Institution, 1988.

Samara, 'Adil. "Letter from the West Bank on the War in Lebanon." In *Khamsin 10*. London: Ithaca Press, 1983. 21–24.

——. "The Political Economy of the West Bank 1967–1987: From Peripheralization to Development." In *Palestine: Profile of an Occupation*. London: Khamsin/Zed Press, 1989. 7–31.

Santos, Boaventura des Sousa. *Toward a New Common Sense: Law, Science, and Politics in the Paradigmatic Transition*. New York: Routledge, 1995.

Sayigh, Rosemary. "The *Mukhabarat* State: Testimony of a Palestinian Woman Prisoner." *Race and Class* 26, no. 2 (autumn 1984): 75–82.

——. *Too Many Enemies: The Palestinian Experience in Lebanon*. London: Zed Press, 1994.

Shammus, Anton. "Palestinians Must Now Master the Art of Forgetting." *New York Times,* 26 December 1993.

Shohat, Ella. Review of *Wedding in Galilee. Middle East Report,* no. 154 (September–October 1988): 44–46.

Silko, Leslie Marmon. *Ceremony.* New York: Viking, 1977.

Soteriou, Dido. *E Mikrasiatiki katastrophe kai i stratigiki tou imperialismou stin Anatoliki Mesogeio* (The Asia Minor catastrophe and the strategy of imperialism in the Eastern Mediterranean). Athens: Kedros, 1975.

——. *Matomena xomata* (Bloodied earth). Athens: Kedros, 1962.

——. *Oi Nekroi perimenoun* (The dead are waiting). Athens: Kedros, 1959.

Spivak, Gayatri Chakravorty. "Can the Subaltern Speak?" In *Marxism and the Interpretation of Culture*, eds. Cary Nelson and Lawrence Grossberg. Urbana: University of Illinois Press, 1988.

"Stranded in Time." With Christopher Hitchens. *Frontiers*. BBC/PBS. WGBH, Boston. 6 May 1990.

Syntagma tis Kypriakis Dimokratias (The Constitution of the Cypriot Republic). Nicosia: Government Publishing House, 1960.

Tornaritis, Criton G. *Cyprus and Its Constitutional and Other Legal Problems*. Nicosia: Proodos, 1977.

——. "The Legal Position of the Church, Especially the Greek-Orthodox Church in the Republic of Cyprus." *Cyprus Today* 28, no. 1 (1990).

Toubia, Nahid, ed. *Women of the Arab World: The Coming Challenge*. London: Zed Press, 1988.

Traboulsi, Fawwaz. "Beirut-Guernica: A City and a Painting." *Middle East Report* 154, 18:5 (September-October 1988): 29–37.

Tucker, Judith. "The War of Numbers." MERIP, nos. 108–9 (September–October 1982): 47–50.

Turkish Cypriot Political Parties, The. Levkosia: Press and Information Office, Cypriot Ministry of the Interior, 1989.

Turner, Bryan S. *Citizenship and Capitalism: The Debate over Reformism*. London: Allen and Unwin, 1986.

'*Urs al-jalīl* (Wedding in Galilee). Dir. Michel Khleifi. Marissa Films, 1987.

Venezis, Ilia. *Mikrasia, xaire* (Asia Minor, goodbye). Athens: Estia, 1974.

——. *To noumero 31,238: To biblio tis aixmalosias* (The number 31,328: The book of captivity). Athens: Estia, 1931.

Vournas, Tasos. *Istoria tis synchronis Ellados (1909–1940)* (History of contemporary Greece [1909–1940]). Athens: Tolidi, 1977.

Worsley, Peter, and Paschalis Kitromilides, eds. *Small States in the Modern World: The Conditions of Survival*. Nicosia: New Cyprus Association, 1979.

Xatzimousis, Pavlos. *Bibliographia 1919–1978: Mikrasiatiki ekstrateia-itta prosfygia* (Bibliography 1919–1978: The Asia Minor expedition—Defeat displacement). Athens: Ermis, 1981.

Xrusoxoou, Iphigenia. *Martyriki poreia (1922–1924)* (Tortured march [1922–1924]). Athens, 1974.

——. *Pyrpolimeni gi (1877–1922)* (The scorched earth [1877–1922]). Athens: Filippoti, 1973/1982.

——. *Xerizomeni genia* (Uprooted generation). Athens, 1977.

Yasin, Mehmet. "The Myth of Our Own Cat." In Elli Paionithou, "*San tous paranomous erastes e pos anakalipsame tin Tourkouypriaki poesi*" (Like illegal lovers, or, how we discovered Turkish Cypriot poetry). In *Kypros: Logotekhnia kai tekhni* (Cyprus: Literature and art). Special issue of *E Leksi* (The Word) 85–86 (June–August 1989) 702–9.

——. "Perishing Cyprus." *Olay* (26 April–17 May 1982). Reprinted: Levksosia Press and Information Office, Cyprus Ministry of the Interior, 1989.

Yasin, Nessié. "Which Half." In Elli Paionithou, "*San tous paranomous erastes e pos anakalipsame tin Tourkouypriaki poiesi*" (Like illegal lovers, or, how we discovered Turkish Cypriot poetry). In *Kypros: Logotekhnia kai tekhni* (Cyprus: Literature and Art). Special issue of *E Leksi* (The Word) 85–86 (June–August 1989) 702–9.

Young, Iris. *Justice and the Politics of Difference.* Princeton, NJ: Princeton University Press, 1990.

Zipes, Jack. Introduction to *The Utopian Function of Art and Literature,* by Ernst Bloch. Trans. Jack Zipes and Frank Mecklenburg Cambridge, MA: MIT Press, 1988.

Index

Mary N. Layoun is Professor of Comparative Literature at the
University
of Wisconsin-Madison and the author of *Travels of a Genre:
The Modern Novel and Ideology.*

Library of Congress Cataloging-in-Publication Data
Layoun, Mary N.
Wedded to the land? : gender, boundaries, and nationalism-in-crisis /
Mary Layoun.
p. cm.—(Post-contemporary interventions)
Includes bibliographical references.
ISBN 0-8223-2507-1 (cloth : alk. paper)
ISBN 0-8223-2545-5 (pbk. : alk. paper)
1. Nationalism and literature—Middle East.   2. Politics and
culture—Middle East.   3. Nationalism in literature.
4. Politics in literature.   I. Title.   II. Series.
PN56.N19 L39 2000   809'.93358—dc21   2001–027926